Your Hand Is a Map of Yourself

Your thumb and fingers, and the lines and mounts of
that represents the macrocosm of your self. Your han
can find the keys for why you do the things you do—

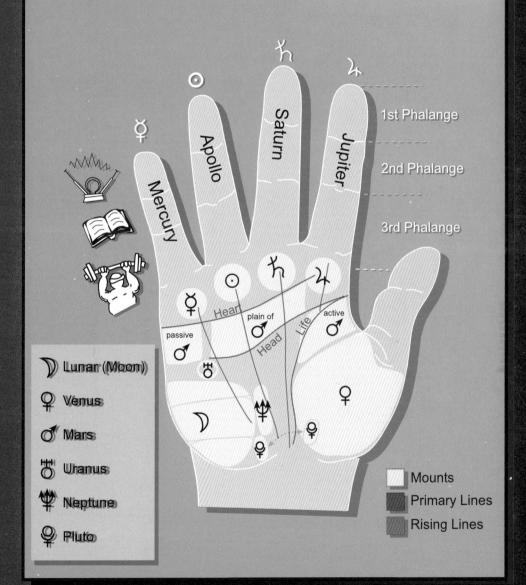

1st Phalange

2nd Phalange

3rd Phalange

Mercury
Apollo
Saturn
Jupiter

Heart
plain of
passive
Head
Life
active

☽ Lunar (Moon)

♀ Venus

♂ Mars

♅ Uranus

♆ Neptune

♇ Pluto

Mounts
Primary Lines
Rising Lines

alpha
books

A Who's Who of the Palm

Each area of the hand is named after a Greek or Roman god, and knowing who these gods are can help you memorize which area represents what. In fact, these names were originally assigned because everyone knew who was whom and could identify these areas' meanings at once.

Mercury is the Roman name for the Greek god, Hermes, and the name of your little finger and the mount below it. Mercury was the most versatile of the gods, responsible for trade, commerce, manual dexterity, and speech (he was also a thief!). Not surprisingly, this area of the hand covers your communication and commerce, as well as your capacity for healing.

Apollo was one of the twelve Olympians, and is the name of your ring finger and the mount below it. Apollo was the sun god, and was responsible for fine arts, music, poetry, and eloquence. Your Apollo is the area of your potential for creativity as well as your vanity.

Saturn, the Roman name for the Greek god Cronus, was the father of the other gods, and is the name for your middle finger and the mount below. This is the area of your rules and responsibilities, how you interact with law and order, and your relationship with your father.

Jupiter is the Roman name for the Greek god Zeus, the ruler of heaven and earth, gods and men. It's also the name for your pointer finger and the mount below it. Your Jupiter finger and mount are the areas of your optimism, leadership potential, charisma, and relationships with those you know well.

Venus is the Roman name of the Greek goddess Aphrodite, the goddess of love, and her mount, found at the base of your thumb, is where you'll find your heart *chakra* and capacity for giving.

Mars is the Roman name for the Greek god Ares, god of war and battle. Your three Mars mounts—active Mars, passive Mars, and the plain of Mars—are the areas of your temper and your temperament, as well as your resilience and assertiveness.

Uranus is the most ancient of gods, the ruler of the sky. In palmistry, the Uranus mount is the area of your inventiveness and how you use your ideals.

Neptune, Poseidon in Greek, rules the sea, and your Neptune mount is where you'll find your urge to build or create on a large scale, as well as the potential for travel as a career.

Piuto, the Greek god of the underworld, is the mount where you'll find your potential for transformation—as well as your relationships with your siblings.

Luna (the Moon), Artemis in Greek, is the goddess of unmarried girls, childbirth, and chastity. This is the area where you'll find your feminine instincts, nurturing and receptivity, your dreams, and your imagination.

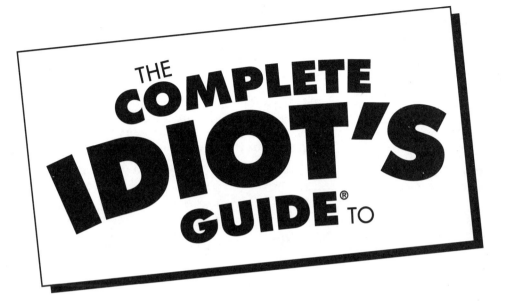

THE COMPLETE IDIOT'S GUIDE® TO

Palmistry

by Robin Gile and Lisa Lenard

alpha books

A Division of Macmillan General Reference
A Pearson Education Macmillan Company
1633 Broadway, 7th Floor, New York NY 10019

Alpha Development Team

Publisher
Kathy Nebenhaus

Editorial Director
Gary M. Krebs

Managing Editor
Bob Shuman

Marketing Brand Manager
Felice Primeau

Acquisitions Editor
Jessica Faust

Assistant Editor
Georgette Blau

Production Team

Book Producer
Lee Ann Chearney/Amaranth

Development Editor
Lynn Northrup

Production Editor
Robyn Burnett

Copy Editor
Susan Aufheimer

Cover Designer
Mike Freeland

Photo Editor
Richard H. Fox

Cartoonist
Jody P. Schaeffer

Illustrator
Kathleen Edwards

Book Designers
Scott Cook and Amy Adams of DesignLab

Indexer
Chris Wilcox

Layout/Proofreading
Marie Kristine Parial-Leonardo
Linda Quigley

Contents at a Glance

Contents

25 Turning Self-Sabotage into Self-Fulfillment   371

26 The Future of the World Is in All of Our Hands   381

Appendices

Foreword

"A quarter of an inch away from madness." This was my introduction to Robin Gile some 13 years ago after he glanced at my hands for the first time. Since then we have shared rides and motel rooms as we worked the psychic fair circuit from Denver to San Diego.

As president of the International Association of Metaphysicians and as a practicing psychic, I have had my hands read by a number of palmists and those who thought they were palmists. Of all of those readings over the past 20-some years there are only two palmists in the United States that I would recommend without qualifications. The first one would be Robin Gile.

Robin has the ability to see nuances in a hand that go right past other palmists. He has told me about things that happened in my past that I had forgotten about until he mentioned them. His insights into what is happening in my life at the time of his palm reading is almost unbelievable. His predictions of upcoming events is uncanny. Now that I have read his book, I find that he also has the ability to communicate his knowledge in a very easy-to-understand fashion (though I am sure his co-author's ability to write has a lot to do with this).

Whether you want to become a professional palmist or just want to gain some insights into your own life, *The Complete Idiot's Guide to Palmistry* is without a doubt the easiest way to accomplish both goals. It gives precise in-depth information very plainly and in a way that is easy to understand. If I were a Human Resources manager I would want to have the knowledge this book conveys. For if you learn what Robin is giving you the opportunity to learn, it will provide you with great insight into others and into yourself.

The Complete Idiot's Guide to Palmistry contains a lifetime of study about the hand and human nature in 26 easy-to-read chapters. I hope you enjoy reading Robin Gile and Lisa Lenard's collaboration as much as I did.

Benjamin Smith

Benjamin Smith is the president and founder of the International Association of Metaphysicians and has been a practicing metaphysician for over 20 years. A psychic and past life regressionist, Smith has been involved in expos and psychic fairs across the American West and Southwest. He is a certified facilitator and trainer of the Essential Peacemaking/ Women & Men gender communication workshops.

Introduction

Oh sure, you're thinking, *palm reading.* A gypsy in a turban or a guy with a goatee intoning, "You will live a long, long life. You will meet a tall, dark stranger."

It's time to get that picture out of your head because, in truth, palmistry is far more than a gypsy's ruse to predict the future. Your hand, in fact, is a microcosm of your self, and everything about you is there for you—and for the experienced palm reader—to see.

Whether it's your emotional nature, how you think, or what you collect, your nature is written in your hand. And palm readers look to far more than your life, head, and heart lines. They look at your thumb, your fingers, and the mounts of your palm—as well as all of these things as a whole.

Are you ready to find out what palmistry's *really* about? If so, *The Complete Idiot's Guide to Palmistry* is for you.

How to Use This Book

The only thing you really need to get started is your own two hands; but we'd like to make a few other recommendations as well. Throughout this book, you'll find suggestions for updating your palmistry notebook, and using an unlined notebook, to sketch your hand and make notes about it. We'll also be talking about other tools the palm reader uses: calipers, rulers, good light, and you may decide to invest in some of these after we discuss them in Chapter 3.

This book is divided into six parts:

Part 1: Your Future's in Your Hands introduces you to palmistry: its history, how archetype and myth can be used to explore your own hands, and how to look at your hands.

Part 2: Let Your Fingers Do the Talking lets your fingers do the walking *and* the talking—we look at the thumb and the other four fingers, the characters in your personal story.

Part 3: I've Got a Line on You is where we look at the lines in your hand. There's more here than just your life, head, and heart lines—and we'll tell you what these lines represent and the stories they tell about you.

Part 4: Ain't No Mount High Enough introduces you to the mounts of the hand, which you can think of as the areas where your story unfolds.

Part 5: Looking for Love, Money, and Happiness is where you get to put what you've learned about palmistry to work. We'll tell you how to look for love, money, and happiness in your hands!

Part 6: The Bigger Picture explores the bigger picture, from self-sabotage to how a generation's hands reflects its possibilities.

Extras

In addition to helping you learn all about palmistry—and yourself—we've added some additional information. Look for these boxes throughout the book for explanations of unfamiliar terms, helpful tips, things to watch out for, and interesting stories about palmistry:

Handy Words to Know

These sidebars define palmistry terms so you can speak the language of hands.

Helping Hands

These useful palmistry tips will help you read palms like a pro.

We Gotta Hand It to You

Here's where we'll be sharing some hand stories to illustrate how palmistry works in the real world.

Hand-le with Care

Forewarned is forearmed, or, in this case, fore-handed. These warnings can help you avoid making mistakes.

Acknowledgments

We'd both like to thank the following people for "lending us their hands": Lee Ann Chearney; her grandmother, Jesse Chearney; B. D. Cook, Kathy Edwards, David Feela, R. Gile, Chris Goold, Connie Jacobs, Joan Green, L. Lenard, Joanie Luhman, Richard Luhman, R.C. Martinez, Bill Ray, Stuart Ray, Vicky Ray, and Pam Smith. We'd also like to acknowledge the following meeting places in Albuquerque for their tables—and coffee: Starbucks at Barnes & Noble; the cafés at Bound to Be Read and Borders; and Gourmet Bagel and Coffee Company.

Robin wishes to thank Lisa Lenard for her unfailing good humor and bad puns, for her ability to appear interested as he digressed into Norse explorers of the Rio Grande Valley and other esoterica and her patience therein, for her support, and of course her ability to bring order to the chaos of his mind.

Robin also thanks his good friend Kathy Edwards for her quick-minded ability to make sense out of scribbled lines on her hand with statements like, "This is genius, that is madness! And here is your husband—or something like that." Her illustrations are possibly fulfilled from her own psychic capacity.

Robin would like to personally dedicate this book to Clerow: *It was 17 years in fruition. Thanks, guy. Know yer better now than ever.* To David, who got well a long time ago but still helps out when asked. To the Brotherhood of Life bookstore and its venerable owner Richard Buhler *and* the stalwart Mr. Dale Boyce, manager. They have given Robin something of his daily bread and more for some years now. To Ben and Darlene and Delores and many others who have listened, and sighed, and answered. And lastly, and mostly, to the legions of clients who spent their time, hope, and money. Robin hopes he gave enough in return. Please believe he was sincere and consistent and always tried to be both positive and truthful.

Once again, Lisa thanks Lee Ann Chearney at Amaranth, for her skill in bringing projects like this together. She'd also like to acknowledge Lynn Northrup and the rest of Macmillan's amazing production staff for their commitment to excellence and knowing the difference between "its" and "it's." Thanks to Kathy Edwards for the awesome drawings—and for the boxes of books. Thanks as always to Bob, Kait, and the creatures. And most of all, many, many thanks to Robin Gile, for making her a believer.

Special Thanks to the Technical Reviewer

The Complete Idiot's Guide to Palmistry was reviewed by an expert who double-checked the accuracy of what you'll learn here to help us ensure that this book gives you everything you need to know about palmistry. Special thanks are extended to Ed Campbell, both for his close reading of this book and for his own invaluable resource, *The Encyclopedia of Palmistry*.

Mr. Campbell is a scientific palmist with over a decade of experience; he frequently lectures at seminars, workshops, and conferences. Mr. Campbell teaches palmistry at the experimental college of the associated students of the University of Washington at Seattle. He also helped to organize the Northwest Hand Institute for the further scientific study of the significance of hand appearances in character, health, environmental, and personal relationship analysis. Mr. Campbell's Web site is **www.edcampbell.com.** Robin would additionally like to personally acknowledge Mr. Campbell's fine work and the great pleasure he takes in the tiniest of disagreements.

Trademarks

All terms mentioned in this book that are known to be or are suspected of being trademarks or service marks have been appropriately capitalized. Alpha Books and Macmillan General Reference cannot attest to the accuracy of this information. Use of a term in this book should not be regarded as affecting the validity of any trademark or service mark.

Part 1
Your Future's in Your Hands

What is palmistry? If you've got a picture in your head of a hand-holding gypsy, think again. Palm reading is as old as humanity itself, and, rather than a method of foretelling the future, its primary use is as a way of exploring the self. Palmists use the microcosm of the hand as a map of the macrocosm of the self, and, once you learn how, you can, too.

I Want to Hold Your Hand

In This Chapter

➤ Your hand is a map that moves

➤ Palmistry is as old as humankind

➤ Learning to read the map of the hand

➤ Common questions palm readers are asked

➤ What your hand can tell you—and what it can't

Does the word "palmistry" conjure up images of gypsy fortune-tellers in dusty carnival tents? Do you think palm reading exists only as a means of telling the future? Did you know that the shape of your hand, your fingers, and the mounds on your palm are as important to palmistry as your life, head, and heart lines?

Palmistry is far more than a way of predicting the future—it's a way of understanding the self. The study of the hand to learn about the self is as old as human curiosity. You don't have to be a gypsy fortune-teller to learn palmistry; with this book, it's in your hands.

Before we begin, we'd like to introduce ourselves. "Robin" is Robin Gile, and he's been reading palms professionally for the past 20 years. "Lisa" is Lisa Lenard, writer and, as you'll soon learn, dilettante extraordinaire.

Your Hand Is a Map That Moves

Let's start with the analogy of a map. What is a map? It's a semantic (symbolic) representation of a territory. The map is not the territory itself, but if you know how to read the map's symbols, you'll find your way to that remote fishing hole, to Wilmington or Warsaw, or to the nearest mall. Most of us don't even think about what a map is and isn't. A map is not the actual places it represents, for example; no one would make that mistake.

Just as a map represents a place, your hand is a map of yourself. Your hand is no more yourself than a map is an actual place, but it is a *representation* of yourself. And the hand, unlike the foldout map you got from the chamber of commerce, is a map that *moves*. That makes your hand rather like state-of-the-art global positioning systems (GPS), which pinpoint where you are globally at any moment in time. The map in your hand can no more remain the same than you can stay in one place, but like that GPS, it can show you precisely where you are at any given moment.

Your hand is a map of a moment.

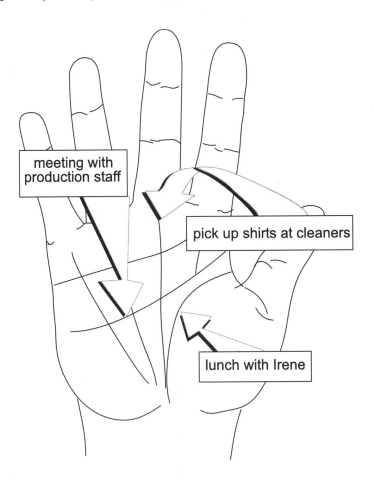

meeting with production staff

pick up shirts at cleaners

lunch with Irene

The map of your hand is a map of a moment—this moment. As your life story progresses and changes, its map, your hand, adjusts to reflect those changes. *Palmistry,* also known as *chiromancy,* is, quite simply, a study of how your hand reflects your life. In fact, you can think of it as the story of you as reflected in your hand. By understanding how the microcosm of the hand represents the macrocosm of the self, a *palm reader* can help you better understand the hows and whys of who you are.

What Is Palmistry?

Before we go any further, let's clear up what palmistry is *not.* It's not an excuse: You can't say you're always late because it's in your hand. The fact that you're always late *is* in your hand, but remember, *the hand reflects the self,* not the other way around.

Second, your hand doesn't cast your future in quick-set concrete. Don't forget, it's a map that moves, and it will change as you do. A short lifeline doesn't mean you should rush out and spend your inheritance (you may need it for that nursing home when you're 90), and any potential you have to be the next Eric Clapton will remain only potential unless you pick up a guitar and practice.

So, what *is* palmistry? It's a way of knowing yourself, and of knowing others. It can help you understand your potentials, fears, talents, and limitations. By studying your hand, you can better see the many sides of yourself. In fact, the hand reflects precisely what it is that makes you unique:

➤ Your individuality

➤ Your emotions

➤ Your talents

➤ Your health

➤ Your strength

➤ Your relationships

➤ Your fears

Handy Words to Know

Palmistry, or **chiromancy,** is a means of understanding the macrocosm of the self through the microcosm of the hand. **Palm readers** are people who have studied how this interrelationship works and can help you better understand yourself by studying your hand.

Helping Hands

Your hand is a map of a moment—but how long that moment is differs from hand to hand, and, within a hand, over time. Some hands move by day, some by the week, some by the month. One woman's hand changed as Robin was reading it!

➤ Your quirks

➤ Your behavioral patterns, from nail biting to your choice in partners

Understanding yourself is the first step toward living your life to the fullest of your potential. Using palmistry to help you understand yourself can actually help you change your future—as we said before, it's in your hands.

A Short History of the Hand

People have been studying hands as long as they've had them—which takes us back to our very beginnings. The hand, after all, is uniquely human, and, as such, has symbolically represented both divine intervention (the Hand of God) and the singularity of the individual. Handprints, in fact, have been found next to drawings on prehistoric cave walls—the original signed prints.

Notice the strong thumb and long Apollo (ring) finger in this simulated cave handprint.

Ancient Greek myth says Hermes (called Mercury in Roman mythology), the multitalented messenger god, was responsible for helping humans understand the maps of their hands. Definitive written testimony comes from Aristotle in 350 B.C.:

"Palmistry is a judgment made of the conditions, inclinations, and fortunes of men and women, from the various lines and characters which nature has imprinted in the hands." And the word *chiromancy*, which is another word for using the palm to tell fortunes, comes from the Greek words for *hand* and *I foretell*.

Palmistry climbed to the peak of its popularity in Europe during the Middle Ages, with the first known book on the subject printed in 1448. During the Renaissance, many French and Italian scholars studied and wrote about chiromancy in depth. During this time the legitimacy of palmistry was never questioned; instead, its ability to reveal the intricacies of the self were taken for granted.

Still, there's always been a stigma associated with palmistry, and, with the dawning of the age of

We Gotta Hand It to You

The Old Testament makes more than passing reference to palmistry. The Book of Job, for example, is literally filled with references to the significance of the individual hand. We're told more than once in no uncertain terms that God makes each hand unique, and that "He sealeth up the hand of every man/ That all men whom He hath made may know it." (37:7)

science, the interest in it, along with other esoteric sciences like astrology and numerology, began to wane. A resurgence of interest occurred in the late 19th and early 20th centuries, and it is largely from texts written during this time that modern palmistry takes its cue. Casimir Stanislas d'Arpentigny, a retired general from Napoleon's army, who made the study of the hand his lifelong passion, lent scholarly observation to its reputation. He was also the first to trace its history to the Hebrew Kabbalah (the Jewish book of mysticism) and ancient Hindu texts.

William G. Benham, author of *The Benham Book of Palmistry* (originally published as *The Laws of Scientific Hand Reading* in 1900), is considered the father of modern palmistry. One of the areas Benham was especially interested in was what the hand can reveal about an individual's health. More important, though, as Hank Stine points out in Newcastle's recent reissue of this book (1988), Benham "turned palmistry from an esoteric art into a codified science with its own laws and principles." Benham applied the rules of scientific experiment to palmistry, lending it much credence in the process.

More recently, there's been another resurgence of interest in palmistry. As more and more people try to fill the spiritual gap rational science has left in their lives, it's only natural that methods of self-discovery like palmistry, which, while scorned by some, served humankind well for thousands of years until they were abandoned by "rational" science, would begin to be re-examined.

How Does It Work?

Your doctor will be the first to tell you that your hand is a reflection of yourself. She'll look at your hand for signs of illness and health, both physical and mental. Like a palm reader, your doctor knows that, among other signs in the hand, areas of redness on the hand may indicate circulatory problems, while yellow may indicate disorders of the liver, and a pink hand indicates a healthy constitution. Chances are, she'll take a good look at your nails too: Are they ridged? Cupped? Blue? All these things can help her determine your health and well-being.

Now that the science fiction of cloning has become a reality, how palmistry works has become much easier for us to understand. Cloning is possible because the whole is represented in each cell, so that one cell can be replicated until the whole is duplicated. Palmistry is possible because you are represented in your hand. *No two hands are alike* because you—and your cells—are unique. The macrocosm is represented in the microcosm. *You* are imprinted in your hand.

Why Does It Work?

Palmistry works because your hand changes as you do. Try this test: The next time someone cuts you off on the freeway, take a look at the fleshy pad where your thumb joins the rest of your hand. Is it swollen and red? If getting cut off made you the least bit angry, it will be reflected in this place, called active Mars (more on the mounts of Mars in Chapter 17).

This is just one example of how your hand changes as you do. Larger changes—such as marriage, children, career moves, even new pets—will also appear as they occur. Interestingly, things that you do as a matter of routine will not necessarily appear on the hand. We'll discuss this in more detail in Chapter 3.

Hand-le with Care

When you do something routinely, it may well not appear in your active hand. For example, what's travel to a truck driver? It won't show up as many travel lines. Similarly, what's money to a bank teller? His money's going to show up in a different place than Bill Gates's.

You Can Learn to Read This Map

How did you learn to drive? Did your father, like Lisa's, take you out to deserted, snowy parking lots on Sunday afternoons to practice skid control? Did your mother white-knuckle you through traffic until you had the proficiency to get your first driver's license? Or did you sit through an eternity of proms-gone-awry films in driver education classes until responsibility was drilled into your skull like a mantra?

Whether you enjoyed them or not, each of those lessons is one of the many that must come together to make you a good driver. Learning palmistry is a lot like learning to drive: It's not enough to know where the gas and brake pedals are, or to understand that red means stop and green means go, to get you the keys to the Jeep.

Just as there are different lessons about driving you can learn from Mom, Dad, and your driver education teacher, there are different lessons you can learn about palmistry. And just as there are subtleties to driving that come only with experience, there are subtleties to understanding the hand. This book will give you both sides of the learning experience.

For example:

➤ Look twice

➤ Look at both hands

➤ Seek additional support from other signs

Oh, Say Can You See?

Beyond the basics you can learn from books like this one, you've got to establish a setting for a good palm reading as well. Four givens are essential to reading palms, and if you haven't got them naturally, you'll have to alter circumstances so they exist. They are:

1. Observation
2. Light
3. No distractions
4. Intuition

Let's take a closer look at each of these factors.

It takes good sight, good light, good concentration, and intuition to read a palm well.

Observation Is All

Observation is more than merely looking at hands: It's about your vision and its clarity; it's about seeing every line and the gradations of every lump and bump, the variations of every color and hue. Lisa learned this early in the writing of this book. "See that grid?" Robin said, pointing to a place on his mount of Venus. Lisa squinted and squinted, glasses on, glasses off. She couldn't see it. Robin got out a magnifying glass. Sure enough, there it was.

You've got to be able to see a palm to read it. Sounds simple, doesn't it? But until Lisa sat down with Robin, she had no idea just how little she was seeing. The major lines on a palm may be quite clear to you, but there are other markings that are just as important to who you are: squares, grids, triangles, and stars, to name but a few (more on these in Chapter 19). Some of these markings may be quite faint, but they're as much a part of the big picture as your life, head, and heart lines. If you can't see them, get thee to an optician!

Once you can make out everything clearly, it's time to hone those powers of observation. It's natural to filter out much of what you see in a day, but to read palms well, you've got to pay attention to everything. To test your powers of observation, we've provided a fine example of Van Gogh's work, *The Starry Night*, in the following photo.

10

What do you see when you look at this painting? Write your thoughts here.

_____

_____

_____

_____

_____

The Starry Night (1889). Oil on canvas. The Museum of Modern Art, New York by Vincent Van Gogh. Acquired through the Lillie P. Bliss Bequest. (Photograph © 1999 The Museum of Modern Art, New, York.)

What did you notice first in this painting? Most people are immediately drawn to the light of the moon in the upper right-hand corner. This is what's called the focal point of the painting, so that's natural. The other stars and the clouds are often what are noticed next. If you were to divide the painting horizontally, the sky would take up the top two thirds, so noting this is natural as well.

Now what else did you note? The tree in the lower right of the painting? The steeple of the church in the center? The houses, some with lights in their windows? The wheat fields? The hills? The mountains? Look at the painting again. What do you see that you didn't notice the first time you looked? Are you surprised at how much you missed? Look at it yet again. What do you see now? Note these things below.

Next, practice looking at something that you see every day, whether it's your kitchen counter or a particular street corner. Look for things that you don't ordinarily notice about this and make a note of them. Then look beyond those details and note what else you see.

Observation is about turning off the "filters" we use to block out what seems nonessential in our day-to-day lives. Observation is about seeing more than the moon and stars in Van Gogh's painting, or the stop sign at your street corner. Observation is one of the four keys to reading palms well. Practice your powers of observation and soon you'll be seeing all sorts of things you hadn't noticed before—including markings in your palm.

You Light Up My Life

You may see 20/20, but if the light isn't right, you'll be whistling in the dark. Good light is essential to reading palms well. You'd be amazed at how much of the light we live with every day is inadequate when it comes to palmistry. Any light that casts shadows, including natural sunlight, is less than ideal. Light that affects coloration won't work either, as color is an important aspect of what the palm reveals. Overhead fixtures can diffuse light rather than concentrate it, and candlelight, while perfect for setting a mood, does little to help a reader see.

So what's a palm reader to do? Invest in a good, direct light source. This can be a $9.99 desktop lamp, provided it will be focused directly on the subject's hand. The best light Robin has found is a small halogen bulb that can be used in a variety of fixtures. For the purposes of palmistry, if you can find a small halogen lamp that you can hold in one hand, you'll be able to take your show on the road, too.

Staying in Focus

Well, you're ready to look carefully and you've got the right light. What else do you need to read palms well? You need to be able to concentrate. We all know how difficult it is to perform a task—from writing that term paper for school to finishing that budget for the quarterly meeting at the office to baking that cross-lattice, apple-pear pie—if you can't concentrate. You wouldn't want to take a final exam in a photocopier room, would you? When reading palms, you'll want to choose a quiet place with a minimum of visual or auditory distractions. So, you'll want to observe the hand closely, see it well under good lighting, and *concentrate!* The next step, intuition, involves putting it all together.

Using Your Intuition

Intuition, according to *Webster's New World Dictionary*, is "the direct knowing or learning of something without the conscious use of reasoning" (3d ed., p. 709). If you're intuitive, you won't need a dictionary to tell you what it is—because it's got nothing to do with words. We like to think of it as a way of knowing and understanding that can't be explained in a rational, scientific way (yet). The word itself comes from the Latin, *intueri*, which means "to see within." Intuition involves knowing without thinking, a direct line from the knowledge to you. Among the words Robin likes to use for intuition are "seeing," "knowing," "gestalt," and "empathetic." One of the things about intuition is that describing it seems to defy language—because it's felt in a nonlinguistic way.

When it comes to reading palms, the lessons we can give you here will take you only so far. One day, you'll be faced with a hand that, according to this and other books, says, "calm and easygoing," while your intuition is saying, "Still waters run deep." Or the fingers say, "Lock away your valuables," and your intuition says, "Trust this person." Whom or what can you trust when this happens? Trust your intuition. It's a big part of being a good reader. Check out *The Complete Idiot's Guide to Being Psychic* for more on tapping into your own psychic intuition.

Handy Words to Know

Intuition is a way of knowing something without a conscious thought process.

Helping Hands

We're all born with intuitive powers, but few of us develop or use them. Like any skill, the more you practice your intuition, the better you'll become at using it. You can practice your intuition by beginning to listen to your "inner voice" or your "gut instincts." These are but two of intuition's many guises. We recommend you keep a journal for your inner voice—it's got much to tell you.

The Five Questions Robin Is Asked the Most

When Robin looks at a hand for the first time, something always strikes him about that hand—and consequently, about that person. It may be a prominent lunar mount (stressed creativity) or a crooked Mercury finger (crooked communication). Sometimes passive Mars is screaming out for vengeance; sometimes Apollo's in the throes of redecorating. (We'll be discussing all these things in upcoming chapters.) But often, Robin doesn't ever get to tell the person these things because most people come to Robin with questions already in hand.

Now, there's nothing wrong with this. Most people tend to think of palmistry as a way of seeing the future, and the questions they ask reflect this. But palmistry's real value lies in its ability to see the past, present, and future—all in one tidy package. Still, we understand that you want to know the answers to the following five questions. It's only human. So we thought we'd give you the questions many people ask Robin, and then, a better way of asking them—of yourself or of a palm reader.

1. Will I be rich?
2. Will I find job/career success?
3. Will I have a happy family life (or other questions about the family)?
4. Am I healthy?
5. WILL I FIND TRUE LOVE?

1 & 2. We're both struck by the fact that these two questions are almost never asked together. It's as if it doesn't occur to people that they can find wealth and happiness in their careers. Or, as if the lottery or Uncle Otto's will are the only ways of getting rich. If you want to be "rich," the best way remains working at a job—and living a life—you truly love. To paraphrase Joseph Campbell, "Follow your bliss, and the money will follow." What does "rich" mean to you, in the end? Robin thinks if your car starts—and it's paid for—you're on your way to achieving wealth. (By the way, if you truly want to know if you're ever going to win the lottery, ask the question in just that way. Lottery winnings do appear in the palm!)

3 & 5. Here's another separation we find a bit curious. Are "true love" and "a happy family life" mutually exclusive? We hope not. It's far better to use your hand as a map to look at your current family situation and determine where and why problems may be occurring. If money burns a hole in your pocket and your spouse is a cautious spender, for example, there's naturally going to be some conflict, but it doesn't have to stand in the way of a happy family life or true love. If, on the other hand, your boyfriend insists he's going to leave his wife just as soon as her psychiatrist says it's safe, maybe you're looking for love in the wrong place.

Ultimately, how happy and loving your relationships are appears in your hands in more ways than one. If you're single, you'll find compatible people in places where you do the things you enjoy doing already. And if you're in a relationship, you know that true love requires as much work as it does candlelight and sweet nothings.

Your hand will show your capabilities for both giving and receiving love, but remember: *Your hand is a map that moves.* You can learn to give more or receive more, or both, once you have the knowledge with which to work.

4. Our health, on the other hand, is something in which we all have a vested interest. After all, everything else more or less depends on it. Yes, the hand can show the potential for major and minor health problems, and yes, it's important to note these so you can take preventative action. But why not ask the question this way in the first place: "What ways are best for me to stay healthy and fit?" For some, this will be high carbs and running; for others, no yeast and meditation. These answers are in your hand—and well worth knowing.

What Your Hands Can Tell You—And What You Can't See

Here's one of the givens of palmistry: You won't see in your hand what you can't see in yourself. In other words, your own hand will tell you only what you want to hear. For this reason, it's never a good idea to read your own palm, although for practice, your own palm is probably the best map you have, since you've got, to some degree, an inside line on its owner.

Hand-le with Care

Sure, you're your own most accessible subject. But you'll never see yourself entirely clearly, and that goes for your palm, too. Consider this a warning, but don't let it stop you from being your own guinea pig.

It takes discipline and detachment to see what's outside your own emotional scope. It isn't impossible to practice these things, but it may be easier to ask another observer for his or her blunt appraisal of your observations of yourself.

Your hand, read by a practiced reader other than yourself, can reveal your deepest secrets to you. So, while it took Robin 10 years to realize that he didn't have square fingers (they're quite conic, or cone-shaped), if he'd listened to another reader sooner, he might have learned a lot more about himself a lot sooner as well. "No!" he said. "I'm not argumentative!"

The moral of the story: Unless you're really good at getting outside yourself (we haven't met that person yet), your own hand's only going to tell you what you want to hear. Let go and hand it over to an objective palm reader who can clue you in on the "real" you.

The Least You Need to Know

➤ Your hand is a map that moves.

➤ Palmistry is as ancient as humanity itself.

➤ Good light, good sight, good concentration, and intuition are the keys to good palm reading.

➤ Unless you're really good at getting outside yourself, your own hand will only tell you what you want to hear. An objective palm reader may do better at revealing your deepest self to you!

Chapter 2

Every Hand Tells a Story

In This Chapter

➤ Finding yourself in your hand

➤ Quiz: How well do you know yourself?

➤ Oh, the stories your hand can tell

➤ Myth and archetype in your hand

The next time you have a bad headache, before you grab that aspirin, take a look at your hands. If you look closely, you'll see a small red, blue, or black dot on the pad just below the first finger of your active hand (your active hand is your right, if you're right-handed; your left, if you're left-handed). In palmistry, this pad is called the mount of Jupiter, and it rules the head, which is why that small dot appears just there. After you take the aspirin and the headache goes away, that small dot will be gone!

Now, don't go knocking yourself in the head to test the truth of this. Just remember to check the next time you feel that telltale throbbing. That small dot is just one example of how what appears in your hand reflects your larger self.

The Hand Is a Microcosm of the Self

As you learned in Chapter 1, the study of the relationship between the hand and the self has a long history. Palmists like Robin know that with every palm they see, more about the hand/self connection is revealed. Until he met a bank robber, for example, Robin had never seen an aggressive thief's hand (Robin meets all kinds of people...). Until he looked at the hand of a paraplegic, he hadn't really studied how the body's parts are—and aren't—reflected in the hand.

Like Robin, the more you study palms, the more you'll come to see how the hand is a microcosm of the self. In fact, we want you to think of the hand as the microcosm and the self as the macrocosm: Everything you've done, everything you may do, everyone you know, and everyone you may know—all this is reflected on your hand. The shape of your hand, for example, can tell an experienced palm reader a wealth of information about your character, while your fingers contain secrets you may be keeping from even yourself.

Once you know which areas of your self are reflected where in your hand, you can begin to use those keys to open doors you hadn't even known existed. Look at the hand in the following figure. We've marked a few of those keys for you. Then look at your own hand and identify the same areas.

The hand holds the keys to many doors of the self.

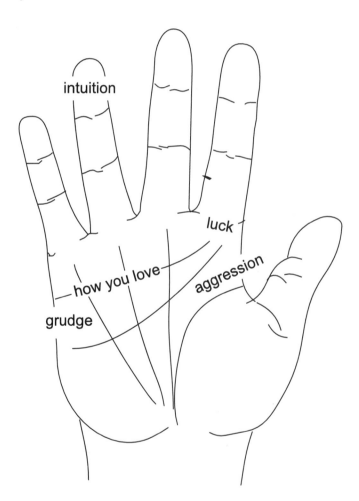

Know Thyself

As the hand, so goes the self. Palmistry, like other esoteric sciences such as astrology, numerology, and the tarot, seeks to help each of us to know ourselves. Astrology uses the birth chart as a metaphor for the individual; numerology explores our relationship to the numbers in our lives; the tarot provides a symbolic tool for uncovering answers we may be hiding from ourselves; and palmistry provides a key for using the hand to reveal our personal mysteries. Palmistry's ability to help you understand yourself allows you to know who you are so you can have the awareness of all your potentials.

Helping Hands

Don't expect to find everything you want to know the first time you look at a hand. Like any science, palmistry takes time, study, and patience to master. It's enough at first to understand that everything about you and around you is reflected in your hand. Soon enough, you'll begin to learn just what's reflected where.

How Well Do You Know Yourself?: A Handy Quiz

Think you know yourself pretty well? If your hand revealed someone who was sometimes argumentative, would you argue with the person who read it that it just wasn't so? Before you begin to read palms, it's important to take a look at what you know about yourself—and what you don't. Just for fun, we've devised a quiz to help you do just that. Pick one answer that best describes you.

1. You walk into a party and realize that you don't know a soul there. You

   (a) walk up to the first person you see and introduce yourself.

   (b) locate and head for the bar.

   (c) stand at the door for a few minutes, then leave.

   (d) would never go to a party by yourself.

2. There are four messages on your answering machine. Whom do you call first?

   (a) your boss about that project

   (b) your mother about that recipe

   (c) your best friend about nothing

   (d) that pesky credit bureau about your Visa bill

3. At the office Christmas party, the person who drew your name has given you *The Complete Idiot's Guide to Palmistry*. You

   (a) immediately open it and begin reading it aloud.

   (b) thank her and put it aside.

   (c) hide it in your desk drawer and sneak looks at it every chance you get.

   (d) take it home so you can read it on your own time.

4. You and your lover see an expensive ring in a store window. Your lover obviously loves it. You

    (a) go into the store immediately and buy it.

    (b) go into the store the next day and buy it.

    (c) commiserate over its cost and walk away.

    (d) do nothing.

5. Your partner gives you the pricey ring you admired together in a store window. You

    (a) express the love and gratitude your lover deserves.

    (b) insist it costs too much and take it back.

    (c) wonder what your partner's trying to hide by giving it to you.

    (d) would never expect such a gesture from your partner.

6. It's 5:30 p.m., and from the look of traffic, you won't be home for another half hour. Finally, your lane begins to move while the next lane remains at a standstill. The person in the car next to you signals to get in front of you. You

    (a) wave the person in.

    (b) keep just little enough space between you and the car in front of you that a car can't get in.

    (c) pretend you don't see the person next to you.

    (d) start to let the car in, then lean on your horn and show the person your middle finger.

7. Your interview for a job for which you're well qualified went very well. You

    (a) know you'll get the job.

    (b) know you won't get the job.

    (c) send a thank you note to the interviewer.

    (d) quit your current job.

8. Another person in your office gets the promotion and raise you were hoping for. She

    (a) deserved it.

    (b) got lucky.

    (c) must be sleeping with the boss.

    (d) worked a lot more overtime than you did, if you're honest about it.

9. Now here's that wallet with $200 that appears in all quizzes like this. What do you do when you find it?

    (a) look inside for a name and number so you can call and return it.

    (b) call, and ask about the reward.

    (c) don't call at all.

    (d) take a $20, then call.

10. You tell your brother you know the best way to get to the wedding, even though he says he knows the best way. Within five minutes, you're hopelessly lost. You

    (a) stop and ask for directions.

    (b) tell your brother you were wrong and ask for his directions.

    (c) keep going and grit your teeth.

    (d) miss the wedding because you're driving in circles.

This quiz doesn't have a score. What it does have is adjectives, which you're going to write down to describe yourself. Use the following key to make your list of adjectives.

Question 1 asks if you're an introvert or an extrovert. Find the letter you selected and then write your adjective here: _____

(a) extrovert

(b) introvert

(c) introvert

(d) introvert

Question 2 asks if you're a doer or a procrastinator. Find the letter you selected and then write your adjective here: _____

(a) doer

(b) procrastinator

(c) procrastinator

(d) doer

Question 3 shows how you feel about New Age ideas. Find the letter you selected and then write your adjective here: _____

(a) skeptic

(b) skeptic

(c) believer

(d) believer

Question 4 addresses how good you are at giving love. Find the letter you selected and then write your adjective here: _____

(a) giver

(b) giver

(c) nongiver

(d) nongiver

Question 5 wants to know if you're good at taking love. Find the letter you selected and then write your adjective here: _____

(a) accepting

(b) codependent

(c) suspicious

(d) cynical

Question 6 examines how you deal with tense situations. Find the letter you selected and then write your adjective here: _____

(a) calm

(b) passive-aggressive

(c) angry

(d) passive-aggressive

Question 7 reveals whether you're an optimist or a pessimist. Find the letter you selected and then write your adjective here: _____

(a) optimist

(b) pessimist

(c) optimist

(d) overoptimistic

Question 8 wants to know whether you believe in luck or hard work. Find the letter you selected and then write your adjective here: _____

(a) believe in luck

(b) believe in hard work

(c) believe in luck

(d) believe in hard work

Question 9 examines your honesty. Find the letter you selected and then write your adjective here: _____

(a) honest

(b) honest

(c) honesty is not your strong point

(d) untrustworthy

Lastly, **question 10** asks whether you're stubborn or flexible. Find the letter you selected and then write your adjective here: _____

(a) flexible

(b) flexible

(c) stubborn

(d) stubborn

Now look at your list of adjectives. Which do you think describe you well? Which do you know are not among your characteristics at all? If you know yourself, all of the adjectives should feel right to you. If you don't, some of them will make you uncomfortable. Go back to those questions and see if you answered them honestly (go on—no one's looking).

If you believe you answered honestly, and yet your adjectives don't feel right to you, you may not like everything your palm has to say about you. Because, among other things, your palm will reveal how you behave in these very areas. Your thumb, for example, can tell much about your flexibility, while the straightness of your little (Mercury) finger can reveal whether you're inclined to tell those little white lies.

We Are the Stories We Tell

What do you say the first time you're introduced to someone? Most people say their name and their occupation, and sometimes, where they're from. Robin, for example, says, "I'm Robin, a psychic and a palm reader." Of course, people always respond, "No, really. What do you do?"

We all use this shorthand to introduce ourselves. And, if the conversation continues, we'll tell stories about ourselves as well. Those stories, the ones we choose to tell, reveal a great deal about us. In the same way, our palms tell the stories we choose to tell—because we're living them.

How the Stories You Tell Reveal More Than You Realize

Do you find yourself telling the same story over and over again in different situations? If you've recently come back from a trip, you may tell everyone you see about how patiently the people in London stood in line for buses, or how friendly and helpful the people in Thailand were—even though they didn't speak English.

The stories you choose to tell are, like your hands, a way of defining yourself. In fact, it's natural to define yourself in this way, and it's interesting to explore just what story you're choosing to tell at any particular time because that story reveals a great deal about you.

If, for example, you've most recently been entertaining friends and coworkers with tales about your African safari, you're also telling them that you're a person who likes adventurous travel. Or maybe you're telling the story about how you beat city hall—a story like that might reveal that you're not afraid to tackle bureaucracies when you know you're right.

In a similar way, your hands tell a great deal about you, too. The shape of a hand alone can reveal a great deal to an experienced palm reader, and we'll discuss this in more detail in the next chapter. But even with no experience reading palms, you can already tell a great deal about someone by that person's hand. To test your knowledge, write down a word or two to describe the nature of each person whose hand has one of the following characteristics:

Cold: _____

Blistered: _____

Chewed fingernails: _____

Long fingers: _____

Clammy: _____

What did you say about cold hands? If your hands are always cold, like Lisa's, you may have written something more positive, such as, "warm heart." If your hands are always warm, you may have a different reaction to cold ones, such as "reserved" or "icy." All of these words have some basis in fact, and are part of how a palm reader learns about a person.

The fact is, it's easier for others to read us than it is to read ourselves. That's because we reveal ourselves to others in many ways: through our gestures, through our choice of words, and through our stories—both those we tell and those our hands tell. Many of our identifying actions and habits are second nature to us; we're not always consciously aware of the messages we send out to others about who we are. But to an objective observer, those actions and habits become the measure of the woman, or man! Most likely, too, we've already got an idea of who we are—and it may not exactly match the facts. And here's where we each begin a journey of self-exploration. When it comes to our hands, we can, at least to some degree, read ourselves—especially if we're willing to open ourselves to what we see there. But, as we mentioned in the previous chapter, you won't see in your hand what you can't see in yourself.

How Your Hand Tells Your Story

Your hand tells your story because each area of the hand reflects an area of the self. And when we say area of the self, we mean every single aspect of a person. In your hand you'll find your strength and doing, pain and tears, comings and goings. There are areas in the hand to tell about your relationships, and others where you'll find your view of the world and whether you're religious. Your pets are there, and your taste in furniture and books. There's nothing in your life, in other words, that can't be found in your hand!

By studying which areas of the hand are about which areas of the self, a palm reader reads the story of you. Just as the letters on this page represent words that you can translate into ideas, the nature of your hand can be translated into a story about you. Learning to read a palm is a lot like learning how to put letters together. All stories, after all, are the sum of their parts.

The following graphic shows some of the ways your hand tells your story. We'll be coming back to this picture again and again, so for now, just notice how every area of your life is represented here.

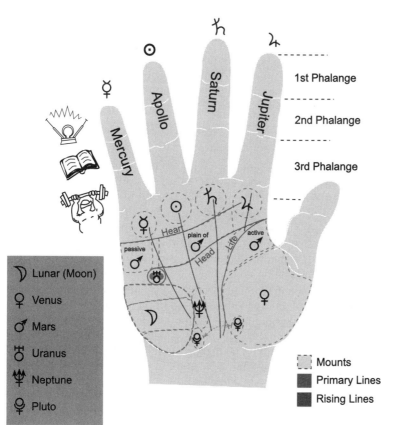

How your hand tells your story.

Why We Tell Stories—and How Stories Work

People have been telling stories as long as they've been reading palms, which is to say, a very, very long time. The reasons for telling stories haven't changed much in all that time, either: We tell stories to explain, to elucidate, to educate, and to entertain. Stories are told as answers to questions, some easily answered, some not so easily. Here are some examples:

To explain:

➤ Why were you late for class?

➤ How did the skunk get its stripe?

➤ Which mount on my palm reveals my ambition?

To elucidate:

➤ Why did the apple fall from the tree?

➤ What's this call to Timbuktu on the phone bill?

➤ How can I tell my head line on my palm from my heart line?

To educate:

➤ Why was the Civil War fought?

➤ Who were your ancestors?

➤ What do my fingers reveal about me?

To entertain:

➤ What happens if a couple whose families are feuding falls in love?

➤ Why did the chicken cross the road?

➤ What's another good reason to learn to read palms?

Stories work because they use narrative to explain, elucidate, educate, or entertain. The narrative can be as simple as "This happened, then that happened," or as complicated as James Joyce's *Ulysses*; it's a way of making sense of things. For example, a narrative answer to the question, "Why were you late for school?" might begin, "Well, first the bus was late so I decided to walk." Or a narrative answer to the question, "How did the skunk get its stripe?" might be a Pepe LePew cartoon. In the same way, when a palm is read, a narrative is created telling its story.

What Do Archetype and Myth Have to Do with Your Hand?

We all have certain stories in common, and when these stories have universal themes they are called *myths*. A myth is a story that provides a way of understanding something that would otherwise be difficult to understand. Myths often explain the unexplainable, such as certain aspects of human nature, why porcupines have quills or beavers have flat tails, or why people die.

Handy Words to Know

An **archetype** is a pattern of both the individual and collective psyches with a universal meaning, such as "hero" or "villain." A **myth** is a story that provides a way of understanding something that would otherwise be difficult to understand.

Every society has its myths, including our own. Some of the myths of the United States include George Washington cutting down that cherry tree, and Abe Lincoln's long walk to return a library book before it was overdue. Each of these stories is a narrative we use to explain certain givens about our society. As a society, for example, we value honesty over evasion, as evidenced by the lesson of both these myths.

When their stories are about more universal themes, such as good and evil, myths are said to contain *archetypes* of either character or motif. According to psychoanalysis pioneer Carl Jung (1875–1961), archetypes are patterns of the individual and collective psyche with universal meaning. A modern example of archetypal characters can be found in the *Star Wars* series, with its clearly defined heroes, villains, magicians, and mentors.

A Myth Is Not a Lie

The first thing you need to understand about myths is that they're not lies. By way of illustration, we'd like to point out certain myths that Westerners more or less take for granted, namely, the stories in the Bible.

Now before you get your hackles up, read what we just said again: A myth is not a lie. A myth is a story told to help people understand what would otherwise be difficult. Taken in this light, it's easy to see the Bible as myth: a way of helping humans understand the complicated.

If any one man can be said to be responsible for our new understanding of the myth in the 20th century, it would be Joseph Campbell (1904–1987). In a 1980s PBS series with Bill Moyers called *The Power of Myth*, Campbell outlined his life's work with comparative mythology. Campbell showed how certain mythological motifs can be found in all societies, such as a:

We Gotta Hand It to You

Sometime around the Renaissance, the meaning of the word "myth" became synonymous with the word "lie." Think about this for a moment and you'll see why the shift occurred: Science, with its rational explanations, sought to re-create the defining narrative, and this could be successfully achieved only if the old narratives were exposed as false. Because the old narratives—from the Bible to Greek mythology to aboriginal origin stories—were myths, their lack of proof was proof of their falseness, according to scientific principles. Unfortunately, out went the baby—spirituality—with the bath water—myth, leaving the spiritual vacuum we're trying to fill at the end of this millennium.

➤ Creation myth

➤ Fall from grace myth

➤ Flood or deluge myth

➤ Star-crossed lovers myth

Campbell also discussed a concept he called "The Hero's Journey," in which a hero (or you!) follows a series of steps to achieve a goal. These steps include:

➤ The call

➤ The initial refusal

➤ The help of a wise advisor

➤ The entrance to the "other world"

➤ Meeting the enemy

➤ Destroying the enemy

➤ Returning victorious to one's home

Myth is important to understand within the context of palmistry because it helps us to understand how our stories connect with the stories of others. If you're less than lucky in love, for example, myth can help you see that you're not alone, that stories have been told throughout the world throughout the ages. We think story and myth are important aspects of the self, and we'll be including some of each as we tell you the stories of your own hand.

An Archetype Is Not a New Kind of Bridge

The scientific definition of archetype, patterns of the individual and collective psyche with universal meaning, may leave you in the dark, so we'd like to give you some examples to better understand this important concept. As we mentioned earlier, Jung pioneered the concept of archetypes, and was the first to label the various archetypal motifs we can find in everything from myths, to dreams, to the tarot, to everyday life. These include:

➤ The hero or heroine

➤ The villain

➤ The trickster

➤ The wise old man

➤ The innocent

➤ The faithful friend

Now, our friends in Hollywood are very aware of how a motif that employs these archetypes will make a powerful connection with an audience, and there are screenwriting books that explain both the hero's journey, and how each of these archetypes fit into this journey. The *Star Wars* series and *The Wizard of Oz* are two easy examples you can use to see how this works. But you can apply these ideas to almost any film. Try *Good Will Hunting* or *Silence of the Lambs*, or any other film with which you are familiar.

But you don't have to take our word for it. Use the following spaces to record how a film of your choice fits into the motif of the hero's journey and how its characters fulfill basic archetypes. Think about what in the film represents "the call," and who is "the faithful friend." Comedy or drama, sci-fi or romance, any movie will help you see how myth and archetype work.

Film: _____

The hero's journey: _____

The call: _____

The initial refusal: _____

The help of a wise advisor: _____

The entrance to the "other world": _____

Meeting the enemy: _____

Destroying the enemy: _____

Returning victorious to one's home: _____

The Archetypes:

The Hero: _____

The Heroine: _____

The Villain: _____

The Trickster: _____

The Wise Old Man: _____

The Innocent: _____

The Faithful Friend: _____

Now that you've seen how Hollywood filmmakers use myth and archetype, we'll tell you *why* they do: because these universal motifs and characters connect with each and every one of us individually. If you've ever had to make a tough decision about anything, chances are you've gone through these steps and enlisted the help or confronted the opposition of this cast of characters.

The story in your hand can't help but employ myth and archetype because myth and archetype are as much a part of you as your hands themselves.

Telling Stories: A Handy Exercise

Throughout this chapter, we've been discussing how the stories you tell can reveal to others what you want them to know about you. Now that you have a better idea of how this works, what story do you think you would tell to someone you'd just met? Use the space below to write what you would say.

_____

_____

_____

_____

_____

Like your stories, your hand is a microcosm of who you are. By reading it, we can reveal our stories to ourselves.

The Least You Need to Know

➤ The hand is a microcosm of the self.

➤ We tell stories to reveal ourselves to others.

➤ We can, with practice, use the hand to reveal ourselves to ourselves.

➤ Archetype and myth are two aspects of humanity's universal stories.

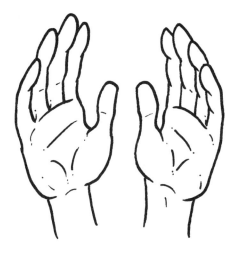

Look, Ma— Two Hands!

Enough about universal stories—we know you want to learn how to read the story of *your* hand. In Part 2, we'll be taking in-depth looks at each area of the hand: the fingers, the lines, the mounts, and your hand's own special geometry. Before we do that, though, we want to introduce you to the entire hand: its size, shape, color, and texture.

The First Things to Look at When Reading Palms

Whether or not you're an experienced palm reader like Robin, something's going to jump out at you about every hand you look at. In some hands, it may be the length of the fingers, while in others you may be struck by the depth of the lines in the hand. Whatever you see first, make a note of it either mentally or in a notebook you keep for just that purpose.

It's good to have a system for reading palms so you don't miss anything. The system will vary from reader to reader, but, because Robin is our expert here, we're going to share the order in which he reads a palm.

Robin's Rules of Order

1. Thumb, then other fingers, including shape, direction (bend), nails

2. The head, heart, and life lines, especially how they lie, color, and texture

3. Other lines of significance and what's strong

4. The mounts: what predominates in strength and talents

5. Both hands: what's strong in the secondary suit

6. Timing: the subject's present age and how soon it is to the next birthday

7. Color, texture, and size

Helping Hands

Robin always takes a good look at the head line to determine how smart his client is. This is important because it determines the way he's going to talk to the client, and how much explaining he'll need to do. Robin says he can tell a client's IQ from her or his palm. In unscientific tests at various coffee places around Albuquerque, where Robin and Lisa met while writing this book, the results were quite impressive.

Hand-le with Care

Perhaps this should be added to Robin's Rules of Order: **Be kind**. You're not going to impress anyone—or communicate with them successfully—by being cruel or insensitive. There are ways of phrasing everything positively, and it's in both your and your client's best interests to do so. Besides, there's no doubt that your own hand has a few traces of imperfection, too. So put your observations in a good light—in more ways than one.

It Takes Two Hands

The next question is naturally, "Which hand do I look at?" The answer is, "Both." As we mentioned briefly in Chapter 2, quick changes will appear in your *active hand* (or dominant hand), which is your right if you're right-handed and left if you're left-handed. But in order to do a thorough reading, both hands should be looked at carefully.

Why? Because your *inactive hand* (or passive hand) contains your destiny or potential, and your active hand the imposition of your will and environment on that destiny. Does this mean your inactive hand doesn't change? No. Much of your destiny changes as you do: If you think of each decision you make as a fork in a road, every fork leads you off in a new direction in which there will be more forks. Every time you make a choice, the possibilities for your destiny change as well.

What if a person's ambidextrous? We hasten to say that true ambidexterity is very, very rare, though many may claim it. There are a number of ways to determine the dominant hand—dowsing with a pendulum, or using your own hand to sense the other's energy, for example. (Dowsing is a method of finding something hidden using a special tool. One can dowse for water, for example, by using a divining rod.)

Like all dowsing tools, a pendulum uses a kind of magnetic energy to make its determination, and will be naturally pulled to the dominant hand. In a similar way, if you're one of those people who can feel another's energy through your own fingers (whether via your active or passive hand), you can use this sense to find the dominant hand as well.

When neither of these methods is available, or if you're truly in doubt, go with the hand the client writes with—and, with the true ambidextrous person, read both hands simultaneously, aspect by aspect.

Measuring Tools: Calipers and Rulers

An experienced palm reader won't need to measure your hand, because her years of experience mean she can eyeball it and know its geometry at once. For those of you less experienced, though, calipers and rulers are important tools for learning how everything from lengths to angles matter when you're reading a palm. If you want to read palms well, it's worth your while to invest in these measuring tools, such as a jeweler's caliper for reading angles, and a ruler. Check for calipers at a jewelry supply or

Handy Words to Know

Your **active (or dominant) hand** is the hand you use to write longhand, stir the soup, hold the phone, punch someone's lights out, or honk your horn: your right, if you're right-handed; your left, if you're left-handed. Your **inactive (or passive) hand** would be the other hand.

We Gotta Hand It to You

Sometimes you'll find someone whose passive hand has deeper and more concise lines than those appearing in his dominant hand. What does this mean? It means that you're holding the hand of a "weekend warrior," someone whose avocation is his or her passion. This can be the systems analyst who plays jazz bass on weekends, or the doctor who heads straight to her dahlias as soon as she gets home. The key here is passion, and if the passion is directed toward something other than the career and its "rational" choices, you'll find it reflected in a dominant passive hand.

Handy Words to Know

Each finger is divided into three **phalanges**, the sections created by the finger's joints. The first phalange, the one with the nail, represents the intuitive, the second the mental, and the third the material.

art supply store. The more palms you look at, the less you'll need these tools, but they're useful at the start.

As we talk about each distinct area of the palm throughout this book, we'll cover its particular proportions. For example, which *phalange* of each finger is longest proportionally determines what styles and strengths you bring to each finger's area of your life (we'll discuss this more in the next chapter). Similarly, the various spaces between fingers, angles of lines, and the height of mounds reveal emphasis or lack of emphasis in those areas.

Some tools of the palmistry trade: the caliper and ruler.

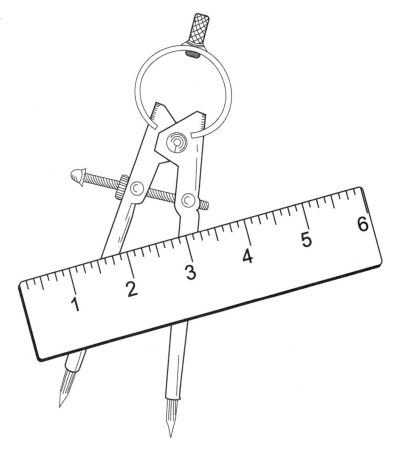

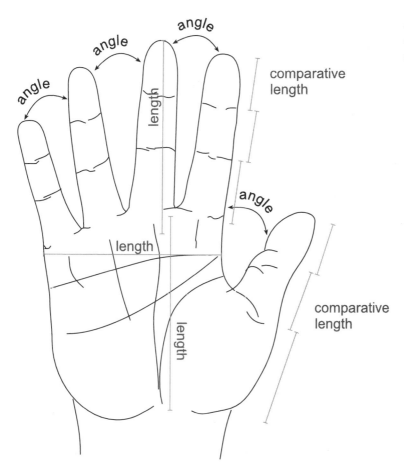

Measuring lengths and angles is an important aspect of reading a palm.

Ch-ch-ch-changes: A Story

Hands change at different rates of speed, but the fastest changing hand Robin ever read was that of a widow with a psychic hand (a hand shape we'll be discussing in a few pages). Her life was in such great transition that her palm changed *as he was reading it!* As she made the decision to leave her weaving and fabric arts behind and pursue writing as her new career, the lines on her Apollo mount (the area of creativity) disappeared, and lines on her Mercury and Lunar mounts (areas of communication and imagination) strengthened. (See Chapters 16 and 18 for our discussion of these mounts.) We hasten to add that this is *highly unusual*, but it does serve to illustrate that hands change at different rates of speed.

Some of the rapid changes you'll find recorded in the hand include rage, acquisition, and desire. Humor will be found in the hand, as will sorrow. Good moods, bad moods, good days, bad days—all of these show concurrent changes in the hand.

Another example: A librarian Robin knew had been working on her dissertation for years. But suddenly, in the weeks immediately after her dissertation had been accepted—but before she received her Ph.D.—her line of success (the Saturn line, which we'll explore in Chapter 14) grew over half an inch!

The Shapes of Hands

Personality classification by hand shape used to be a given of palmistry, but, like just about everything else these days, it's now understood that personality can never be quite so cut and dried. Robin, in fact, gives hand shape a relatively low ranking on his list of important things to look for (you'll note it doesn't even appear on Robin's Rules of Order we listed earlier). Nonetheless, the shape of the hand is one of the first impressions you'll receive of the person whose palm you are about to read. As such, we feel it's important to at least cover the basics of this aspect of palmistry.

According to traditional palmistry, hands come in one of seven shapes, each depicting a specific personality type. The classification system we outline in the following table comes directly from d'Arpentigny, whom we mentioned in Chapter 1. While we feel the personality characteristics we've listed for each hand are far too reductive (limited in scope), we're showing them here for convenience, and for fun:

Type of Hand	Traditional Personality Characteristics
Elementary	Nature-loving, hands-on, physical, plodding
Practical	Pragmatic, patient, mobile, active, persevering
Spatulate	Confident, competent, can-do
Conic	Imaginative, creative, sometimes impractical, the dilettante, sometimes lazy physically
Philosophical	Intellectual, cultural, extroverted, extravagant, mentally motivated to be physical
Psychic	Spiritual, mystic, contemplative, idealistic, seldom physically strong
Mixed	The odd duck, the mosaic, not consistent

The truth is, hardly anyone has a hand that's entirely elementary or singularly psychic. In fact, when you look at other palmistry books, you may be hard-pressed to figure out which hand is yours. For that reason, our drawings are going to exaggerate the specific characteristics of each hand shape so that you can see which of that shape's qualities your own hand has. We'll bet your hand, like most Americans', is mostly conic or mixed, but let's take each hand separately.

The Elementary Hand

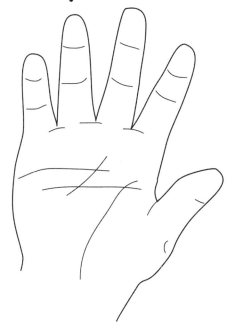

The elementary hand.

Characteristics

Hand shape: Large, somewhat club-like

Fingers: Short and stubby, fingernail wider than long, square tips

Palm: Rough-textured like a slab of wood

Appearance: Coarse

Lines: Very few clear ones, generally straight, not often long, except life line

Keywords

Earthy

Hard-working

Nature-loving

Tireless

Stubborn

Astrological sign: Taurus

Some books, such as Cheiro's *Language of the Hand*, actually call this the lowest type of hand. This reflects 19th century class distinctions, where those who worked with their hands were considered lower than those who worked with their minds. We call it snobbishness. And it ain't necessarily so.

True, the elementary hand, with its short fingers with square tips and solid palm, is the hand of someone who works with his or her hands. But today we know you've got to be as smart to work with your hands as to teach at the university (in some ways, smarter). If you're someone who works outside, likes to weed your garden, tinker with your car, or refinish your furniture, you've probably got some elements of the elementary hand.

People with elementary hands tend to like routine rather than change, and they can be stubborn if you try to change their habits or their minds. But they're also strong, reliable workers, and they have a way with everything from your pets to your garden. It's here you'll find the truck driver, the miner, the gardener, and the plumber, as well as the lapidarist (an expert in cutting and engraving precious stones) and the kennel master.

The Practical Hand

The practical hand.

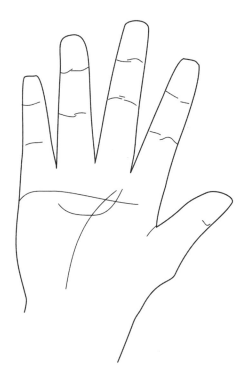

Characteristics

Hand shape: Square

Fingers: Short and square—or not, with square tips

Palm: Square to slightly long

Appearance: Smooth

Lines: Deep and directed (not random)

Keywords

Consistent

Down-to-earth

Patient

Honest

Precise

Decisive

Astrological signs: Capricorn, Virgo, some Aries

If you want a good organizer, you need look no further than someone with a practical hand. Here you'll often find architects and teachers, people, in other words, who can both make plans and build on them. They're even-tempered, pragmatic, and reliable—and usually achieve their goals.

This is also often the hand of the successful businessperson—who'll still have a life outside the office. That's because this hand reflects a balanced, practical nature, and the energy to see a project from start to finish. When you see a practical hand, be assured that this is a person on whom you can depend. Still, while the practical hand is somewhat creative, it's not particularly inventive. Do you see the difference?

The practical hand indicates someone who'll set realistic goals but at the same time is somewhat independent. Not neurotically so—his or her head line won't be too long. Here you'll find the nurse, the teacher, the middle manager—people who are good at what they do.

The Spatulate Hand

The spatulate hand.

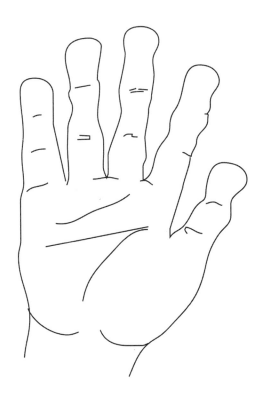

Characteristics

Hand shape: Square, sometimes broader at the base of fingers, occasionally wider than long

Fingers: Reasonably long, often knotty joints and flattened tips

Palm: Reasonably thick

Appearance: Medium-framed (not frail)

Lines: Deep and well cut

Keywords

Social, well-liked

Confident

Competent

Mechanical

A three-dimensional visualizer

Astrological signs: Sagittarius, Gemini, Capricorn

Here's the person who can fix anything (here's Lisa's husband Bob), the can-do, competent, confident guy or gal who can pick up a shovel or put out the fires on a daily basis (now Lisa's quoting from Bob's resume). Not only is the spatulate hand the one you'll find on construction managers like Bob, but it's also the hand of the natural musician—also like Bob, who's a hell of a guitar player.

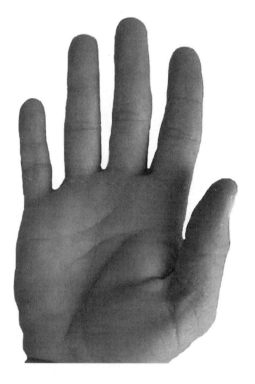

Here's Bob's hand, a good example of a spatulate hand.

As long as we've got a specific model in mind here, let's give some specific examples of what he's like. When you give Bob directions, he'll be drawing a map as you give them, rather than writing the directions themselves. That's because he's a 3-D visualizer. In fact, he doesn't see things visually in his head (this is very hard for Lisa to understand, since she can't visualize it!) but rather graphically. In one particularly romantic moment, when Lisa asked him what he sees when he thinks of her, he said he sees a "blob"!

Okay, so they're not the romantic type. Their other assets more than make up for it: Your car will run like a top; your computer bugs will be a thing of the past; your windows will open and close without a hitch; and you'll never need an appliance repairperson. You'll have to look elsewhere for this superperson, though; Lisa's not giving up Bob!

The Conic Hand

The conic hand.

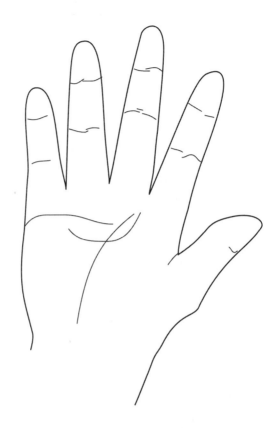

Characteristics

Hand shape: Wider at the base than at the fingers

Fingers: Long, smooth, sometimes somewhat pointed tips—truncated cones

Palm: Well-proportioned, with some flesh

Appearance: Soft, light, always graceful

Lines: Not straight, vary from hand to hand, but probably full of lines

Keywords

Creative

Original

Passionate

Sensitive

Instinctive

Risk taker

Astrological signs: Cancer, Libra

Sometimes called the artistic hand, the conic hand is found more often than any other type these days. That's because women often have hands that are for the most part conic, which also goes a long way toward explaining the negative connotations of the keywords listed in traditional palmistry books, such as "inconstant," "impulsive," "emotional," and "sensation-seeking." Oh, those women, such flighty, undependable creatures…yeah, right.

In reality, people with conic hands have a variety of interests. Another (more feminine?) way of expressing the spatulate hand: Those with conic hands take great pleasure in things of beauty and are often good at creating beauty themselves, whether it's watercolor, landscape design, or home decorating. People with conic hands make good lawyers, too, because they're good listeners, both generous and sympathetic.

You'll often find a piece of flesh on the ball of the fingers of conic hands that means these people like variety, and can become bored if things get too monotonous for them. But with their great imaginations, they can always daydream if they're bored!

The Philosophical Hand

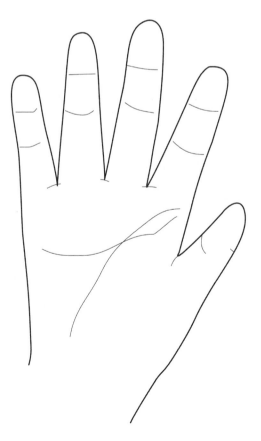

The philosophical hand.

Characteristics

Hand shape: Long

Fingers: Long, sometimes pointed, with obvious joints and fleshy tips

Palm: Long, broad in center, narrow at base and fingers

Appearance: Firm but not hard, receptive

Lines: Many, deep

Keywords

Scholarly

Analyzer

Diplomatic

Cultural

Extravagant

Reclusive

Astrological signs: Sagittarius, Aquarius, Capricorn with heavy Saturn

Here's the hand of the career philosopher, and people whose interests are more mental than physical. In fact, you could call this hand the opposite of the practical hand, and you'd be pretty close to the mark. These are the patrons of the arts, the film critics and book reviewers, the seekers and inventors.

People with philosophical hands are more concerned with principles and ideas than with material success or pleasure. They're not especially practical (you'll find the absent-minded professor at home here), but this is the hand of the creator and the reformer, so practicality isn't what's called for.

Those with philosophical hands like luxury, but they're not all that attached to it. This is the scientist in the field, the person who fixes or improves upon the ideas of others. Patient and analytical, the philosophical hand gets to the bottom of things so they can rise to the top.

The Psychic Hand

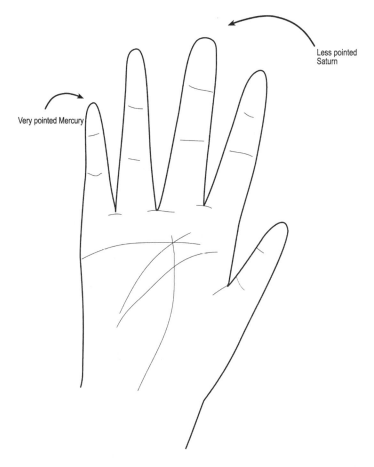

The psychic hand.

Less pointed Saturn

Very pointed Mercury

Characteristics

Hand shape: Long and slender

Fingers: Long with smooth joints or pronounced joints (can go either way)

Palm: Long, narrow, oval, thin

Appearance: Smooth and pale

Lines: Full of lines

Keywords

Idealistic

Contemplative

Imaginative

Handy Words to Know

When a hand has a **psychic overlay**, you'll find certain features of the psychic hand, such as long, antenna-like fingers, a branching head line (as well as secondary lines), and very fine skin texture, overlaid on another hand type. Together, these features add sensitivity to the otherwise everyday hand.

Intuitive

Psychic

Seldom strong for long, sometimes overwhelmed

Astrological signs: Aquarius, Pisces

More often found in the Orient than in Western cultures, the pure psychic hand is very rare. The name itself implies a purity of thought rarely found in anyone who has been exposed to late 20th century life in any way, so it's most likely found in a nunnery or monastery or other reclusive lifestyles.

Still, you may come across aspects of this hand in the most surprising places. People with psychic hands are visionary and forward thinking, and are often many years, if not decades, ahead of their time. They intuitively understand a universality that is more difficult for others, and don't let day-to-day details affect them in the least.

More often, you will see hands with a *psychic overlay*. This allows the psychic hand enough of a dose of practicality to exist in today's world; it makes them "real" as opposed to "pure," a good thing. Still, practical these people are not. But they are our prophets and dreamers, and we should respect and honor them.

The Mixed Hand

The mixed hand.

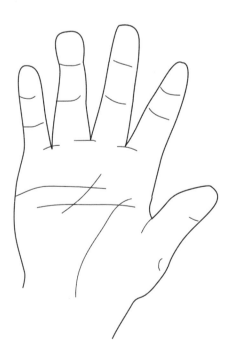

Characteristics

Hand shape: Often square, occasionally elemental

Fingers: Vary from finger to finger, Jupiter (index) finger somewhat pointed or conical

Palm: Mounds well-accentuated, frequently somewhat flat

Appearance: Often with spatulate Apollo (ring) finger

Lines: Vary, seldom consistent

Keywords

Adaptable

Versatile

Mobile

Sociable and friendly

Jack (and Jill) of all trades

Hidden sides

Astrological signs: Gemini, Cancer, Aries, Pisces

Very few of us in this culture of homogenized mixed races have pure hand types. If anything dominates, it's practical and conic hands, but to a degree, we all have mixed hand types: Our culture demands a certain degree of generalization from us all.

A truly mixed hand is both obvious and extreme. The fingers are remarkably different from one another, for example, or seem as if they belong to an entirely different palm. You might find, for example, long pointed fingers on an elemental palm.

With such a mixture, flitter or flirt, the mixed-hand person never stays in one place for long. Which way is the wind blowing? The mixed-hand person is likely to move in that direction. We hate to call them fickle, but, well, they're not afraid to change direction if it suits their purposes. At times they can also form odd alliances, depending on their purpose.

You're far more likely to find tact here than honesty, and it's hard to nail down any specific occupational likelihoods for people so likely to change occupation at the drop of a hat. Let's call them flexible. Let's call them dabblers. Let's not call them exactly dependable—though they can be a whole lot of fun.

Yes, But How Does It *Feel?*

Okay, so you've noted the shape of your subject's hand. What now? When you first meet someone, you shake his or her hand. You probably notice if the hand feels warm or cold, damp or dry, strong or weak, flexible or rigid, rough or smooth. As you've probably guessed, all of these characteristics reveal a good deal about the hand, and, consequently, about the person to whom the hand belongs. Before you launch into an in-depth reading of the palm, getting the feel of your subject's hand is another important first impression.

Feel the hand itself. A handshake is a good way to do this: It won't put subjects on their guard or make them feel uncomfortable. Then, as you begin to read the palm, you'll touch it more, and begin to make some larger determinations about how it feels. But don't go overboard. You don't need to be a "hand holder."

Hand-le with Care

Americans in particular are very conscious of their comfort zones, areas within which those they don't know may not enter. In other cultures, people stand much closer to each other, but Americans require a good arm's length to feel at ease. Congruent to this, most of us find it off-putting when someone touches our hand, but that's exactly what a good palm reader must do to check the consistency of the flesh and the texture of the skin.

Pressure, Pressure, Pressure

We're all under pressure, and our hands are no exception. How your hand reacts to pressure is a good indication of how you react to pressure as well. If you're like a little teapot, slowly coming to a boil and then blowing your top, your hand's going to show a red dot on the head line, an inflated active Mars mount (see Chapter 17), or, possibly, active perspiration.

As many hands as Robin has touched, it's no surprise that he's developed some categories about their responses to pressure. Rather than give you his conclusions, though, we thought we'd give you that list and let you fill in the blanks about each pressure category. As you'll see, Robin's come up with some pretty self-descriptive words. But first, what do you think these various textures might represent?

Tissue paper _____

Mud _____

"Jell-O" _____

Full balloon _____

Deflated balloon _____

I am a rock; I am an island _____

Basically, there are two things that are of primary importance when it comes to how a hand reacts to pressure: Does it respond? And does it bounce back? A hand like a rock isn't going to respond as a "Jell-O" hand will, and, similarly, a mud hand's more likely to stay sunk than a full balloon. Tissue paper is frail, easily impressed, and nonresilient. In fact, it could pay to suggest a tissue paper client have his kidneys checked, as this can indicate some trouble in that area.

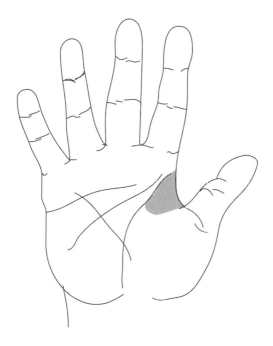

Anger in the hand: an inflated active Mars mount.

Another thing you'll note as you apply light pressure to a hand is how its color changes, and how long it takes for its natural color to return. This is a good indication of a client's circulation, and hence, his or her health.

More than anything else, what your skin's reaction to pressure is revealing is your energy at that particular moment. In his book *The Benham Book of Palmistry,* William G. Benham divides hands into four categories: flabby, soft, elastic, and hard, which you can easily match up with Robin's categories listed earlier. But what do these mean in terms of your energy? To find out, take a look at the following table.

Pressure Category	Energy Level
Flabby	Prefers rest to exertion
Soft	Deficient in energy, energy can be strengthened with planning and forethought
Elastic	Active, healthy, well-directed
Hard	Very active—a manual laborer

What Color Is Your Hand?

We've all got different colored skin. Black, white, yellow, red: Even within those broad categories there are endless variations of pigmentation. It's part of what makes each of us unique and special.

As with other aspects of the hand, the more hands you look at, the more you'll be able to understand how various pigmentations manifest on various colors of skin. On Oriental hands, for example, there are very distinct pinks and greys, as well as a darker pigmentation that shows a certain focus. There are also warmer and cooler tones within each pigmentation, and, with practice, you'll notice that within every color of hand you'll find a pink, white, green, grey, black, and blue.

A hand's relative color is an indicator of health. Not only is the client's circulation shown, but every other part of his or her physiognomy as well. Remember, too, that each color is a variation on the skin's natural color, so that "pink" on an African-American hand can appear quite different from "pink" on a Caucasian one.

Pigmentation	Possible Indications
Pale or white	Poor circulation
Pink	Relative good health
Red	Intensity and vitality—someone who doesn't do things in a half-baked way
Yellow	Can indicate a variety of ailments, depending on where the yellow appears. Can relate to liver or bile problems
Green	Envy, challenge of self-control, being in the wrong mind set
Blue	Difficulty with circulation or the heart, depression
Black	Lack of enthusiasm for struggle, dark thoughts, deeds, unsuccessful conclusions, failure, finality
Mottled	Emotional ups-and-downs, inconstancy, unfixed mind

All hands have variations of color within them, and with practice, you'll begin to notice not only a hand's relative coloring but its own variations as well. You'll learn that a red inner Mars mount (near the center of the palm, see Chapter 17) can indicate anger, for example. A blue tint to the lunar mount (on the heel of the hand, see Chapter 18) can mean, aside from a poor environment, quite literally, "the blues."

Cold Hands, Warm Heart?

Most hands you'll touch will be warm and moist without being too hot or clammy. That's because warm hands indicate a good, healthy physiology, which is how most of us feel, most of the time.

Some hands, though (like those typing these words) are nearly always cold. Robin says this can be a sign of chronic instability, or not having enough strength to face daily challenges—but you should check the head line before you make such a blanket statement. In Lisa's case, it's more about just plain lousy circulation, and yes, her feet are usually cold, too (just ask Bob).

When hands feel clammy to the touch, there's a lot of stress that's come to the surface. A clammy hand indicates a nervous person, though whether the nervousness is of a passing nature or a more permanent one is determined in other areas of the hand, such as the Mercury (baby) finger and mount. Sometimes this person is just nervous about getting his or her palm read, after all.

What Your Skin Is Saying

Some skin is rough and some skin is smooth, and, as you've probably guessed, the texture of your skin is important. The old palmistry books say that smooth skin means refinement and coarse skin indicates, well, coarseness, but it's much more important to study the skin relative to the rest of the hand to determine its message.

When you feel a hand's texture, in other words, you're looking for the out-of-the-ordinary rather than the ordinary. Very smooth skin, with a shiny, slippery feel, for example, can indicate a mineral deficiency or sometimes, quite literally, a slippery nature. Very coarse skin can indicate stress, such as trauma or abuse. If the skin isn't particularly noteworthy in these ways, you can move on to its thickness.

The words "thick skinned" and "thin skinned" are actually a better analogy for understanding skin texture. The best way of determining thickness is to pinch the skin on the back of the hand. On a thickness scale of 1 to 10, 1 would be leather and 10 would be tissue paper, with leather being self-focused and tissue paper being perceptive and receptive.

Thick	Denim	Cotton	Silk	Tissue Paper
1 2 self-focused	3 4	5 6	7 8	9 10 perceptive

Women naturally have thinner skin than men, but the ideal hand for both women and men is both resilient and somewhat thin skinned. Too thick a skin can mean one is dogmatic, while too thin a skin can indicate oversensitivity. Interestingly, the texture of the skin is generally an indication of the type of work that a person does.

A teacher, for example, probably has skin that's about a 6 on the thickness scale. That's because he or she needs to be sensitive and receptive to the needs of students, but not entirely open—the teacher's still got to be in charge, in other words. Police officers will have thicker skin. After all, they are exposed to aggression and confrontation far too often, and have to be thick skinned to keep it from getting to them.

When skin is actively shedding from an area of the hand, it's an indication that you're actively processing something in that particular area of your life. Eczema or hives on the thumb side of your Jupiter (index) finger, for example, can mean you're dealing with the challenge of prominence in a social leadership role. This might be as simple as a report to the PTA, or being the spokesperson for the annual Girl Scout Cookie drive, but it's going to show up on your Jupiter.

Hand-le with Care

When skin loss is chronic in the hand, it's an indication of someone who may be feeling very out of place or uncomfortable with his life role, though this may not be as complex as it sounds. A simple answer, such as "change jobs" or "get a divorce," may be adequate to rectify the situation!

Some Handy Anatomy

Palm readers aren't the only ones who get a feel for your hands. Physicians regularly examine your hands as a part of any general physical examination. Doctors look for just about the same things: flexibility, color, strength, nail condition, and texture. The hand has 27 bones and is the most flexible structure in the human skeleton. There are eight bones in the carpus, your wrist; five in the metacarpus, the middle part of the hand (including the long bones that run from the wrist to the base of the fingers); and fourteen in the phalangeal section, your fingers.

Remember that when your doctor shakes your hand, he or she is also gauging your muscle tone, range of motion, and warmth for circulation. In Chinese medicine, the pulse and circulation are integral diagnostic tools and close attention is paid to the hand and wrist. Blood flows through the hand by the radial artery located on the thumb side of the wrist and the ulnar artery located on the Mercury (little finger) side of the wrist. The nerves running through the hand, the radial, ulnar, and median, govern its motion and feeling.

The half-moon shape at the base of your nail is called the lunula; it's crossed by the skin of the cuticle. In medi-speak, a lack of oxygen in the blood that creates blue nails is called cyanosis and can be a sign of a heart or respiratory condition. Brittle or ridged nails can be a symptom of iron deficiency anemia. Pitting and a separation of the nail from its nail bed are common in psoriasis. Yellow or discolored nails may be a result of nicotine staining or an aftereffect of the pigment in nail polish. Nails are made of keratin, the same protein in skin and hair. Yellow can also indicate too much carrot juice or sometimes jaundice.

A Hand in Your Future: Keep a Journal

It's time *you* started observing hands. First, you should get a notebook and create a journal you'll devote to just this purpose. The more you learn about hands, the more you're going to notice them, and you'll want to write down what you notice. A few weeks into this book, Lisa went to hear a speaker whose audience was largely writers, and she was struck by the number of square fingertips she saw (her own are conic).

You may also want to include drawings in your journal. Even if you're not artistic, quick drawings can nonetheless serve as visual cues to remember what you've noticed.

You'll start to notice certain hands in certain places as well, and observation is the skilled palmist's secret tool. The more you notice, the more you learn; the more you learn, the more you know. Every hand you see is another lesson—a hand in your future, so to speak.

The Least You Need to Know

➤ Develop a regular order of how you look at a hand.

➤ Look at both hands when reading palms.

➤ Various lengths and angles are important to note.

➤ Different types of people have differently shaped hands.

➤ How hands feel can be keys to physical traits.

➤ The more hands you look at, the more you'll learn.

Part 2
Let Your Fingers Do the Talking

Your fingers—including the thumb, Mercury, Apollo, Saturn, and Jupiter—are the characters in your own particular story. Each finger is divided into three phalanges that cover the intuitive, mental, and material worlds. Your fingers can reveal why you behave the way you do, why you collect the things you do, and where your creativity will fully flower.

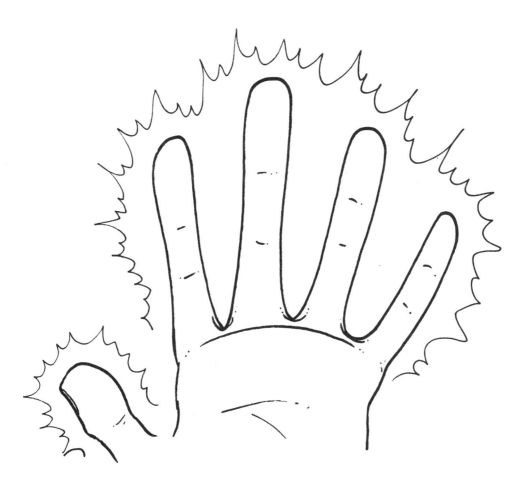

Chapter 4

Every Finger Tells a Story

In This Chapter

➤ What your fingers are saying about you

➤ Long fingers and short fingers

➤ Straight fingers and crooked fingers

➤ Are you active or passive?

➤ Smooth thinkers and deliberators

➤ Fingertips and fingernails—the tip of the iceberg

Every finger tells a story, because every finger is a character in your story. There's your thumb revealing your stubbornness; your Jupiter (index) finger, your sociability; your Saturn (middle) finger, your conformity; your Apollo (ring) finger, your creativity; and your Mercury (baby) finger, your way of communicating.

A palm reader's going to look at your thumb and fingers together and separately, and, by the time she has, you're going to have some solid characters peopling your story. And every character is *you*.

What Your Palmist Knows at First Sight

"Let me see your thumb." That's the first thing your palm reader's going to say to you after shaking your hand to get a first impression of the feel of it. Not your life line, not the size of your hand or its shape. Why the thumb? Because character-wise, your

Helping Hands

Let's explain what we mean by "honest in your inclinations." A crooked Mercury can mean that when you see that priceless antique lamp for $3.00 at a yard sale, you're going to grab it. A straight Mercury means you're going to tell the owner how much it's worth.

thumb is equal to your will, and the bigger it is, the more strong-willed you are. If the force of will demonstrated by the thumb isn't balanced by the length of the other fingers, you can bet there's some control issues going on. Your thumb also governs your logic, love, and vitality, as well as your strength of character. All this makes it clear that your thumb's more than a mere finger, and, in fact, it's technically not, as we discuss in Chapter 5.

Right off the bat, a palm reader will know if you're going to challenge him or listen to what he's got to say—just by looking at your thumb. He'll also see whether your fingers are crooked or straight, and, if they're crooked, which way they're leaning. The slant of your Mercury (baby) finger, for example, is an indication of how honest you are in your inclinations.

In addition, a swift glance at the fingers can tell an experienced palm reader which areas are currently accentuated in your life—and why. Any finger that's prominent or accentuated in some way—whether it's by diminution or largeness—indicates there's an issue in that area of your life that's being accentuated—or avoided. You can run, but you can't hide—your fingers will tell the story even when you won't!

Okay, before reading any further, hold out your hand, palm up. Just hold it out in the same way that you'd offer it to the palm reader. Now, hold that position and read on.

Hold Out Your Hand

"Hold out your hand." Inquisitive folks, these palm readers, aren't they? First they want to see your thumb, now they want you to hold out your hand. Why? Because the way you extend your hand reveals your own inquisitive nature.

People usually extend their hand in one of four ways:

➤ *The Claw.* Yup, just what it sounds like, ready to reach out and snatch something. The Claw doesn't want his hand read, and he may be greedy besides. There's not a high level of trust here because, with his grasping nature, the claw doesn't want to share in either direction.

➤ *The Paddle.* With the fingers held tightly together, the Paddle's still not entirely open to the idea of having her palm read. Sure, something might come of it, but nothing's going to be given away and nothing's going to be extreme, either. Robin equates the Paddle to "first-date syndrome": Should I trust you? You show me.

Hand-le with Care

Sometimes, arthritis has crippled a hand to a degree that a person can't show you more than a claw. In this case, give 'em some slack. The person may be ready, willing, and able despite the way that individual extended his or her hand.

➤ *The Fan.* This hand's so open, it's held taut, with the lines outlined sharply in relief. Not only is the Fan open and receptive, she'll help you with your reading. "Oh, that must be my cousin Clyde," she'll say. When you're given a Fan to read, be sure to find something dramatic and exciting in her hand to share with her—there'll be lots to choose from.

➤ *The Natural.* You don't need a picture of this one. Some people extend their hands in a natural and relaxed way, with the fingers not clenched.

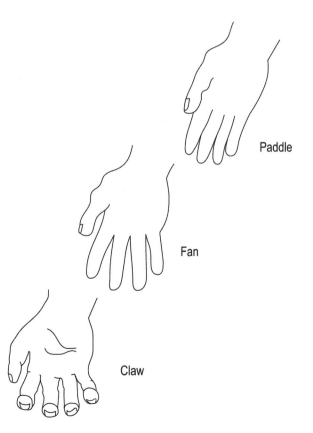

Top to bottom: the Paddle, Fan, and Claw.

Paddle

Fan

Claw

A Who's Who of the Fingers

We've alluded to Apollo, we've mentioned Mercury, we may even have said something about Saturn or made a joke about Jupiter. But now it's time for you to see just who's who when it comes to your fingers.

Meet your fingers: Mercury (the little finger), Apollo (the ring finger), Saturn (the middle finger), Jupiter (the index finger), and the thumb. The astrological symbol for each planet appears above each finger.

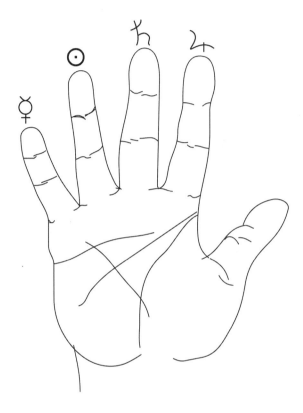

Aside from your thumb, which, as we mentioned earlier, is an indicator of your flexibility, each of your four fingers has a name—and character—based on Greek mythology. And, like any character, each finger has a distinct personality.

➤ First, there's **Jupiter**, the god of luck and fortune, pointing the way. Your Jupiter (index) finger rules your wisdom, leadership qualities, and optimism, as well as your self-esteem. Jupiter's about your relationship to yourself, and to people at a personal level.

➤ Next to Jupiter, standing tall, is **Saturn**, father of the gods, and the finger in charge of rules and regulations. It's here you'll find your father or father figures, as well as the way you discipline yourself and others. This is the finger of conformity (after all, it's in the middle!); think of your Saturn as your relationship to the law—in all its manifestations.

➤ Your ring finger is called your **Apollo** finger, after the Greek god of the sun, and it's here you'll find your creative pursuits and idealism. Your Apollo will show whether you're a performer before the spotlights or behind the scenes, how well you're liked, and the level of your intensity (like the sun). Apollo, in other words, is about your relationship to expression.

➤ Your smallest finger (the baby) plays an equally important role. It's your **Mercury** finger, and, as the finger in charge of the mind, it rules how you communicate, your intuition—and your approach to sex. In addition, it's on your Mercury that you'll find your approach to business and how you talk to others. Think of your Mercury as your relationship to people at the nonpersonal (public, that is) level.

A Closer Look at the Fingers

So now you know their Greek names (and why they've got Greek names in the first place). But there's a lot more to each finger than its name and personality. Palm readers look at each finger's length—both singularly and relative to the other fingers. They divide each finger into three phalanges, the sections that are created by the finger's joints. They look at the joints themselves, to see if they're smooth or knotted.

We Gotta Hand It to You

Why Greek names? Up until the end of 19th century, every man who went to school (unfortunately, there were far fewer educated women back then—just read Virginia Woolf's *A Room of Her Own*, if you don't believe us) learned Greek mythology as a matter of course (pun intended). Every scholar, young and old, could immediately recognize the archetype represented by a particular Greek god's name. Jupiter was equated with optimism; Saturn with rules and regulations; Apollo with the arts; and Mercury with communication. In its way, the use of Greek god names was a kind of shorthand; it's just that it's not the kind we generally learn anymore. Still, you'll find if you do learn this shorthand, it will serve you well in not just palmistry, but in astrology and astronomy as well. Not to mention at cocktail parties!

Palm readers also look to see if your fingers are crooked or straight, and, if they're crooked, which way they're leaning. They'll look at the various markings on your fingers to see which areas of your life are being affected in what ways. The distances between your fingers matter, too, as do the shapes of both your fingertips and your fingernails. Lastly, the nails themselves provide important clues about your health—both mental and physical. Clearly, there's a lot of weight on those little guys—let's give 'em a hand.

Phalanges: Strength in Sections

Take a look at your fingers. See how each is divided into three sections? (The third section of the thumb (a part of the palm) is the mount of Venus, which we'll talk about in depth in the next chapter.) As we mentioned, those sections are called phalanges, and the relative size of each phalange reveals your strengths and weaknesses within the area that finger rules.

➤ The first phalange—the section that includes the fingertip—is the area of your psychic intuition. Depending on the shape of its tip (we'll discuss tip shapes a little later in this chapter), your first phalange reveals how you express yourself intuitively. Robin likes to call the first phalange "the antenna," and it's a good analogy. Here you'll find what you receive—and what you return.

➤ The second phalange represents your mental capacities. Here is your logic and your rational side, as well as your patience. The breadth of your second phalange reveals your mental scope.

➤ The third, or bottom, phalange, is the area of your materiality. Here you'll find your attachment to the material world, as well as your physical energy. Concrete activity can be found on the third phalange, the realm of the material world.

When well-proportioned, on a scale of 10, the first phalange's length will represent $2^1/_2$; the second $3^1/_2$; and the third 4 (go back to consult the figure on page 35). Of course, the length of each phalange varies from finger to finger and from person to person—it's part of what makes each of us unique. We should add that you'll seldom see phalanges proportioned this way; most of us have quite different proportions.

The three phalanges of the fingers.

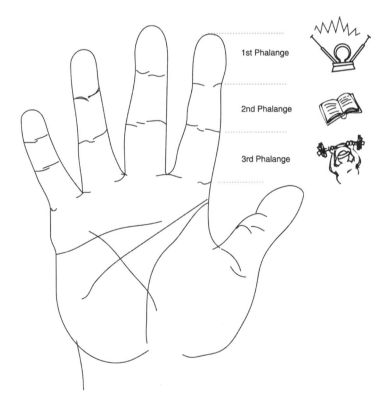

1st Phalange

2nd Phalange

3rd Phalange

As we explore the fingers in Chapters 5 through 9, we'll discuss what the length of the phalanges mean for each finger.

How Long Are Your Fingers?

Get out your calipers—it's time to measure the fingers. In the well-proportioned hand, Jupiter will reach to the bottom of Saturn's nail; Saturn is often a half-nail longer than Apollo; Apollo can reach to the bottom of Saturn's nail; and Mercury will reach to Apollo's first joint. If you're thoroughly confused, use the following illustration as a guide.

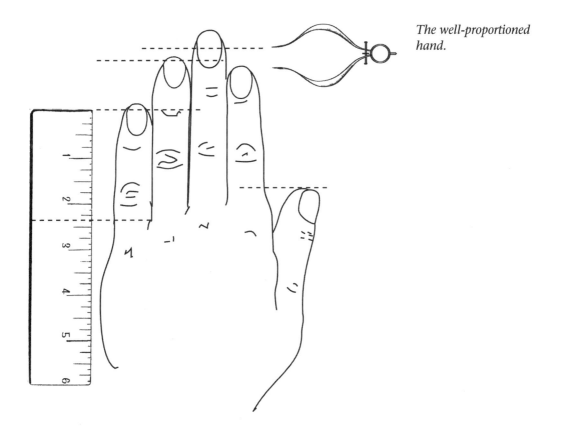

The well-proportioned hand.

The majority of hands resemble this one, but quite a few may have some eccentricities of their own. Let's look at some of these eccentricities one at a time to show you what we mean.

If your Jupiter (index) finger reaches past the bottom of Saturn's nail—what is called a Napoleonic Jupiter—you've probably got some extra ego. A Napoleonic Jupiter challenges Saturn, which means it wants to dominate. You'll often find this configuration in athletes or very ambitious types, as well as natural leaders.

63

Helping Hands

A Napoleonic Jupiter is so-called because Napoleon (a leader who challenged world order for decades) himself supposedly had a Jupiter finger that was longer than his Saturn finger. Maybe that's why he kept his hand tucked into his waistcoat when posing for posterity.

If your Jupiter is short, you're probably not a leader. There may, in fact, be some self-esteem issues that need to be addressed, the concern of which can be determined still more in other areas of the hand.

Napoleonic Jupiters notwithstanding, Saturn, the middle finger, is almost always the longest finger. It's also the one most likely to be injured, both because of this position, and because Saturn is about discipline.

An extreme Saturn can be as much as a full nail longer than Apollo. This indicates a love of detail, and energy that is directed into solitary pursuits. You may find a researcher when you find a long Saturn. Accentuated, Saturn can indicate a patriarch or a hermit. And if Saturn is long while the other fingers are short, it can be an indication of extremes.

Your Apollo (ring) finger is generally the same length as your Jupiter finger, but is set higher. It should surpass the bottom of Saturn's nail, and if it's longer than that, it indicates a good aesthetic sense, as you might find in an appraiser. This can also be the performer, as it indicates charisma. It can indicate superficiality, but that's okay, because a long Apollo means you'll live long and prosper, Vulcan or not. A long Apollo is lucky.

When your Mercury (or little finger) is long and straight, you're a pillar of your particular community, a professional's professional such as the underwriter's underwriter, or the teacher's teacher. In its well-proportioned form, Mercury reaches the first phalange of Apollo. When it's short and straight, it may mean proud and poor—someone who's not given to commerce or business oriented.

Throwing Out Those Curves

There are plenty of people with straight fingers, but there are just as many of us with crooked ones. Which direction those curves are going can reveal a great deal about whether you're an introvert or an extrovert—or both.

Using the following illustrations as a guide, draw an imaginary (or real, as Robin does with his ever-present ballpoint pen) line vertically down the center of your hand. This line will pass right down the middle of your Saturn finger.

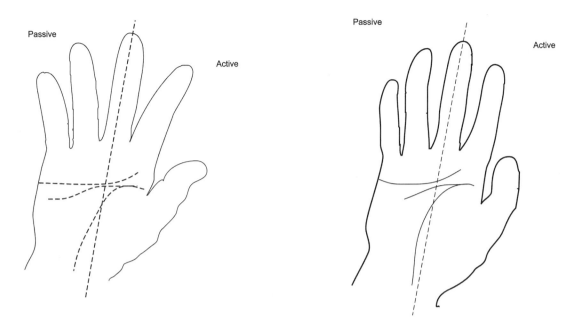

Finding the fingers' curves. Note how the fingers on each hand have different curves.

As you'll note, the side of the hand with Mercury, Apollo, and half your Saturn finger is the passive side, and the side with the thumb, Jupiter, and the other half of your Saturn is your active side. Now, look to see if any of your fingers are leaning, and, if so, in which direction they're leaning. If they're curved toward the active side, the activities ruled by those fingers are extroverted; if they're curved toward the passive side, they're introverted. But let's make this a little simpler by looking at each finger individually.

Active Fingers	Indications
Thumb (away from the hand)	Very social and expressed, generous
Jupiter	A joiner, very social, high profile
Saturn	Neighborhood Watch commander, possibly had an overly influential father, strong sense of being responsible
Apollo	The ham (yeah, but where's the talent?), the stage mom, clothes horse, always has a joke to share
Mercury	A businessperson, strong communication skills, perhaps in media, or a teacher

Passive Fingers	Indications
Thumb (close to hand)	Pragmatic, circumspect, unexpressed, understated
Jupiter	Some inherent shyness, natural humility; possibility of limited expression (stutter?)
Saturn	The philosophical outlaw
Apollo	Obscure taste in art and music (the accordion aficionado); unusual expression in taste
Mercury	A statement of obscurity, eccentricity toward society (the nudist?)

Helping Hands

What if you've got a hand like Lisa's, with the active fingers pointed toward the introvert side and the passive fingers toward the extrovert side? Well, according to Robin, you've got a writer: There's the need to explore what's inside (the active leaning toward the passive), and the need to express it (the passive leaning toward the active).

Tiny Signs in Little Lines

You'll sometimes find some sketching on the fingers themselves. These small tracery lines can be horizontal or vertical. Small dots, crosses, triangles, squares, or grids are also present, and, rarely, circles and ovals. We like to think of these little lines as footnotes, and where on the finger they appear indicates the area they're affecting. Like everything on your hand, these can change.

➤ *Dot.* Depending on its color, a dot indicates a high or low point. A blue dot is a low point, while black is very low. A red dot, indicates an abundance of energy in that area; a white dot, inspiration or energy to use if you choose.

➤ *Circle.* A circle represents a challenge that may become a blessing in disguise. These lessons are often karmic opportunities, so once learned, like all completed lessons, they offer much benefit.

➤ *Oval.* Ovals represent a similar energy to the circle's karmic one, only this time the lesson is more easily assimilated because the oval is a female type of energy.

➤ *Cross.* Here's some needed help from outside. Because the help is from someone else, though, it can sometimes take the form of criticism, but think of it as constructive criticism, helping you to modify your path of action.

➤ *Triangle.* Triangles are karmic gift certificates—but they're only good at the particular "store" where they appear. Karmic boons, they're beneficent, but their reach is narrow.

➤ *Square.* Squares are stepping stones, a level of assistance and support to use in conjunction with logic to move to the next square.

➤ *Grid.* Grids have more lines than tic-tac-toe (which is more likely a cross or a square); grids create multiple squares, not just one. They're seldom seen in a positive light because they indicate a need for much work in the area in which they appear. Grid lessons must be repeated several times, but that's often because we can't find a fresh approach to them. As such, they're sometimes a sign of an area that's being overused.

➤ *Horizontal line.* As you might suspect, horizontal lines literally cut or limit the energy across the area they affect. A horizontal line across the middle phalange of Saturn, for example, might indicate a need to learn to limit one's obsessive energy or other self-imposed limits.

➤ *Vertical line.* The vertical line accentuates an area. Parallel vertical lines add stability and greater balance. More than two vertical lines can be more chancy because they indicate a potential scattering of energy.

Marks on the fingers.

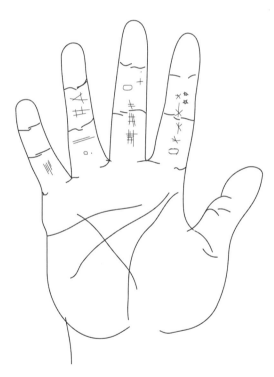

Joints: How Smooth Is Your Thinking?

You can determine the smoothness or knottiness of your joints by actually running your hands along the sides of your fingers. Yes, your fingers may appear to have knotty joints, but when you run your finger along them, you'll find them smoother than you

Helping Hands

A knotted upper joint can mean that the person holds onto ideas; while a knot on the middle joint can mean he's more likely to hold onto material possessions.

think. We all have something at each joint, but it's the extreme knots that we refer to as "knotty." Often, longer fingers have the smoothest joints and shorter fingers the knottiest ones.

The smoother the joint, the smoother the thinking. The smoothest joints indicate those who make intuitive leaps.

Knotty joints, on the other hand, indicate deliberate decision makers. Knotty-jointed folks analyze every angle before making a decision, and are often worriers to boot. If the joints are so knotty that the phalanges between them appear to have "waists," the thinking is often too complex—and the decision is often not made in a timely fashion.

The "waisted" finger.

Distance to Cross

The spacing between the fingers indicates where you've got some work to do. To determine if there's space between your fingers, hold your palm, fingers together, up to the light. Does any light show through at the bottom between any two fingers? That's where your work hasn't been completed yet.

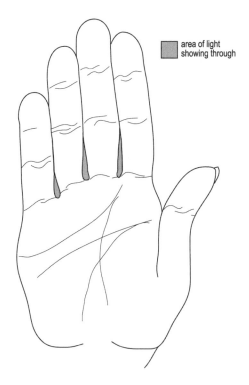

area of light
showing through

Light between the fingers indicates work in an area of your life that needs to be completed.

➤ *Light between Saturn and Apollo.* Something's going on between your discipline versus your creativity. Are you avoiding the easel, the notebook, or the piano? It will show up as a gap here.

➤ *Light between Saturn and Jupiter.* Here the difficulty's with fulfilling promises, especially to yourself. This can, for example, be that diet that you're going to start this Monday for sure.

➤ *Light between Apollo and Mercury.* There's more than one possible explanation for this gap. You may need to learn to treat others with constancy and politeness, or to free yourself from prejudice. Basically, a gap here indicates you're not entirely aware of others' needs and feelings. No gap here means you're an empath!

The Shapes of Your Fingertips

Like the hand itself, fingertips have different shapes. Nearly all fingertips are square, spatulate, conic, or mixed, though pointed fingertips are possible as well. Hand shape and fingertip shape are two very distinct areas, and it's not uncommon to find conic fingertips on a square hand, or even on an elemental one.

Fingertip shapes.

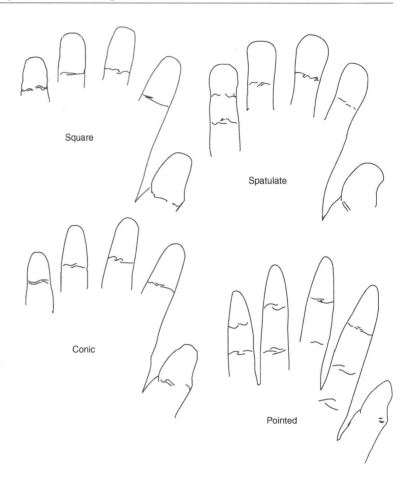

Fingertip shape relates to your practicality. The more pointed your fingertip, the more idealistic and sensitive you are. Palmistry pioneer William G. Benham suggested that this is because more of the life force can enter through pointed fingers. You be the judge. The main question to ask about fingertip shape is whether you use it well—or whether it uses you.

Square Tips: Everybody Needs the Farmer

Square fingertips indicate systematic practicality. These are ordered people, with a place for everything—and everything in its place. They'll get up at the same time each morning and go to bed after a set routine at the same time each night. Followers of routine and custom, they need routine to feel comfortable and successful. They're steady, somewhat uninspired folk—but they always know where to find everything.

Spatulate Tips: Hands On, Can Do

Spatulate fingertips belong to the realist. These are the common-sense people, those who are always practical. Constantly in motion, people with spatulate (broad or rounded) fingertips are active, energetic, inventive, and skilled in all that they do—they're the ones who know how to use every tool. You can think of people with spatulate fingertips as "everyday people." They're great to have around—and they will use their hands.

Conic Tips: The Pragmatic in All of Us

Conic fingertips are found most often on women's hands, and indicate the quick-thinking, intuitive, artistic person. Conic fingertips don't care much for routine or operating systems, but they are creative and talented. More idealistic than pragmatic, people with conic fingertips rely on impression rather than analysis, and while they are "can-do," they'll frequently choose the course of least resistance.

Mixed Tips: A Little Bit of This, a Little Bit of That

Mixed fingertips are what most of us have—some slightly square or spatulate, some slightly conic, maybe even one a little pointed (most likely our Jupiter, which tends to be more pointed than the rest anyway). There are a number of reasons for this, the main one being we're all mutts. But remember, mutts are resourceful survivors—and the smartest dogs around. (Just ask Sadie and Too, who rule the roost at Lisa's house. If we could read their pads, their tips would surely be mixed!)

Oddly mixed fingertips—say, one of each shape—represent the odd duck. Here you'll find the lost soul from the mainstream, the person who just can't find himself—because he's going in too many directions.

And Then There Are Nails

Nails are important! Not only do they indicate your current health, both physical and mental, they immediately show a palm reader a great deal about your self-esteem and how you relate to others. We like to think of the quality of the nails as an indication of how well-tuned the engine is. When was the last time you had *your* oil changed?

Helping Hands

Pointed fingertips are an extreme of the conic. These are people with their heads literally in the clouds—the poet, the dreamer, the prophet. It's almost as if these people don't belong on Earth, and it takes a solidly grounded square-fingertip person to hold them there.

Nail Shapes

Nails can be grouped into one of four general shapes: square, rectangle, oval, and almond. Use the following illustration to note the appearance of each.

Fingernail shapes progress from left to right: square, rectangle, oval, almond.

➤ The **square nail** is as long as it is wide, and has a definitely square appearance to it. The square nail indicates excellent strength, but also a lack of foresightedness. The wider the nail, the healthier the subject. Here you'll find great physical stamina, and not-so-great common sense.

➤ The **rectangle nail**, longer than it is wide, indicates someone who's very forceful and sometimes driven. People with rectangular nails are smart, and there's guidance behind their drive to succeed. At the same time, though, people whose nails are longer than they are wide may not think things through. Sometimes, in fact, impulse can be too strong—and trouble results.

➤ The **oval nail**, by far the most common type, indicates good overall balance. These are people who've earned the qualities of compromise and function well within society. They're not extremists—they're most of us.

➤ The **almond nail**, pointed at its tip, indicates great beauty—but not a great deal of healthiness. Think of the almond nail as the hothouse flower: It needs a special environment to survive, but when it has it, it can thrive.

Are You a Biter or a Decorator?

We've all seen people with beautifully painted long nails (maybe we *are* people with beautifully painted long nails), and we've also seen those whose nails are short and well manicured without drawing attention to themselves. Then there are those nails that are chewed to the quick—as well as those that aren't even real.

Like everything else about the fingers, extremes in nails indicate extremes in character, while more middle-of-the-road nails indicate more balanced people. Whether you're a biter or a decorator reveals more about you than you may realize.

Long, pointed, painted fingernails may seem to indicate an artistic sort, but in reality they may be masking a lack of self-esteem. Like hair and makeup that draws attention to the self, long fingernails are sometimes a way of preening the surface to cover up what we think is lacking underneath. But the key word here is "think"—you're never as lacking as you think.

Bitten nails are also indicators of a lack of self-esteem, but in this case, it's not as masked as in long, decorated fingernails. Bitten nails are there for all the world to see—and they show someone who lets worries and fears take control. Nail biters are indulging in self-criticism and might-have-beens, instead of taking the bull by the horns.

The well-balanced nail is neither long nor short, neither bitten nor overly decorated (although a little light polish does not a peacock make). The half-moons at the nails' bases are clearly seen, and the skin around the nail is neither red nor ragged. But enough about that—I've got to go cut my nails.

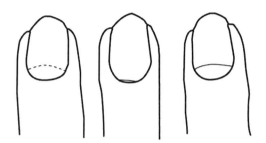

The moons of the fingernails.

How Many Reps Can Your Nails Do?

Take a moment now to feel your nails. That's right—run a fingertip along your nails. How do they feel? Smooth? Ridged? Rough? Dished (concave rather than convex)? How your nails feel is a letter to you from your nails—about your health.

Smooth nails indicate overall good health and stamina, as you might expect. Color plays a role here as well: The pinker the nail, the healthier the subject. Nails that are blue at the base can mean there's a poor oxygen supply. In that case, the subject could benefit from really breathing—deeply and regularly. *The Complete Idiot's Guide to Meditation* may help, too.

Vertical ridges, rather like corduroy, are a sign of stress, and sometimes of old injuries that never healed correctly. A fine-tuning of one's mineral intake (adding some B complex, gelatin, or protein as needed) can do wonders to help smooth out these ridges.

Nails that are dished indicate poor circulation, or a presence of heavy metals within the system. A subject with dished nails probably needs a vacation, or, at the very least, a physical flush of the system. Dark and convex nails may indicate lung problems. Remember, though, your palm reader's not a doctor—so be sure to get that second opinion.

Like everything about your hand, your nails and fingers change as you do. That includes smoothing out your nails by being aware of your health—and taking care of yourself.

The shape and opacity of nails may vary considerably between individuals. Healthy color should be a variation of pink. Dark-skinned subjects may exhibit pigment deposits or bands on their nails; however, the sudden appearance of such bands on light-skinned persons is not healthy. Vertical bands are a normal variant that may have a number of different causes, including age, stress, diet, and injury. A ripple across the width of the nail may indicate injury, and is frequently found on the thumb.

Finding Your Finger Profile: An Exercise

As we've already mentioned, reading your own palm can be harder than reading someone else's. But you're also the most accessible subject you've got, and you've got to start somewhere. For that reason, we'd like you to start with your own hand, and to do that, you'll need a piece of paper, a pen or pencil, and a ruler.

Place your hand flat on the piece of paper and trace it. Before you lift it from the page, lightly mark each joint next to each finger. These markings will help you determine the length of each phalange.

Now lift your hand and look at the hand you've drawn. In this chapter, we've concentrated on the fingers, and that's what you should look at, too. Go back through each section of this chapter and make notes on what we say about your finger profile.

If you've already started a palmistry journal with your observations about hands, as we suggested in Chapter 3, add this exercise. If you haven't started that journal until now, this can be your first page: Your Finger Profile. It's the beginning of a map of your self.

The Least You Need to Know

➤ The longer the finger, the stronger that area's influence.

➤ The lean of your fingers indicates whether you're active or passive.

➤ Your joints indicate whether you're a smooth thinker or a deliberator.

➤ Your fingertips reveal how practical—or impractical—you are.

➤ Your nails are indicators of health—both physical and mental.

Chapter 5

There's Nothing Like a Thumb

In This Chapter

➤ Nothing's as important as your thumb

➤ How much will and drive does your thumb have?

➤ A measure of your generosity

➤ A willingness to compromise

➤ Where to find your love, logic, and will

Palmistry pioneer d'Arpentigny once said, "The thumb individualizes the man," and, sexism aside, this phrase summarizes as well as any the singular importance of this most human of digits. In India, in fact, there are palm readers who read only the thumb, so well does it reveal the basics about a person, and gypsy palm readers say if they can read only one thing about a hand, they would choose to read the thumb.

Think for a moment about what your thumb can do. First of all, it can oppose each of the other fingers, touching them tip to tip. It can help you add a pinch of salt, pick up a needle from a haystack, turn a key in a lock, or hold the phone. In fact, only the chimpanzee's thumb approaches the dexterity of a human's, so it's no surprise that this most human of features would also reveal human nature. There is, in truth, nothing like a thumb.

The Most Important Digit

Think of your thumb as the force of will that empowers everything and you've got a good overall description of this most important digit. When your palm reader looks at your thumb, some of things she knows about you include:

➤ Your willpower

➤ Your generosity

➤ Your flexibility

➤ Your capacity for compromise

➤ Your ability to hold onto a goal

➤ Your subtlety

➤ The quality of thought that goes into your actions

➤ Aspects of your self-esteem

➤ Aspects of your self-doubt

From this list, it's easy to see why palm readers call the thumb much more than a mere finger. In fact, you've got your whole world in your thumb—from the strength of your will that's found in your thumb's first phalange, to the capacity of compromise that's found in its second, to the love you have to give that's found in the third.

The Volume and Length of the Thumb

Right off the bat, your thumb's volume and length reveal the force of your will. The average thumb reaches near the middle of the third (bottom) phalange of the Jupiter (index) finger. If it reaches beyond the middle of the third phalange, it's considered long, while if it doesn't get beyond the bottom of the third phalange, it's considered short. Of course, there are variants in where the thumb is set. We'll be discussing this shortly.

Left to right: average thumb, long thumb, short thumb.

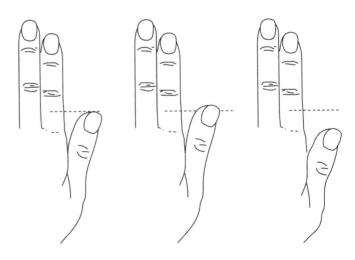

If you've got an average-length thumb, you're strong-willed without being stubborn, rational without being rigid, and tenacious without being clingy. When it comes to thumbs, in fact, "average" means healthy and well-adjusted.

If your thumb is longer than average, chances are you're full of vitality and enterprise, and need to be in authority, or, at the very least, prefer to work unsupervised. Independent long-thumbed folks may also be stubborn, overbearing, or insist on having their way. This is, however, the thumb of the born leader, the doer, someone who can make a difference. These are the people who need precisely those qualities, so a little stubbornness can go a long way.

If your thumb is shorter than average, you may not try as hard to get what you want—but that won't be what's important to you anyway. A short thumb indicates a more sentimental nature, someone who's more interested in the romantic side of things than the pragmatic. A short thumb can also indicate a follower, whether it's someone who follows directions well or prefers to settle into those situations that are offered. This includes being offered a career rather than finding one that's truly desired—taking what's accessible, in other words.

Hand–le with Care

Don't think that a short thumb means short-changed. Remember, the world needs poets as well as presidents. Or maybe a poet president wouldn't be a bad idea—look at Vaclav Havel of the Czech Republic (actually, we'd like a look at his thumb).

The Tip of the Thumb

Modern palm readers believe that the shape of the fingertips, and in particular the thumb's tip, is more important than the shape of the hand. To take a closer look at this, let's review the classifications here, and then relate them directly to the thumb.

Shape of Thumb Tip	Characteristics
Square	Practical, down-to-earth, follows routine, not often sensitive or expressed
Spatulate	Hands-on, can-do, everyday person, sometimes workaholic

continues

continued

Shape of Thumb Tip	Characteristics
Conic	Quick thinking, sensitive, artistic, not always very committed
Pointed	Intuitive and dreamy, possibly subtle or unexpressed (unheard), can be manipulative (passive aggressive)

Because the first phalange of the thumb rules the will (more about the thumb's phalanges in just a few pages), these tip shapes are applied directly to how you exercise your will. The heavier the thumb tip, the stronger the will, although, as with anything on the hand, a good reader will always look at other factors before drawing conclusions about your will and expression and yourself in the world from just the thumb tip alone.

In addition, the thumb's placement and role means it's possible for it to have a shape different from the other fingers. You'll probably very rarely see a hammered Saturn, for example, or a Mercury with a flattened tip. But these are both fairly common configurations for a thumb.

➤ A hammered thumb indicates difficulty in holding goals as well as a demanding ego.

➤ A flat tip can be either a manipulator or motivator of others, depending on other factors.

➤ A murderer's thumb shows too much force of will, which can result in impulsive actions. It's important to note that murderers' thumbs can be genetic, so just 'cause you've got one doesn't mean you'll end up in the slammer—but you would have to learn self-discipline and control of your force of will.

Top to bottom: hammered thumb, murderer's thumb (front and side view), flat-tipped thumb.

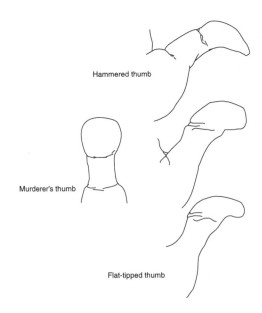

Hammered thumb

Murderer's thumb

Flat-tipped thumb

The Set of the Thumb

The set of the thumb involves two things. First, you'll want to note where on the hand the thumb actually sits, which used to be a judgment of intelligence but is now used to read degree of caution. Second, notice the angle the thumb naturally makes with the side of the hand toward Jupiter (index) finger, which is called the angle of generosity. Let's look at each of these in a little more depth.

You Take the High Road, and I'll Take the Low Road

In its most natural "setting," a thumb will sit at mid-hand, but you'll find plenty of thumbs that are set either higher or lower than this average (we'll discuss the set of a finger in more detail in the next chapter). Different 19th century interpretations exist for high-set and low-set thumbs, including that the higher the set, the lower the intelligence; or the lower the set, the greater the caution. Like we find a lot of those 19th century interpretations, we find these to be just a little too simplistic for the late 20th and early 21st centuries.

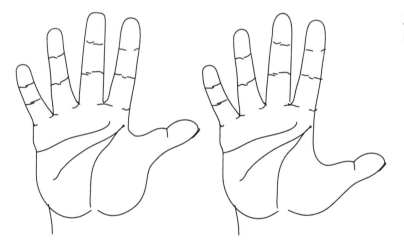

Left to right: a high-set thumb; a low-set thumb.

In fact, what Robin's discovered among the thousands of hands he's studied is that the higher set and more narrow the thumb is, the more specialized the person. Not only that, he's noticed that stronger thumbs are low set, but high-set thumbs have clearer direction. Lisa's low-set thumb is one of the reasons he calls her (affectionately, we hope) "the dilettante"—it's not that she's undirected; it's more that she's just interested in so many things. That's because low-set thumbs indicate what Robin calls the "generalist."

What should be clear is that, unlike those 19th-century interpretations, Robin's aren't good or bad—or class conscious. There's nothing wrong with specialization. And, Lisa's quick to add, there's nothing wrong with being a dilettante, either.

How Generous Are You?

For the next thumb measurement, hold your hand out naturally, palm up, and note the angle that's made between the thumb and the Jupiter (index) finger. Most thumbs create an angle of about 45 degrees or a little less, which creates a nice balance between self-interest and generosity. Palmists call this angle the *angle of generosity*, and it measures how you relate to others.

The angle of generosity. Top: average; center: narrow; bottom: wide.

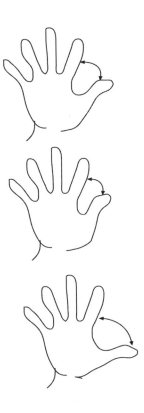

Handy Words to Know

The **angle of generosity**, measured between the thumb and the Jupiter finger, reveals how you relate to others.

A thumb with an angle stronger than 90 degrees seems very generous—and unlikely to acquire great wealth, unless the person's so talented that he'll learn to live with loads of dough. Even thus "loaded," much will be shared with a generous thumb—just plain "generous," the thumb can't help it.

An average angle of generosity means you'll "neither a borrower nor a lender be." You're practical and giving, but you're not going to be taken advantage of. Most of us fall into this category—willing to share, but pragmatic at the same time. We won't be giving the farm away to the next hobo who shows up, in other words.

The wider the angle of generosity, the more giving you're likely to be. Of course, a very wide angle can indicate a pushover, or someone who's just a wee bit too generous, while if the angle's more narrow, it indicates caution, and yes, when it's hugged tightly to the hand, stinginess. Like all that's revealed in the hand, though, there may be a very good reason you're less than trusting of others. And other factors in the hand may mitigate this as well.

How Stubborn Are You?

Next, take the first phalange of your thumb and try to bend it back. Does it bend back easily or resist the pull? Or, to put it another way, have you got a piece of licorice or a steel rod? The flexibility or inflexibility of your thumb is, as you may have guessed, an indication of *your* flexibility or inflexibility. Here's your ability to compromise—not to give in, but compromise. There's a big difference.

That piece of licorice is more correctly (and kindly) called a supple thumb. It has no problem bending over backwards, and that's its problem—it will bend over backwards. People with very supple thumbs may be extravagant and eccentric, and they'll tend to shift with the wind. They're also, we hasten to add, generally quite happy, bright, active, and daring people. A little flexibility is a good thing—it's too much that can be a problem.

That steel rod, on the other hand, is called a stiff thumb, and, like the supple thumb, its name implies its nature. A thumb that won't bend at all says stubborn, stubborn, stubborn, but just a little bit of give indicates good old-fashioned common sense. Stiff thumbs don't compromise because they have a straight-ahead approach. They also know that slow and steady wins the race, that it's best to put your money away for a rainy day, and that the early bird catches the worm (they also know a good cliché when they see one).

You're probably fortunate if this first phalange joint has at least some flexibility. That's because this indicates a capacity to adjust and compromise—to go with the flow, in other words. The capacity to make some adjustments with the changes life offers, after all, makes life easier all the way around. Too stiff a thumb can lead, quite literally, to a stiff neck. Take it from two stiff-thumbed folks who know!

Bend Me, Shape Me

Now, let's test your resilience. Take your poor abused thumb yet again and push down on the pad at the top of the first phalange. The first phalange is the one with your nail on it; the second's the one that connects the thumb to the palm; and the third is also your mount of Venus, which we'll talk about shortly. Is the pad at the top of the thumb's first phalange spongy? Does it bounce right back or just lie there and play dead? Or is there no give at all?

The resilience of your thumb pad is a good indication of your own resilience. If it's flat to begin with, you're probably a wee bit set in your ways (or possibly a little tired), while a fleshy pad indicates an extravagant nature. If, after you give it a push, it springs right back, you spring back from adversity, too, but if it just lies there and doesn't bounce back, your stamina is probably not up to snuff.

Like everything about your hand, this can change, so it's worth paying attention and watching your strength when your resiliency is not as good as it should be. And, if your normally springy thumb suddenly doesn't bounce back, a little herbal preventative maintenance, such as echinacea, ginseng, or goldenseal, could be in order as well.

Phalange Is Not a Dirty Word

Among them, the thumb's three phalanges cover just about everything: The first phalange represents your will and expression; the second, your logic and power of thought; and the third, the mount of Venus, your love and warmth for others. Think of it this way: If logic weren't there to mediate between will and love, who knows what would happen?

The following illustration shows you which phalange is which.

The phalanges of the thumb.

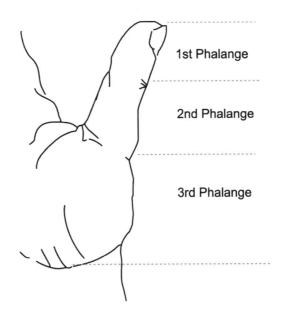

1st Phalange

2nd Phalange

3rd Phalange

When studying the phalanges, a palm reader looks at their shapes and relative lengths, as well as the shape of the thumb tip itself. Taken together, these three elements of the thumb paint a picture of your will, logic, and how your love motivates you; in other words, how you live in your world.

The Shape of the Thumb

Because the shape of the thumb is determined by the phalanges' relative lengths and shapes, we've saved that to talk about now. Thumbs come in as many shapes and sizes as people do, so it should come as no surprise that the shape of your thumb can reveal a lot about your will and logic. Take a look at the variety of thumbs in the following illustration.

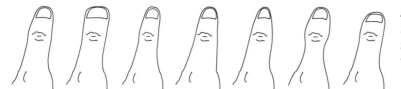

Some thumb shapes, left to right: conic, broad, narrow, tapered, pointed, waisted, hammered.

The shape of the thumb reveals how well your will and logic work together (or don't work together), and is determined by looking at the length and shape of the individual phalanges as well as at the tip of the thumb. In general, the wider the thumb, the more practical the person; the narrower the thumb, the more sensitive the person. But, as you'll soon find out, there's nothing general about what the thumb reveals.

The First Phalange

The first phalange of the thumb is the home of your will, and if it's longer than the second phalange, your will outweighs your reason. This means that you sometimes may insist on having your way without quite knowing why, or that you may have a bit of a temper. You may, in fact, be quite forceful in your opinions, although those opinions don't always have logic or reason to back them up. Some actions, with a long first phalange of the thumb, will be without substantiation, but the force of will carries them through.

Conversely, a short first phalange can indicate a lack of follow-through, or, for that matter, a lack of "beginning-through." Because the first phalange is where we find the power to act on our reasoning, if it's deficient, we may live far more in the world of words than action.

When the first and second phalanges are approximately the same length (or the second is just a bit longer), will and reason are balanced, which means there is judgment and determination in equal amounts, logic without vacillation, reason without tyranny.

Nothing can be accomplished without the force of will, whether it be the writing of a book, the building of a bridge, or the marriage of two people. Will is what accomplishes the goals of the second phalange—reason—and the third phalange—love. A good balance among the three assures a good balance in life as well.

Lengths of the first phalange.

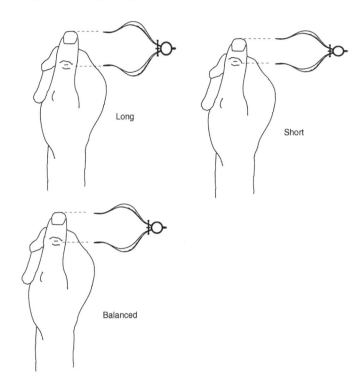

Long

Short

Balanced

The Second Phalange

The second phalange is where you'll find your intellect—your left brain approach to all you do. A well-balanced second phalange designates directed thinking—the kind you use playing chess, each move well thought out and considered, each step logically following the next. The second phalange represents an aspect of your inherent ability to learn.

The second phalange is the phalange of reason and logic, but if it's much longer than the first phalange, the thinking will take the place of action. Good ideas abound here, but actually taking action on them isn't likely unless there's something in the first phalange (such as it being well-fleshed or otherwise strong) to spur them on.

When the second phalange is dominant without being extreme, its owner has good judgment. It balances will and love, recognizing both but keeping them tempered with good sense. Think of it this way: Will and love without reason between them has been the subject of far too many tragedies.

An overly long second phalange indicates someone who may become so overwhelmed by the details that the whole job never gets done. That's because this represents thinking without adequate decisiveness, which can result in endless vacillation and self-doubt.

A short second phalange may indicate a lack of forethought and a rush to action. A short second phalange, in fact, often indicates someone who should look before she leaps.

Hand-le with Care

Sometimes the second phalange is so short that the person is incapable of making a decision. It's hard to lead people like this; they'll stand forever on the fence, leaning whichever way the wind is blowing. These folks are unlikely to take the personal initiative to explore their lives, and seldom break away to new ideas or professions.

If there's a horizontal line on the second phalange, this same capacity for self-doubt and self-criticism can be healthfully used. A repetition of this line, though, would be too much of the same. In this case, a little bit goes a long way.

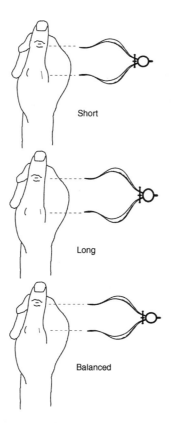

Short

Long

Balanced

Lengths of the second phalange.

The Third Phalange: Does Love Make the World Go 'Round?

When is a mount a phalange? When it's the mount of Venus, the third phalange of the thumb. How can this be? Take a moment to wiggle your thumb, bending it toward the other fingers. Notice how the mount of Venus behaves just as the third phalange of the other fingers, bending toward the hand? It's a phalange...it's a mount...it's Supermount!

Left to right: under-accentuated third phalange, well-balanced third phalange, very full third phalange.

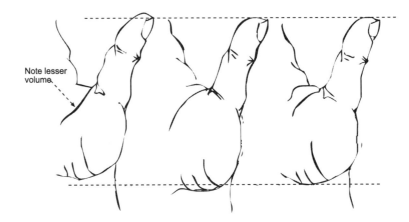

Note lesser volume.

But seriously, the mount of Venus's dual role is entirely fitting. As the thumb's third phalange, it's the home of love and passion—and, as we all know, love, whether sweet and kind or self-indulgent and embittered, motivates us all. If the length of the thumb's third phalange is equal to or greater than the length of the other two phalanges combined, then your love rules both your will and logic, and you're an incurable romantic. Of course, this can also mean that you're healthy emotionally, since to love and be loved is to live and survive. As we all know, "It's better to have loved and lost than to have never loved at all...."

Think of the mount of Venus as a representation of your appetite for life and material things, as well as your desires. Here you'll find your passion, too—that is, the warmth and depth of your feelings.

Because the third phalange is also a *mount*, we've got to look at it as we would a mount. Mounts are judged by a number of factors: their height and firmness, their width, and the markings (if any) that appear there. We'll be talking about the mount of Venus again, as a mount, in Chapter 17. But here, let's look at it as the third part of the thumb's equation, which you can write as: *will + reason + love = you*.

The Heart Chakra on Your Hand

The mount of Venus is defined by the life line, which we'll discuss in detail in Chapter 13. The life line is the one that extends on the palm from about the thumb's second phalange to the wrist. The more sweeping the arc of the life line, the wider (and usually, higher) the mount of Venus, while a life line that hugs the thumb means this third phalange will be narrow and confined. Simply put, the wider the third phalange, the wider the expression of the heart.

You can think of the mount of Venus as the heart *chakra* in your hand. In yoga, the chakras are considered the psycho-spiritual centers of the body's energy, and the heart chakra is the spiritual center for love. The chakras store and release prana, or the life breath. Stimulating the chakras to release the prana that flows through the spine is a lifetime study for many yogis! The chakras complement the brain, nervous system, and musculoskeletal system of Western medicine. The heart chakra, located behind your heart, is also called the Venus chakra. Note that we are giving the definitions of "chakra" and "prana" as they are used in the practice of yoga, not as they may be defined in the practice of any of the other Eastern arts.

The following table lists all seven chakra locations, their colors, the aspects of being human with which each is associated, and their planets, according to yoga tradition.

Handy Words to Know

Mounts are the areas of the palm where the action of your life unfolds. These include the mounts of the fingers, which share the respective fingers' energy, and the mounts of the palm: Venus, Mars, Uranus, Neptune, and Pluto. We'll be discussing mounts in detail in Part 4.

Handy Words to Know

The heart or Venus **chakra** is the center of the seven psycho-spiritual areas of energy in the body. The Venus chakra is the area of compassion and emotions.

Chakra	Location	Color	Association
First	Base of the spine	Red	Physical body, Saturn
Second	Area of the womb and genitals	Orange	Creativity, Jupiter
Third	Solar plexus	Yellow	The will, Mars
Fourth	Heart	Green	Emotion, Venus
Fifth	Throat	Blue	Communication and interpersonal connection, Mercury

continues

continued

Chakra	Location	Color	Association
Sixth	"Third eye" (center of forehead)	Indigo	Thought and intuition, Sun
Seventh	Crown of the head	Ultraviolet	The higher self, enlightenment, Thousand Petaled Lotus

According to yoga, the chakras are psycho-spiritual energy centers that store the life energy within the spine. This energy, called prana, is released by activating the chakras by performing yoga poses, meditation, and breathing exercises. (Illustration by Wendy Frost.)

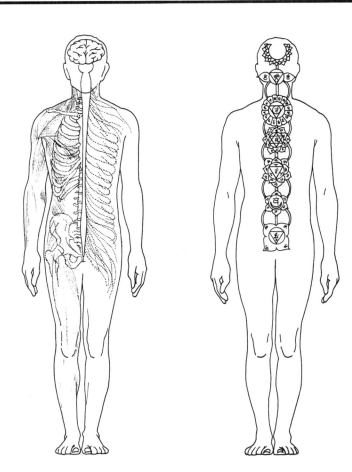

If you'd like to learn more about the heart chakra or the other six chakras, you'll find all that and more in *The Complete Idiot's Guide to Yoga.*

When the third phalange of the thumb is the longest of the three phalanges, the person is said to have a Venusian character. This means he or she has a good heart (both literally and figuratively), which in turn means good looks, good health, and a warm disposition. A high, firm mount of Venus indicates a passionate and resilient nature, a survivor in the face of tribulation and tragedy. Overdeveloped, though, it can mean that the heart rules the mind and the will, which can lead to foolish sentimentality.

A healthy third phalange is full, somewhat inflated, not unduly marked with grids, has a warm color, and isn't board-like, but resilient. All this means a healthy attraction to others, so strong first and second phalanges are equally important to keep this tempered with logic and will. It indicates, too, a sympathetic nature, someone whose care for others naturally means others will care for him as well.

When the third phalange is weaker, that is, flat, hard, and deflated, control issues are at work. Whether the control is being exerted by the will or the intellect is found by looking at the first and second phalanges of the thumb, but whichever is in command, the heart chakra suffers as a result. A narrow third phalange can indicate psychological or physical difficulties with sex, and if the mount is low and flat, the person will seem cold and unresponsive. Interestingly, the celibate might have a full third phalange—but it's expressed with food or other life pleasures and luxuries. There's more to physical pleasure than just sex, we remind you.

We Gotta Hand It to You

It's time for the "sad movie" test. Do you like sad movies? Do you cry at sad movies? Do you seek out sad movies when you're already feeling a little blue? Do sad movies give you permission to cry your heart out when your life asks for discretion? If you answered "yes" to all of the above, your third phalange may have a blue shadow on it, which indicates a need to lament. A depression on the mount of Venus will also indicate an emotional and regretful area in the heart, or, in other words, love lost.

Are You a Giver or a Taker?

Your capacity for giving and taking is really a matter of math: 1 full mount of Venus + 1 widely angled thumb = 2. When this equation appears in the hand, the person is seldom alone in life, and even if the person is alone, he or she is not that way for long. That's because this individual's life is generally full of people and people projects. When the giving equals the taking, companionship abounds.

Is the Love You Take Equal to the Love You Make?

Can you receive love as well as give it? Fewer of us are really as good at being receivers as we might think. Math is involved in this equation as well, but in this case your palm reader looks to both your thumb and your lunar mount (which we'll discuss in Chapter 18).

For example, there may be control issues going on when there's a wide angle of generosity and a strong second phalange joint, which can mean stubbornness. Sometimes manipulation is at work when there's a hammered thumb and a depleted lunar mount. Chapter 21 is all about love, so if you'd like to know more, we'll see you there.

Even Cowgirls Get the Blues: Some Thumb Stories

In Tom Robbin's 1970s classic, *Even Cowgirls Get the Blues*, the heroine, Cissy, is a beautiful woman with unusually large thumbs. Knowing what you now do about thumbs, what would you conclude about Cissy? Well, for starters, that she will (and must) find her equal.

Unusually large thumbs aside, Robin has again and again found the thumb to be the barometer of a person. For example, there's "Frank the Flower." Frank's thumb was too long and too full on top, with many lines that were so long they reached the life line, while his oddly bent third phalange was very short.

Frank was clever—especially when it came to living high off others. Living on welfare wasn't enough—he was also getting paid to go to school, and had a job through Social Services. While at work, he hurt his back, and was given disability on top of the benefits he was already receiving. Frank created his own undoing by bragging about how many different agencies were funding his lifestyle. When last seen, he was selling burglar alarms.

Then there was Rita. Pretty, smart, and capable, she had a large right thumb—and a much smaller left thumb. Now Rita was right-handed, so her capacity to lead was in conflict with her lack of confidence, and she often put herself in positions where her authority and independence were at decided odds. This was reflected in the battle of her thumbs as well.

A well-proportioned thumb will be found as the foundation of many a deliberate soul who's unwilling to fail. It's neither genius nor luck nor good fortune, but loving tolerance for fellow humans, consistency, and persistence as seen in the mount of Venus, the second phalange of intellect, and the first phalange of will, that's the dynamic that creates success for many, many people.

Which Thumb Are You?

As you can see, your thumb reveals an enormous variety of things about you—and it's time to apply these things specifically to your thumb. To do this, draw your thumb in your notebook, being sure to note its angle of generosity, shape, the length and shape of its phalanges, its nail and tip shape.

Once you've got your sketch, go back through this chapter and make some notes about what we have to say about your thumb. Are you surprised? You probably will be, in some ways. We don't always like what our thumb has to say about us—but it knows whereof it speaks. Pay attention!

The Least You Need to Know

➤ The thumb is the most important digit in palmistry.

➤ The length of the thumb is a measure of will and intellect.

➤ The angle of the thumb is a measure of generosity.

➤ The flexibility of the thumb is a measure of ability to compromise.

➤ The phalanges of the thumb exercise love, logic, and will.

Chapter 6

Your Mercury Finger: How You Communicate

In This Chapter

➤ Mercury: communication, commerce, impersonal relationships, medicine, and healing

➤ How clever are you?

➤ Finding your tact

➤ The ways you communicate and conduct your business

➤ Express yourself!

It may be called the "little finger," but your Mercury finger doesn't play a small role in your life. In fact, this digit holds the key to everything about communication and commerce in your life: your career, your business relationships, and your ways of communicating with others, including your use of the media and your potential to heal.

People with a strong Mercury can be healers or hypochondriacs, lawyers or liars, writers or publishers, physicians or psychics. In this chapter, we'll attempt to untangle the many sides of Mercury, and help you discover how *you* communicate.

Taking Care of Business, Healing, and Teaching

Mercury is nothing if not versatile, and those with a strong *Mercury finger* can be successful as anything from doctors to writers to palm readers (or any combination thereof). Lawyers and businesspeople also use strong Mercury tendencies to their advantage, and good public speakers are Mercury-influenced as well.

Just as yoga's heart or Venus chakra relates to the thumb's mount of Venus, its throat or Mercury chakra relates to the Mercury finger. Yoga's Mercury chakra is located in the throat and is the psycho-spiritual seat of communication. In astrology, Mercury is also the planet governing communications. When the planet Mercury goes retrograde (appears to be moving backwards), prepare for everything to take twice as long while communication glitches are resolved!

The Jupiter finger is for inspiration and Apollo's for showmanship, but no other finger combines so many different aspects into such a compact package as Mercury. In fact, Mercury is versatile precisely because your versatility itself is located here. Mercury the god was versatile, so it's only natural the finger bearing his name would cover a lot of territory.

Because Mercury covers so much territory, it also represents a wide variety of personal styles. In addition to communication and commerce, intellect and intuition are both at home here, each trait combining with the others in myriad ways that make you unique. How? Let's begin by taking Mercury apart—so that we can put it all together.

The Length of the Mercury Finger

The length of your Mercury finger is an indication of how clever you are. Do you have the gift of gab or are you the strong, silent type? Are you someone who's more comfortable in a familiar milieu rather than in the spotlight?

The average Mercury finger reaches to the bottom of Apollo's nail. Now, Mercury's not next to the Jupiter (index) finger, it's next to Apollo, the ring finger, which is just one good reason for using your ruler to measure its length. Another reason is that many peoples' Mercury fingers are *set* lower than their other fingers, with the third phalange's bottom well below the other fingers. Mercury should be measured by its length rather than its set (we'll be talking about its set a little later on) to determine whether it's average, long, or short.

When Mercury is longer than average, it can indicate someone who's "too clever by far." These people can't help but make money—but they may not have too many lasting personal relationships. But Mercury's main aspect in relationships are the impersonal ones, such as that with the mailman or your Internet server's help line, so a longer Mercury doesn't translate to friendship as a longer Jupiter does. In addition, the dominant phalange of Mercury is just as important as Mercury's overall length because this determines in which sphere of Mercury the emphasis is found.

A shorter Mercury can indicate a person who's not necessarily skilled in the art of communication; perhaps the gift of gab doesn't come easily. People with short Mercury fingers often prefer to stick close to home, not just because of the geographical comfort zone but because it's where they prefer to practice their skills. And while they may be in business, they don't necessarily have a flair for it: It's just what they do.

If you find a Mercury finger that's especially short (that is, no longer than the second joint of Jupiter), it could indicate a very definite lack of breadth or depth, someone who, in the days before political correctness, might have been called a hick or a rube. Let's call it instead hometown pride. (Lisa once lived in a county in rural Nebraska where many of the women, in their 90s, had never even been out of the county. Not to Grand Island, certainly not to Lincoln or Omaha. Short, short Mercuries—little tiny comfort zone.)

We Gotta Hand It to You

Mercury is named for the winged messenger god, whose areas of responsibility include wealth, trade, travel, commerce, manual dexterity, eloquence, androgyny, rapidity of thought, thievery, the wind, *and* protection of the animal kingdom (busy guy, that Mercury!). Among his many accomplishments, Mercury invented the lyre and the winged sandals, stole Apollo's cattle, and discovered fire. Further, he supposedly did all this in the first 24 hours of his life. It's easy to see why the word "Mercurian" is synonymous with the word "versatile."

Bottom to top: Average, short, and long Mercury.

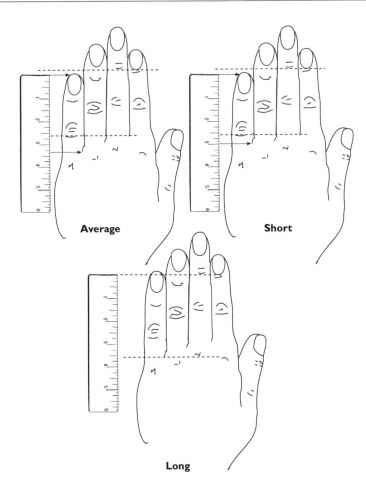

Average

Short

Long

The Set of the Mercury Finger

More often than any of the other fingers, Mercury may be low *set* on the hand. The set of the fingers is measured along an imaginary horizontal line at their base, and, in an evenly set hand, the bottom of each finger's third phalange would be roughly aligned horizontally with the other fingers'. Fingers that fall below this line are said to be *low set*, while fingers that begin above it are called *high set*.

Different palmistry books put forth different theories about a low-set, or dropped, Mercury. The one thing that all these theories seem to have in common, however, is the concept of deprivation. One book suggests that the subject will have repeated setbacks in his life: He'll rise to the top, only to fall again to the bottom, over and over again. Another theory, which we'll call the Freudian approach, proposes that there may be problems with the opposite sex arising from childhood difficulties with the mother or father.

Robin's take on the low-set Mercury brings another intriguing possibility into the picture. Robin has found that the low-set Mercury is an indication of an economic status that was lower than one's peers' during one's childhood. Perhaps not surprisingly, this is often a source of embarrassment to clients, and so is often vehemently denied when Robin first brings it up. In many cases, though, the client has later admitted that Robin was right.

A high-set Mercury is extremely rare. If you do come across one, whether the person's name is Sam Walton in commerce or Clyde Barrow in crime, Ted Turner in media or Christian Barnhard in medicine, that person will be profound in his or her particular Mercury talent. A high-set Mercury points to particular skill in one's chosen realm—and we'd bet these folks would have one.

Handy Words to Know

The **set** of a finger refers to its placement along an imaginary horizontal line drawn across the base of the fingers. The bottom of each finger's third phalange in an evenly set hand would be aligned horizontally with the other fingers. Fingers that fall below this line are said to be **low set,** while fingers that begin above it are called **high set.**

A low-set Mercury, a high-set Saturn.

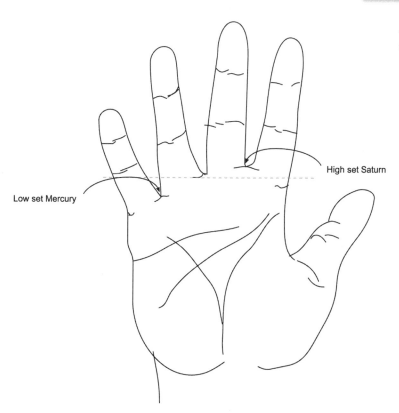

High set Saturn

Low set Mercury

The Leanings of the Mercury Finger

The shape of the Mercury finger takes into account a number of aspects: the relative thickness of each phalange, whether the finger is straight or leaning, and the width of the finger relative to its length. We'll address the phalanges and their lengths in their individual sections a bit later on. For now, let's take a look at which way Mercury's leaning.

Whether Mercury's crooked or straight is a measure of honesty, in all its various manifestations. Dishonesty, we must note at once, comes in many degrees and forms, from the gentle tact of "saying something nice" to the outright crimes of theft and perjury. Honesty, too, takes many forms, from George Washington's "I cannot tell a lie" to a child's "Mrs. Smith has a big nose." Most of us fall somewhere between the extremes of honesty and dishonesty—it's part of what makes us human.

Top, straight Mercury; middle, Mercury leaning away from Apollo; bottom, Mercury leaning toward Apollo.

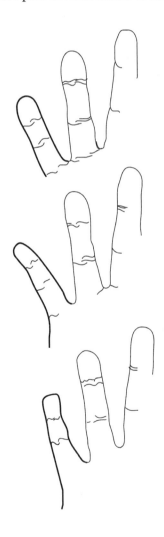

A short and crooked Mercury finger, whether leaning toward or away from the Apollo finger, indicates a, let us say, "challenge" with honesty. The degrees of this lean include a gentle bending toward Apollo, which indicates tact, and a gentle bending away from Apollo, which indicates someone whose passion is outside society's accepted norms, as well as the need to criticize society's ills.

Hand-le with Care

There's a difference between a leaning finger and a crooked or bent one. While a lean indicates an inclination, a bend can mean more serious issues with the finger toward which it leans, and can indicate a quality of extremes, seldom desirable ones.

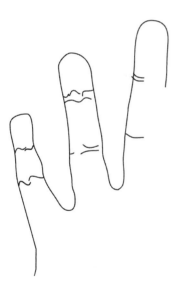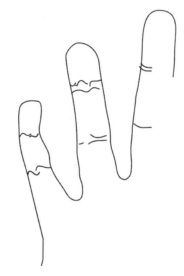

Mercury leaning toward Apollo (left); Mercury bent toward Apollo (right).

If your Mercury leans like a slender willow toward your Apollo finger, you've got good instincts about people. That's because you're a shrewd observer, someone who learns by watching, and knows that a little bit of tact and kid gloves go a long way. You may also be an alert businessperson, aware of the impact of others (such as trends and taste) on how your business prospers.

If that same slender willow bends the other way, away from your Apollo finger, you may well be what we'll call a "gentle eccentric." Maybe you're a snake breeder, a weekend nudist, or collector of newspaper clippings about eccentric people, but your passion lies outside what the rest of society is doing at the moment. Good for you!

If the lean away from Apollo is pronounced and extreme, the antisocial eccentricity may be more extreme as well. Role-playing games may be important—or playing the Grinch at Christmas. A Mercury leaning away from Apollo may belong to the solitary backpacker, the elitist, the self-published poet, or the psylocibin mushroom aficionado....

When Mercury is straight, the person's straight as well—like a Girl or Boy Scout, "straight, honest, and square"—which means that this person's a very poor liar. Fortunately, the straight Mercury knows it and makes no attempt to lie about anything, which in turn means he or she can sometimes be, well, tactless, when a social lie would probably be a better idea. (Graceful remark: "That tie looks great with that suit, unique and original!" Tactless Mercury: "A tie with flying pigs on it? What are you thinking?")

Because straight Mercury is often coupled with a pointed tip, you'll often find a level of idealism here as well: People who believe in the truth and hope of dreams, in other words. In this case, you'll find the social activist, the conservationist, the animal rights activist—the humanitarian with a mission.

The Angle of the Mercury Finger

To determine the angle of the Mercury finger, spread the hand open in a fan. The distance between Mercury and Apollo should be roughly equal to the distance between Apollo and Saturn, and the distance between Saturn and Jupiter.

The angle between Mercury and Apollo is called the *angle of eccentricity*, and it measures if, and how much, your behavior departs from what society considers the norm.

Handy Words to Know

The **angle of eccentricity**, measured between the Mercury and Apollo fingers, determines how much, if any, a person's behavior departs from what society considers the norm.

If the angles between each set of fingers are roughly equal, you're probably not especially eccentric or dramatic in your appearance or in the way you interact with society. Your house isn't going to be painted violet or chartreuse, you're probably not wearing leather and chains; you're comfortable, in other words, within what's accepted as normal within society.

A Mercury finger that's set slightly apart from the other fingers without being extreme indicates what we'll call acceptable eccentricity. Perhaps you eat cold pizza for breakfast every morning or talk like a walking dictionary, complete with punctuation. You may insist on certain regularities that others consider odd, but they certainly don't interfere with your functioning well within society.

Top to bottom: no angle of Mercury, balanced angles between fingers, wide angle of Mercury.

If your Mercury cocks far out from the other fingers, at an angle of 45 degrees or more, your eccentric behavior may depart from the norm to an unusual degree. Maybe you wear your kilt to work instead of a business suit, or maybe you're living in a yurt in southwest Colorado, but your distinct way of expressing yourself is an important aspect of who you are.

When the angle between the Mercury and Apollo fingers is very narrow, the person will have a chronic need for company and companionship. This person will very seldom be found alone.

A Look at the Mercury Phalanges

As with all of the fingers, each Mercury phalange covers a specific area, as you'll see in the following illustration. The first phalange in Mercury, the intuitive, reveals your sensitivity and inherent abilities. The second phalange, the mental, shows who and how you mind. The third phalange, the material, shows your knack for business communication.

The Mercury phalanges. The first phalange reveals your sensitivity and inherent style; the second phalange, who and how you mind; and the third phalange, your knack and use for business communication.

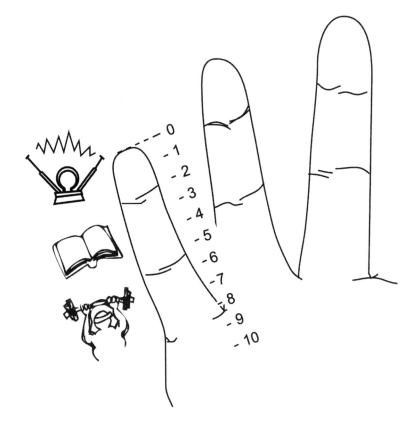

Get out your ruler and measure each phalange of Mercury. Many palmists feel that the ideal proportions, on a scale of 10, would be $2^1/_2$ for the first phalange, $3^1/_2$ for the second phalange, and 4 for the third phalange, but you're much more likely to find anything but this ratio. You'll probably find one phalange slightly longer or shorter than the others, although it's fairly common to find one phalange noticeably longer or shorter. Which phalange is longest and which is shortest reveal a great deal about your potentials and pitfalls for commerce and communication. Let's find out what.

The First Phalange

The first phalange of Mercury reveals your sensitivity and inherent abilities. In assessing its potential you should always take into account the shape of the fingertip as well, which we'll be discussing in a moment.

The longer the first phalange, the more intuitive the person is regarding communication. The longer first phalange is often found in the psychic. It's also a sign of the student or researcher, the person who communicates through learning, in other words. If the first phalange is extremely long, the subject is capable of great feats of expression, either in the written word or as an orator, and is very perceptive as well.

If the first phalange is noticeably shorter than the other phalanges, there's intelligence, but you're more likely to find the procrastinator or the last-minute improviser. These people do have good imaginations, though, which can come in handy for saving them from themselves when they get behind.

The Second Phalange

The second phalange of Mercury is the area of your mental approach to communication and commerce, and when it's strong and long, you're probably talking to the philosopher, who communicates in the realm of ideas. When the second phalange is the longest, a person is careful—even calculating—in his approach to his affairs and the affairs of others. There's a lively mind at play here, and it loves playing with ideas.

A short second phalange of Mercury indicates a degree of shyness. These people often appear aloof, proud, or even arrogant—and they don't care if they do. Interestingly, they often favor other species over their own (human, that is), so you'll often find a short second phalange of Mercury at dog shows and equestrian events. The mind is strong, but it doesn't always connect to other humans in a meaningful way. In this case, the arrogance is hiding the shyness.

At its best, the second phalange will be slightly longer than the first phalange and slightly smaller than the third phalange. People with this configuration will have a healthy degree of thought, evaluation, and planning directed toward their interactions with others and how they communicate, without being impractical or letting their imaginations get the better of them.

Hand-le with Care

On Mercury, strong vertical lines add strength to its positive aspects of mentality, thought, and imagination. Strong horizontal lines represent doubt within one's mental processes, which can translate to a practiced rather than natural approach to how one relates to others in business and other more impersonal settings.

The Third Phalange

How you relate materially to business and communication can be found on the third phalange of your Mercury, and both its length and fullness are factors to take into account in its evaluation. Do you need the corner office with a window to work to the fullest of your potential, or will any corner, anywhere, do? If you've got a longer, plumper Mercury, you're probably reading this in your room with a view.

The longer the third phalange of Mercury, the more likely it is that your office is outside your home, while the shorter it is, the less likely you are to have even bought an answering machine for your home office yet. We're exaggerating just a bit here to make our point: The third phalange of Mercury is the business side of yourself you show to the world.

A short third phalange of Mercury isn't much concerned with appearances when it comes to business and communications. This has nothing to do with how good you are at what you do—we're talking about the material aspect here, remember: How things look. Lisa's found that when it comes to massage therapists, for example, a less overtly clinical-looking office may be a decided asset in putting clients at ease. In her experience, the most effective massage therapists seem to have funky little offices added on to their houses, or they come to your house with massage table in hand!

A longer third phalange of Mercury, however, means that there is likely to be a well-tended reception area at the therapist's office entrance, and an attention to detail in planning out everything from the furniture to the carpeting to the view. The office may be called by its clinic name; the selection of herbal teas will come from a tea bar instead of the massage therapist's kitchen; the towels will be embroidered with the name of the clinic. You'll often find longer third phalanges in fingers of people who know that appearances matter when it comes to power—both attaining it and retaining it.

Helping Hands

Fleshy fingertips—that is, an unusual amount of flesh on the balls of the fingers—can be found with any and every fingertip type, but are fairly rare. They can indicate a meddle-some overachiever, or someone with perfectionist tendencies.

Mercury Fingertips

Here's our communicating tip, and we mean that quite literally. The shape of the Mercury fingertip is all about communication style. Are you a talker or the more quiet type? Are you better with the spoken word or the written word?

In addition, the shape of your Mercury fingertip can be a key to finding the career choice that best matches your potential. All that in a little fingertip? We kid you not.

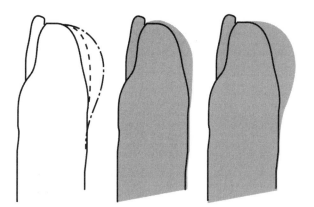

Fleshy tips.

Square Mercury

Someone with square Mercury fingertips may not say much, but that's because linguistic talent is not her strong suit. If this was your teacher, she may have had a good command of the subject matter but a not-so-good way of presenting it. Snore... You remember that one?

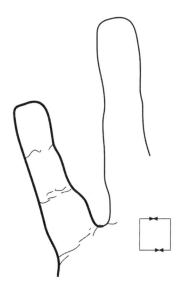

Square Mercury fingertip.

People with square Mercury fingertips aren't ones to make vague or imprecise statements; they say what they mean—when they say it. You'll often find them as the second-in-command—the foreman, for example—or the trusted right-hand man or woman. While they can be successful small businesspeople because they're competent without being risk takers and direct without being excitable, you won't often find them out in front of the crowd. In other words, people with square Mercury fingertips, won't be the best small businesspeople, but they can do it. After all, a little risk-taking is the name of the game when it comes to being a successful entrepreneur.

It can be frustrating for square Mercury fingertips to have to vary their routine or system, so they're at their best when things go according to plan—which they will, when they're around.

Spatulate Mercury

With a spatulate tip, Mercury's a hands-on type of person. Here's someone interested in the *tools* of communication and how they work: the radio engineer, the computer hardware consultant, the ham radio operator, the model airplane builder.

Spatulate Mercury
fingertip.

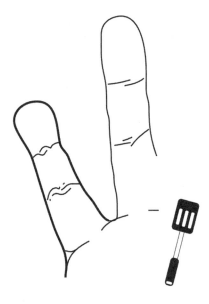

People with spatulate Mercury fingertips are readily accepted into society because they're so darned useful. They can fix anything from phones to faxes, and they'll learn about different ways of communicating, such as American Sign Language (ASL), just because it's there.

Spatulate Mercury's method of communication is tactile and tool-oriented rather than verbal. Remember that spatulate fingertips in general draw things in order to see them, so for them, the phrase "building communications" has a literal connotation.

Conic Mercury

People with conic Mercury fingertips are seldom at a loss for words. They're always finding yet another way to say something, and consequently are the great explainers among us. People with conic Mercury fingertips often wear several "hats" in their personal lives and are found in a variety of work roles.

Facile and agile, people with conic Mercury fingertips can move through various segments of society without a hitch. With their linguistic bent, you'll find them displaying their communication skills in a variety of ways—from chitchat to letters to the editor. You may find people with conic Mercury, with their knack for talk, in sales, but in fact you'll find these clever and resourceful people anywhere—and in all of us.

The person with a conic Mercury will frequently moonlight, or hold down more than one job. Many times, if they are not in a health field, they're around it, whether as the receptionist or the bookkeeper. It should also come as no surprise that conic Mercuries make great teachers.

We Gotta Hand It to You

Lisa's mother-in-law likes to tell the story of the first radio she and her husband ever gave to their son Bob when he was about five years old. He took it straight to his room, and, when they went to check on him an hour later, they discovered that he'd taken it completely apart on his bed. Why? Because he wanted to see all the parts that made it work. Yup—spatulate Mercury tip. Bob smiles indulgently when his mother tells this story but claims he has no recollection of it. However, when he takes things apart these days, it's because he wants to see all the parts—or make Lisa's Explorer run more efficiently.

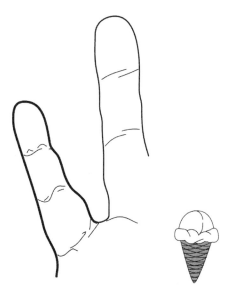

Conic Mercury fingertip.

Pointed Mercury

Pointed Mercury is considered an extreme of conic Mercury—communication taken to unusual extremes. For example, poets often have pointed Mercury fingertips. There's a sensitivity to precision of communication here, and a tendency toward specialization as well.

People with pointed Mercury fingertips may feel they've never found their niche in society, but this is often because they'll embrace some small aspect of something and then dodge away as soon as they feel it taking hold. This fickleness is as much about fear of belonging as fear of becoming overly committed.

Sensitive and articulate, people with pointed Mercury fingertips can be, to put it politically correctly, truth-challenged. That's because a person with a pointed Mercury understands the difference between "fact" and "truth," as well as how each can serve his or her own purposes. Someone with a pointed Mercury will tell others what he feels others want to hear—no matter what it's got to do with the truth. It's his sensitivity, in other words, that makes him tinker with the truth—not some inherent dishonesty.

Picture This: Some Mercury Stories

When we put Mercury's styles together, we find everyone from the nudist to the executive; but that should come as no surprise now that you've learned just how versatile this little finger is. One aspect of Mercury can be found in that great English teacher you had—you know, the one with whom half the students fell in love and the other half took advantage of? His strong but low-set Mercury meant he couldn't connect to the class as a whole, but that on an individual basis, he couldn't help but set hearts aflutter.

Pointed Mercury fingertip.

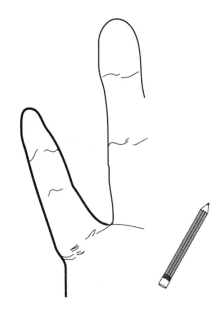

One of the more memorable Mercury fingers that Robin encountered belonged to a young man named Paul. His Mercury bent toward Apollo, and he had the natural appreciation of beauty that such a lean would indicate. So much so, that he couldn't help stealing whatever he saw that caught his fancy—Paul was a kleptomaniac.

In addition, Paul's first phalange was pointed but diminished, his second phalange was deficient, and his third phalange was, well, fat. He wasn't a liar, or even, really, dishonest. He did, though, tell people what he thought they wanted to hear, and he couldn't keep his promises. All this because of his crooked Mercury, with its most unusual phalanges—a sure sign of a less-than-honest nature.

Mercury craves challenge in the moment and a degree of intensity when it's strong. A surgeon would generally have a well-articulated Mercury with good phalange balance, for example, though the discerning line can be very fine. One of the best Mercuries Robin ever saw led its talented owner to drift through a half dozen careers, some quite specialized. It was the eccentric angle of his Mercury, leaning away from Apollo, and the fact that it was quite low set, that perhaps made this individual find lasting satisfaction as a blackjack dealer.

Actors, writers, and businesspeople often have a Mercury finger that's slightly apart from the other fingers. This, remember, is called the angle of eccentricity, and so it's our conclusion that certain careers require a certain amount of eccentricity for success. We're looking at our own hands now—and we both have a nicely coquettish gap between our Mercury and Apollo. Is this a requirement for writers and palm readers? Of course not. But it can't hurt.

Which Mercury Are You?

Take out your notebook and trace your Mercury finger, being especially careful to note the length of the phalanges and its shape. You should also pay attention to its set in relation to the other fingers, as well as its angle of eccentricity.

After you've got a reasonable facsimile of your Mercury, go back through this chapter and make notes about what we say about it. There will probably be some surprises as well as many things you already knew. And there will be things you may have known but never considered as well. That's what palmistry is all about: self-discovery.

The Least You Need to Know

➤ Your Mercury reveals your communication and commerce.

➤ The length of your Mercury is an indication of cleverness.

➤ The lean of your Mercury is an indication of tact.

➤ The dominant phalange of your Mercury reveals potentials and pitfalls for commerce and communication.

➤ The tip of your Mercury shows how you express yourself.

Your Apollo Finger: Oh, You Beautiful You

Apollo is the finger of the sun, brightest light of our world. This is where you'll find your creativity and appreciation of all things beautiful. But not only does your Apollo (or ring) finger reveal if you've got a knack for the dramatic, it shows your flair—whether it's as a collector of modern art or as a postmodern artist.

Here's where your sense of style and your sense of the spotlight reside; your sensitivity to creativity—and your sensitivity to creative types. Your Apollo finger is the heart of the matter, because, after all, the sun rules the heart.

Musicians, Actors...and Fortune-Tellers

It's no accident that if we wear only one ring, we wear it on our *Apollo finger*. That's because the ring finger is where we understand the value of adornment—and whether that ring is simple or elaborate can reveal nearly as much as the finger itself.

Handy Words to Know

The **Apollo finger** is the third finger on the hand, also known as the ring finger. Your Apollo is where you'll find your approaches to creativity and all things artistic.

We Gotta Hand It to You

To illustrate just how varied the manifestation of creative expression can be, we'd like to introduce you to a classic Apollonian: Alexander the Great (356–323 B.C.). That's right, this legendary military leader, who changed the political and social face of the world, led by charisma and dramatic personal example— pure Apollo creative expression. It's said Alexander's Apollo finger was unusually long, and we don't doubt it.

If you're a musician, actor, or fortune-teller, chances are your Apollo is the dominant finger. But creativity takes many forms, so we prefer to refer to your Apollo as the finger of your self-expression. If you're a designer, artist, or dancer, your Apollo is where it's going to show the most. But your Apollo also reveals your creative approach to accounting (hopefully, not *too* creative), acquisition, or designer accents.

The various measurements of the Apollo finger gauge the many different aspects of your creative expression. The length, for example, shows your tendency to take risks, while the shape is indicative of your detail orientation. Apollo's angle is a measure of taste, and which phalange is dominant shows in just what realms your tastes lie. Lastly, there's the Apollo fingertip, which reveals how you interact with the realm of creativity itself—whether as artist or patron of the arts.

The Length of the Apollo Finger

The average Apollo finger is about the same length as the Jupiter finger, and both should ideally extend to just above the bottom of Saturn's nail. A good balance between Apollo and Jupiter equals a good balance between creativity and ambition—which for an artist is a good thing to have. In fact, those whose strong Apollo fingers coupled with strong Jupiter fingers are often the more successful artists because they understand self-promotion as well as the creative urge.

The Apollonian may be the acrobat, the artist, or the actor, all people who represent the very heart of theater and performance. On the Apollo finger you'll also find the orator, the singer, and the musician, as well as the means by which these people capture our attention— and hold it—in the first place. Whether designer, seamstress, or window dresser, Apollo's committed to making something look good, or allowing something to look its best. This means that the sculptor, architect, or engineer is expressing her Apollonian urges as well.

When Apollo is long (that is, longer than Jupiter by at least half a nail, or reaching past the halfway point of Saturn's nail), an artistic temperament is clearly evident—though that same temperament may keep the person from consistent artistic expression. The inconsistency or perfectionism of a long Apollo can lead to a desire to retreat into a fantasy world, which is fine for the artist, so long as she returns once in a while.

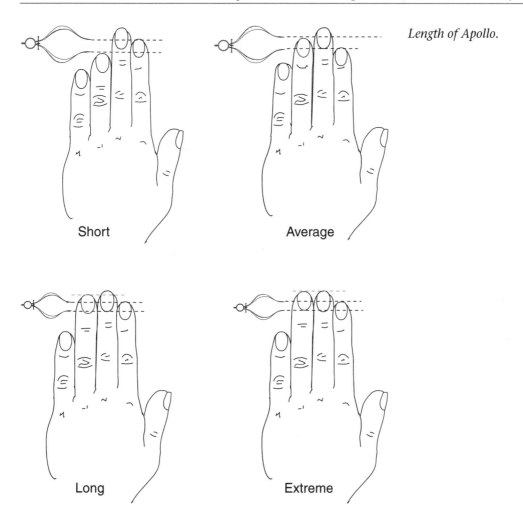

Length of Apollo.

Short

Average

Long

Extreme

Extreme Apollo, nearly equal to the length of Saturn, has a chronic need for an audience. These people have an innate sense of style that actually lends itself to professional performance and appearance. They're individualistic—but they don't always do well alone. In other words, they fully expect applause for their unique approach—and these are often the people you'll never see without their entourage. Because they don't always get the recognition they feel they deserve, people with extreme Apollo fingers will have their highs and lows. Although no one can be in the spotlight forever, someone with an extreme Apollo nonetheless truly believes he can.

In long Apollo, you'll find the risk taker, the person who pushes himself to extremes—the gambler, for example. In fact, this type can be found on the hands of many brief, fiery lives: The legendary actor James Dean, to name but one of these, had an extreme Apollo finger. Still, it's possible for someone with an extreme Apollo to live a full life

We Gotta Hand It to You

In truth, there's an Apollonian in us all, but when Apollo is strong and dominant, it can lend itself to an overbearing or transitory nature. This could translate to the charismatic actor or musician who doesn't live to fulfill his or her promise, or the artist whose flame shoots high—but only briefly. When Apollo is supported by other strengths in the hand, however, you'll find the consistent and ongoing application of creativity that makes a lasting impact in society.

and complete his destiny, albeit with more than the usual amount of highs and lows: Witness long-lived (and brilliant!) architect Frank Lloyd Wright.

While a person with too much strength in the Apollo finger needs acclaim and recognition in order to function, if there's not a strength in the Apollo finger, creativity won't be the driving force. There may be chronic shyness when an Apollo is less-than-average length, especially in front of an audience, and chances are fine arts aren't going to motivate the person in any significant way. People with short Apollo fingers may not, say, *appreciate* the difference between sautéed and fried.

While people with short Apollo fingers may well be educated regarding good taste, an education is all it's going to be. The gut appreciation of fine things— the capability of being moved to tears by a musical composition or masterpiece on canvas—just isn't going to be there.

The Shape of the Apollo Finger

Do you hate details? Do you like to linger over the nuances of brush strokes in a painting, or do you hurry on to the next picture? The shape of your Apollo finger reveals a great deal about how you appreciate things of beauty.

When the Apollo finger is full and fleshy, there's not a particular specialty or creative discipline where the talent lies. What you'll find instead is an attraction to many different fields, a flitting here and there, so to speak. There's a sensual nature here, but there's not necessarily any control of it.

A smooth, graceful Apollo finger indicates an active appreciation and taste in one particular realm of the creative arts. Let's be specific about this: This is the lover of kinetic sculpture, for example—who can't understand why someone would want to carve a statue out of marble. This is the classical composer to whom bluegrass is a cacophony not fit for the human ear. Someone with a smooth Apollo has strong tastes, but while his preferences are not really very unusual, he'll think they're the only genre worth loving.

If the Apollo finger is waisted, or bony, in appearance, the person's going to be detail oriented. This is someone more likely to be caught up in nuance than the bigger picture—that brush-stroke inspector we talked about earlier. In a writer, for example, this would be the Flaubert, polishing each word to perfection before moving on to the next word. Not someone who'd meet a publisher's rush delivery schedule, needless to say.

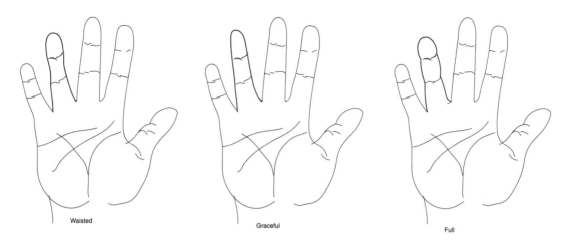

Waisted   Graceful   Full

Left to right: waisted Apollo, graceful Apollo, full, fleshy Apollo.

The Angle of the Apollo Finger

Which way does Apollo lean? Apollo's direction is an indication of one's taste in art and expression. If the lean is toward Saturn, that taste is in a socially acceptable direction; toward Mercury, it's socially more obscure. To illustrate: A Mercury leaner may collect tattoos or antique whips, while a Saturn leaner won't collect anything that's not pragmatic, money-oriented, or hasn't "fallen in her lap."

When the Apollo finger is straight, the person's taste is more difficult to define. A straight Apollo finger indicates someone who's her own person, when it comes to the arts. When the Apollo's straight, in fact, we look to other parts of the hand to determine the person's style. Is it dance? Architecture? Music? Taxidermy? Part of the answer will lie in the shape of Apollo: If it's graceful and sensual—whether or not it's actively creative—the person has a deep appreciation for, and definite opinions about, the artistic realms.

A Look at the Apollo Phalanges

Once again, it's time to get out your ruler and measure each phalange of Apollo. Many palmists feel that the ideal proportions, on a scale of 10, are $2^1/_2$ for the first phalange, $3^1/_2$ for the second phalange, and 4 for the third phalange, but, as with the Mercury finger, you're much more likely to find anything *but* this ratio. You'll probably find one phalange slightly longer or shorter than the others, in fact, although it's fairly common to find one phalange noticeably longer or shorter.

Which phalange is longest and which is shortest reveal a great deal about your creativity and artistic inclinations: the *ways* you're creative, in other words. How are you creative? What's the best way for you to express your creativity? What kinds of creative endeavors do you appreciate? Are you a participant or a patron of the arts?

The phalanges of Apollo. The first phalange reveals your sensitivity to creativity; the second phalange, your mental approach to creativity; and the third phalange, your material approach to creativity.

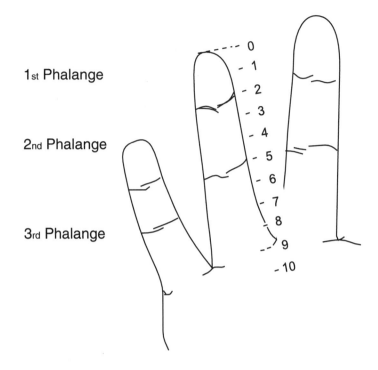

1st Phalange

2nd Phalange

3rd Phalange

0
1
2
3
4
5
6
7
8
9
10

The first phalange of Apollo covers the intuitive realms of creativity; the second phalange, the mental realms; and the third phalange, the material realms. Between the three of them, they've got creativity covered.

The First Phalange

The first phalange of Apollo is an indicator of your sensitivity to creativity. An active, creative individual will almost certainly have a relatively long first phalange of Apollo, with very resilient flesh on the pad at its tip. Resiliency is an important aspect of creativity, and the most creative among us will bounce back from setbacks almost effortlessly. Well, almost.

When the first phalange of Apollo is short, you'll find someone who appreciates things of a more technical nature, such as the lover of history or science, rather than someone who's moved by a sonata or swayed by a sunset. At the same time, a person with a short first phalange may well be someone who understands the monetary value of art, and so will appreciate its return on investment—even if he can't quite get a handle on what the art "means."

Hand-le with Care

Sometimes, you'll find the first phalange of a creative person with flesh that just doesn't spring back as it should. This lack of resiliency is a direct result of creative burnout—they've exhausted their creative energy by working too hard. Like all kinds of burnout, this is a temporary setback. When the first phalange returns to a flexible, resilient state, it's time to get back to work. Setbacks are just that—setbacks. They're not permanent by any means.

When the first phalange of Apollo is extremely long, the person's quite likely to be moved to tears by music, art, dance—or that amazing Beaujolais. There's a danger here of letting the instincts carry one too far—a long first phalange is often found on the compulsive gambler, for example—but there's also the possibility of extraordinary creativity as well. A long first phalange isn't a prerequisite for creativity, but it is an indicator.

The Second Phalange

The second phalange of Apollo shows how we mentally and intellectually approach the creative process. This includes our appreciation of the creative process, as well as what we expect from the plot of a book. Do you like unexpected turns of plot, never knowing what's going to happen when you turn the page? If so, most likely you've got a long second phalange of Apollo. If, you prefer a more traditional approach, where the bad guy always gets it in the end, your second phalange of Apollo is probably shorter. Your second Apollo phalange, in other words, reveals your plot of choice.

Helping Hands

A long second phalange of Apollo can be found on the historian who understands that history is an art form. There's an immersion in detail that adds to and enriches the appreciation of the art form— putting the art form itself on a sort of pedestal.

When the second phalange of Apollo is long, there's a love of detail, nuance, and subtlety. People with a long second phalange of Apollo appreciate stories with recurring characters, as well as an abundance of detail. These are the folks who've not only read *Lord of the Rings*, but Tolkien's appendixes to that series as well. We're talking obsessive here—the people who know where Bilbo was born, and what he was doing on August 2nd.

With a short second phalange of Apollo, a person may possess a deep appreciation of vibrancy of activity, intensity of color, or extremes of contrast, such as can be found in a dessert like baked Alaska, say, or short-sprint racing. In other words, a short second phalange of Apollo indicates a tendency toward narrow scope and specialization, such as a love of country-western music or kinetic sculpture.

People with short second Apollo phalanges may be attracted to certain genres, but they won't notice that the mysteries they love are all written by the same author. Or, they may become absolutely passionate about an individual performer or artist without noticing that the artist has peers or contemporaries. We call this "The Elvis Fan Syndrome."

When the second phalange of Apollo is of average length, you're likely to express your own taste without being overinfluenced by what's popular. You read what you like rather than what everyone else is reading, Oprah notwithstanding. Your pursuit of your interests is both prudent and healthy—not obsessive, in other words, as it might be with a long second phalange, and not specialized, as it might be with a short one.

We Gotta Hand It to You

When the second phalange of Apollo is long and the third phalange is short, you've got the sports statistician. You know, the guy who knows the box scores of every Yankee that ever played? There's this immersion in detail plus this attention to minutiae that combines to create, well, specialization. Extreme specialization. Of course, Roger Maris's 61 in 61 doesn't mean much now that Mark McGwire's had his way. But we digress.

The Third Phalange

The third phalange of Apollo relates to our taste in the material world and how we express ourselves in that material world. It's concerned with the art of the game, rather than the game itself. When we look at the third phalange, we look not only at length but at width. When the third phalange is well balanced, we're apt to find the patron of the arts rather than the creator.

A short, thin third phalange of Apollo belongs to the minimalist, and by that we mean the collector who can carry his collection with him—angels on heads of pins, for example, or, on a more earthly plane, matchbooks. This is the guy with the baseball cards, the gal with the thimbles. Think small, in other words.

It's important to note that a thin third phalange of Apollo indicates a person who won't let her interests run rampant over her life. If that third phalange is full, though, she may be obsessive about her passion.

If the third phalange is of moderate size and the second phalange is also balanced, you've got the discriminating hobbyist. This may be the guy (like Robin) with attractive aquariums, with multi-colored snakes, and lizards in every room, or the woman with an extensive musical library. The important thing to note here is that the creativity in this case is as patron and participant, though it may not be the "performer," per se.

A short and full third phalange of Apollo indicates earthy tastes. You may find your collector of taxidermy here, or the guys with the pyramid of beer cans. Martha Stewart they're not. "Martha who?" they ask.

Vanity is the name of the game when the third phalange of Apollo is long, and Robin's never met someone with a long third phalange of Apollo who didn't have an educated opinion about food. In fact, if yours is also full and fleshy, you're probably an epicure.

Another interesting aspect of someone with a large third phalange is that she most likely won't live in very small quarters, and certainly won't be happy in an efficiency apartment. When the long third phalange of Apollo is also slender, the person won't own much in the way of possessions—but she still won't be happy in, say, a subcompact car.

Apollo Fingertips

The Apollo fingertips reveal how you interact within the realm of creativity and the arts. Are you a dabbler within many creative fields or is your creativity focused on one realm? Are you a musician or a painter? Do you sing or play an instrument? Do you prefer to work with your hands or with tools? The Apollo fingertip can answer all of these questions and more.

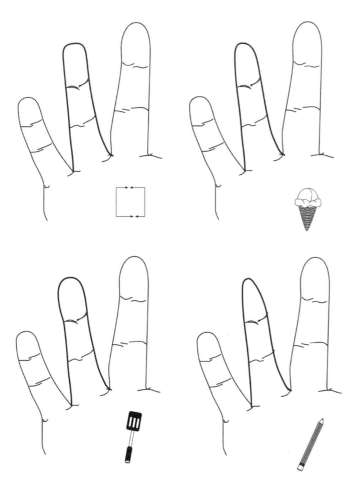

Square Apollo, spatulate Apollo, conic Apollo, pointed Apollo.

Square Apollo

It's rare to have a square Apollo tip, but it's not at all undesirable. A square fingertip on the Apollo finger simply means that the creative endeavor is of a more pragmatic nature, such as architecture or engineering. Whatever the creative venture of the square-tipped Apollo, though, it should have lasting power—square-tipped Apollo isn't easily changed to other venues.

This fingertip lends itself to the natural musician and singer. It also represents the pragmatic inventor, refining the work of others to make it useful. The person with a square-tipped Apollo is, above all, drawn to the more stable forms of creativity—and the talent doesn't dominate his life. With a square tip, Apollo has the balance of the practical along with the creativity.

Spatulate Apollo

The spatulate-tipped Apollo person is very handy. He's a quick study who picks up techniques and styles rapidly and seemingly effortlessly. There's a ready musicianship here, too: Three months of practice will sound like three years when a spatulate Apollo picks up the guitar. Unfortunately, spatulate Apollo doesn't always take it any further.

The person with a spatulate-tipped Apollo is a natural with tools and tends to think three-dimensionally. Just because they're quick studies, though, don't think they're glib or quick with words. Words, in fact, are not their forte, and they'd just as soon draw a diagram as explain something verbally.

Conic Apollo

A person with conical Apollo tips is a practitioner to whom everything comes easily, be it art, music, or acting. Sometimes she will take an overseer role, such as director or editor, but artistic creation is the first name here.

If the third phalange of a conic-tipped Apollo is full and long, you may find someone who takes a technical approach to creativity, such as working in the darkroom, providing the costumes, or being a pastry chef. This fingertip type doesn't encourage undue specialization, although there can be perfection issues if the fingertips are long. No, really, that frosting looks lovely to us...

Pointed Apollo

A pointed Apollo finger can be an indication of the dilettante, the person who's so acutely appreciative of all things beautiful that he can't focus on one specific area. When Robin sees a pointed Apollo, he'll often suggest limits to the person: "You should focus on pastels and acrylics," or "Stick to the keyboard and the flute," or "Why not limit yourself to the quatrain and the lyric poem?"

For people with pointed Apollos, many disciplines of the arts are a breeze. The problem is, there's not enough depth within any of these disciplines because they all come so easily. Those who don't have pointed Apollos are often frustrated when they see the works of these gifted souls. People with pointed Apollos produce their creations seemingly almost without effort, while the people whose fingers aren't pointed achieve the same level only through blood, sweat, and tears.

Unless the person with a pointed Apollo has a very functional and disciplined support system, her gifts will frequently be lost to her lack of focus and direction. Less pointed-fingered folk may cry at the loss, but they may also be secretly overjoyed that the person with the pointed Apollo has crashed and burned.

Beauty and the Beast: Some Apollo Stories

Let's talk about the self-destructive artist—the person who flies high and then dies. True, in less dramatic fields of art, such as sculpting, you'll find people who frequently drift in and out of activity, or who apply their talents in other creative venues. But we're talking here about more dramatic Apollo. Remember: Apollo, which represents the Sun, is naturally the stuff of light, and those with strong Apollo energies must be handled with discretion and even insulation by those around it as well as by its participants.

This means that, uninsulated, Apollo, like Icarus who flew too close to the sun, will crash and burn. Some possible examples: James Dean, Marilyn Monroe, Jimi Hendrix, Jim Morrison, River Phoenix...you get the picture.

We hasten to add that Apollonian incorrigibility doesn't necessarily take the form of self-destruction. Hey, there's always self-sabotage. Think of the promising young male actor (there's one in every generation), whose tendency to pick a fight—or purchase illegal drugs—has been his undoing.

Robin's met more than one gifted performer, singer, or charismatic athlete who, upon arriving at the brink of success and witnessing its multifaceted and chaotic demands, chose to step back and enjoy a lesser recognition instead. While he initially felt this was a waste of a "gift," over time, Robin's come to appreciate that these people haven't made such bad choices after all.

Which Apollo Are You?

It's once again time to take out your notebook and sketch the finger we've discussed in this chapter. Be sure to note the length of the phalanges, as well as the shape of the finger. Then, go back through the chapter and make some notes on what we have to say about *your* Apollo—and about your creativity.

The Least You Need to Know

➤ Your Apollo finger reveals your artistic side.

➤ The shape of your Apollo finger shows your knack for detail.

➤ The angle of your Apollo finger reveals your taste.

➤ The Apollo phalanges show your appreciation for the arts.

➤ The Apollo fingertip shows how you interact with the realm of creativity.

Chapter 8

Your Saturn Finger: Rules and Regulations

In This Chapter

➤ Your Saturn finger: structure, boundaries, order, and karma

➤ The length of your Saturn finger: how you're responsible

➤ The shape of your Saturn finger: your attitude toward discipline

➤ The Saturn phalanges: how you deal with authority

➤ Your Saturn fingertips: your practicality

Someone's got to bring a sobering influence, lay down the law, and remind you of your responsibilities. This thankless role belongs to your Saturn (or middle) finger, the big guy on the block. Mercury communicates, Apollo creates, and then Saturn draws the line. It's here you'll find your attitude toward discipline and the way you deal with authority, as well as your karmic responsibilities.

Don't let Saturn scare you, though—we all need some boundaries and rules, after all. Think of your Saturn finger as The Enforcer if you must, but thank it occasionally for performing this often thankless role, too.

Property and Responsibility

Commonly the longest finger in the hand, Saturn is often called the conscience of the hand or the karmic enforcer because of its prominence. Your *Saturn finger* shows how you relate to the law within society, your nervous system, skeletal system, and spine. In addition, Saturn exhibits your responsibilities, in some cases your possessions, and to some degree your relationship with your father or the male parenting figure in your life. We call him *Mister* Saturn.

Handy Words to Know

Your **Saturn finger**, the middle finger on your hand, is where you'll find structure, boundaries, and order. Saturn is also called the conscience of the hand or the karmic enforcer.

From its length, which shows how you're responsible, to its tip, a measure of your practicality, Saturn is one commanding finger. But, after all, Saturn was the father of the gods.

The Length of the Saturn Finger

Saturn generally extends the length of its own fingernail beyond Jupiter and at least a half a fingernail beyond Apollo. A longer Saturn may indicate an extremely deliberate and serious nature, and, at times, a degree of melancholy. There may be attention to the law, research, or another deep and practical study, such as chemistry or metallurgy. When you realize a long Saturn is the natural realm of the lawyer, the judge, and the surveyor, you begin to see how much it is synonymous with authority. And Saturn's appetite for history means there's an appreciation for antiquities as well.

Length of Saturn.

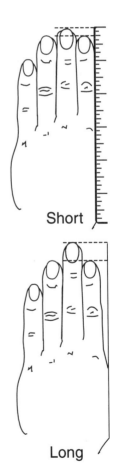

Short

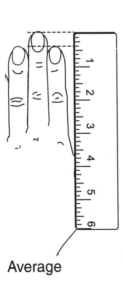

Average

Long

124

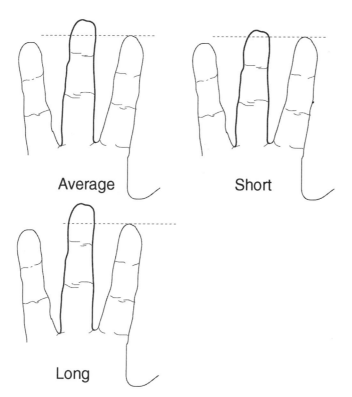

More length of Saturn.

Average

Short

Long

Saturn is short when it appears "challenged" by Apollo and Jupiter; or, in other words, when both fingers approach Saturn's length. The Saturn finger (assuming it hasn't been shortened by an accident) should be considered "short" when only 25 percent of its nail extends past the Apollo finger. However, it's possible that the Apollo finger is long, rather than the Saturn finger being short. How do you know? The simple answer is to compare the Apollo finger to the Jupiter finger. The Apollo finger should be only a little longer, if at all, than the Jupiter finger.

The short Saturn might be described as a ship without a rudder. People with short Saturn fingers frequently attach themselves to individuals with a more defined (and occasionally pedantic) path, and, by accepting these other peoples' projected plans, they may, in fact, do very well.

Helping Hands

Abraham Lincoln is the archetypal Saturn figure. He had a tough life: He lost his favorite son, his wife went mad, he didn't win many elections (except when it *really* mattered!), and he came from an extremely unfortunate and dysfunctional background. Even on Lincoln's long frame, his long Saturn finger couldn't go unnoticed.

Hand-le with Care

If both the Apollo and Jupiter fingers are long, and Saturn is comparatively short, you've got the makings of the charismatic outlaw. Billy the Kid's just one example.

The person with a short Saturn, unfortunately, may not always have a deep respect for the law. With a tendency to not hold onto assets or property or to see long-range potentials, someone with a short Saturn finger may, quite literally, "take the money and run."

A normal Saturn finger usually indicates someone who has a healthy relationship with the male parenting figure, or with the dominant disciplining parent. There is an appreciation for land, property, and investment—without a miserly or greedy acquisitive nature. People with normal-length Saturn fingers also appreciate dignity, discipline, and order. After all, the normal Saturn finger defines the center of the hand—it's the balance beam personified (in a finger).

The Shape of the Saturn Finger

Whether Saturn's straight or leaning reveals your feelings about both law and order, and a straight Saturn indicates an understanding and respect for the law, boundaries, and discipline.

When Saturn bends toward Jupiter, it can be very useful for the self-made person, because it can indicate a personal level of discipline, such as can be found in the athlete or performer who works long and hard to achieve his goals. In addition, the Jupiter-leaning Saturn may have a quality of personal ruthlessness. You might find this in the self-promoting politician, for example.

When Saturn leans toward Apollo, you may have found the "philosophical outlaw." Rather than an indication of a person with illegal or even eccentric behavior, this is a sign of someone who has great sympathy for the underdog and is willing to support unpopular or not entirely accepted concepts.

For example, passive Saturn (which we discussed in Chapter 4) might be a Libertarian or animal rights activist, a freedom rider in the 1950s, or women's suffragette at the turn of the century. What's key to the philosophical outlaw is that she's intellectually aware of and alert to some aspect of injustice or inequality within the world—and generally has both opinion and activity about that issue.

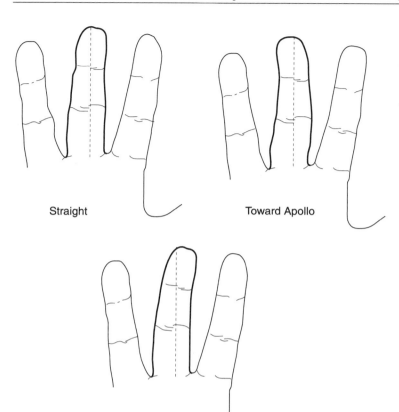

Straight

Toward Apollo

Toward Jupiter

Lean of Saturn: straight Saturn finger, Saturn leaning toward Apollo, Saturn leaning toward Jupiter.

The Angle of the Saturn Finger

An isolated Saturn, with broad or noticeable spaces between the Saturn finger and both the Jupiter and Apollo fingers, may indicate someone with a preference for privacy. These people may have a separate den, study, or workshop, and although they may also have husbands, wives, or business partners, they'll do a significant amount of their work alone. Don't try to make the isolated Saturn a member of the team—he prefers to work on his own.

Isolated Saturn fingers are often found among some, though not all, people who've chosen to live lives of religious isolation. You'll also find isolated Saturn fingers among people who've lost their freedom to some degree, whether they reside in a prison, mental institution, or are physically challenged in some way.

Helping Hands

The next time you meet a forest ranger, night watchman, lighthouse tender, hermit farmer, or anyone else who's chosen a solitary life, physically separated from society, check for aspects of the isolated Saturn in the hand.

A Saturn without gaps or openings between Jupiter and Apollo is common, and minimizes the singular or isolated aspects of this finger. Even if the Saturn finger itself is strong, and the person thus values privacy in her lifestyle or personal choices, you'll still find her having a reasonably active social life and some sort of connection with others. Even the most devoted computer aficionado has her e-mail, after all.

A Look at the Saturn Phalanges

It's once again time to get out your ruler and measure each phalange of Saturn. As with Mercury and Apollo, on a scale of 10, the first phalange should be about $2^1/_2$; the second phalange, $3^1/_2$; and the third should equal about 4. Note that this is a ratio, not a measurement—if you do find 10-inch fingers, call us at once!

As usual, you're likely to find that most hands fall outside this ratio. You'll probably find one phalange slightly longer or shorter than others, although it's fairly common to find one phalange noticeably longer or shorter. Which phalange is longest and which is shortest shows how you deal with boundaries, advice, and authority.

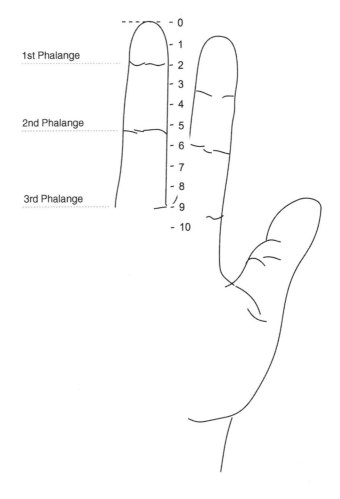

The Saturn phalanges. The first phalange reveals your attitude toward boundaries; the second phalange, your approach to Saturn's world; and the third phalange, your role within society.

Your first phalange represents how you work with and perceive your role within the realm of boundaries, rules, conscience, and commitments. The second phalange reveals your mind's willingness to grapple with the very complex world of Saturn, that is, research, hard science, and material laws, such as those of physics and chemistry. Your third phalange shows your role within society as a law abider, law enforcer, and property owner, and it's here you'll find how you express discipline to others and to yourself.

The First Phalange

How do you work with and perceive your role within boundaries, rules, conscience, and commitments? To answer this question, palm readers look to the first phalange of your Saturn finger.

The person with a short first phalange of Saturn probably won't have a deep and reverent appreciation for the status quo—this could be the revolutionary and the philosopher. In addition, the spiritual sense may be challenged by the length of the other fingers, resulting in someone without a strong spiritual base.

A person with a short first phalange of Saturn may well have had a loving, nurturing, and supportive father, but the father may not have had strong opinions or he may have demanded conformity. In a physical sense, we should note, a short first phalange of Saturn may indicate someone with an agile and to some degree youthful physical appearance.

On the contrary, a long first phalange of Saturn can indicate someone who appreciates nuances of laws, mores, and rules, as well as their interpretations; for example, the concept of legal precedent and its powers. In addition, it's unusual to find someone with a long Saturn who challenges his father's rule. In fact, it's been Robin's experience that such a person lives in a patriarchal system that includes an active and influential grandfather as well.

A long first phalange of Saturn may indicate a nervous sensitivity, or an acuteness of receptivity in the senses. This is not always pleasant, but, Saturn-like, may be frequently suffered in silence. If coupled with pronounced knuckles on the Saturn finger (as opposed to the smooth Saturn finger), a long first phalange of Saturn can also indicate problems in the nervous system.

A medium-length first phalange of Saturn indicates the capacity to live within the laws of society as well as to some degree with the mores of society. It's not that such people don't break laws or challenge their neighbors' sense of propriety, but that they won't do such things in an acute way. The medium-length first phalange of Saturn also points to a strong physical constitution and so, of course, is very desirable for a long and comfortable life, especially where the nervous system is concerned.

Helping Hands

It is possible to find someone with a long second phalange of Saturn who is not surrounded by books. Robin's seen two. One of them was totally auditory, and had an extensive library of music; the other was illiterate.

The Second Phalange

The second phalange of Saturn reveals your mind and its willingness to grapple with everything from hard science to the law.

When the second phalange of Saturn is short, the person's willingness to apply mental energy to problem solving may not be strong. There may be a need to seek an expert or call on a friend when clear and rational informational input or advice is called for. In addition, there's an impatience with complex legal issues and intricate and detailed stories, as well as a lack of appreciation for the intricacies of a chess game.

Never, however, underestimate short second phalange Saturn folks: They almost always have compensating aspects of intuition or insight that serve them just as well as meticulous mental dissection.

The person with a long second phalange of Saturn may be recognized as headstrong with self-determining behavior, which is often based on one's own intelligence, research, and decision-making processes. The person with an articulated second phalange of Saturn may not be a quick thinker; but, whether his joints are smooth or knotty, generally he thinks well and makes good decisions.

When the second phalange of Saturn is long, you'll discover a love of minutiae and details. Here you'll find the person who plays chess or engages in any other endeavor where strength and depth of thought process is necessary for success. The person with a long second phalange of Saturn generally has strong self-confidence in areas where mental acuity is needed. In addition, it's rare to meet a person with a long second phalange of Saturn who doesn't have an appreciation of and interest in history.

Because it's not overly long or short, the balanced second phalange of Saturn may be more difficult to define. Yes, the bookworm is an example of an abundant mental energy, while the illiterate or semiliterate could represent mental energy that's not being used. Perhaps the best definition of the balanced second phalange of Saturn might be a need to know, without having a compulsion or obsession to know everything.

The Third Phalange

The third phalange of Saturn is a statement about your personal style and inclination as you are expressed in the world. If the third phalange is long and not heavily fleshed, we'd assume that the individual has a tidy but rather drab wardrobe, possibly lending itself to minimalism and understatement, though shabbiness or untidiness probably won't be tolerated.

A long third phalange can be a drill sergeant when it comes to self-discipline, with a concurrent need to enforce discipline over others. It's like those vegetarians who, unlike "normal" vegetarians like Lisa, become fanatic in their attempts to convert everyone else to their meatless ways.

From another perspective, the long but full and heavily fleshed third phalange of Saturn may indicate someone whose wardrobe is still conservative, while at the same time more complete, involving a wider variety of styles, colors, and uses of contrast.

The person with a long third phalange of Saturn is often unusually aware of and sensitive to appearances and the opinions of others, particularly those who are perceived to be in positions of authority. If the third phalange is full and fleshy, as well as long, there is a tendency to be perceived in one's own mind as an individual whose opinion is important in matters where the subject of style, appearance, and social acceptability are examined. We call this one "Mr. Know-It-All."

We Gotta Hand It to You

The individual who wears a uniform in her work generally has an accentuated Saturn, whether it's long and full, medium and full, or short and full. In addition, if the third phalange of Saturn has rising vertical lines on it, the quality of conformity is expressed through an attachment to a group identity, namely, the uniform.

When the third phalange of Saturn is long but not full, you've probably discovered someone to whom less is more. Other aspects of the hand, however, might indicate that, although he knows what appropriate and acceptable behaviors are, he may choose not to express his opinion, even when asked. Robin's research has found that these minimalists frequently have complex rules or modes for behavior, though where they are founded remains unclear.

The short third phalange of Saturn isn't so much eccentricity as a simple lack of attention to the material world—the absent-minded professor, for example, who has lost touch with the subtle aspects of what society sees as adequate conformity.

If the third phalange is both short and full, others may perceive the person's behavior as eccentric, though the individual may say that she likes bright colors and sees no reason not to indulge that preference. The fact that she may choose to shop at thrift stores is to her a convenience, a money-saving device, or an opportunity for entertainment, and she'll see nothing unusual in how or why she shops that way. In fact, she won't even give a hoot.

A short third phalange of Saturn doesn't lend itself well to permanency of employment, or, to a lesser degree, to permanency of geographic location. A short third phalange of Saturn also lacking in flesh can indicate a minimalist, who may see austerity and lack of attachment to the material world as an asset. There will be

Helping Hands

The sailor or truck driver for whom travel is a vocation may have a long third phalange of Saturn because he's attached himself to the vocation, rather than because he's geographically mobile. This geographic mobility is different from the guy who works in a snack shop in Des Moines for a few months, then in a transmission shop in Santa Cruz, who's much more likely to have a short second phalange of Saturn.

some degree of self-discipline in this individual, but he may tend to be the passive recipient of his environment rather than an active participant in what happens to him. In other words, his self-discipline won't have a lasting effect.

A short, full third phalange of Saturn is expressed through some attachment to the material world. Paul, for example, was a bona fide, oath-taking, vow-committed pursuer of Zen philosophy who lived in a monastery. His only two notable possessions were, beyond a minimum of clothing and toiletries, an electronic keyboard and a state-of-the-art bicycle. Paul's third phalange was quite short and full, an aspect that also served him well in his previous career as a plumber, where he dealt with a pragmatic necessity of civilized human existence.

The balanced and moderate third phalange of Saturn is, thankfully, quite common. Balance in terms of length as well as a moderate degree of flesh in the third phalange gives one the opportunity to live with dignity and a useful place in society—without extremes that can be demanding. Balanced third phalange Saturn people have the flexibility to express many roles and wear many hats within their lifetimes.

Self-discipline, which may be either lacking or overexpressed in the short full third phalange of Saturn, or become an obsession in the long thin third phalange Saturn, is both a tool and a challenge to moderate third phalange Saturn development. Self-discipline seems to be adequate and available, but it is, unfortunately, all too frequently temporary with the moderate third phalange: "Of course, I can always start that diet again *next* Monday..."

Saturn Fingertips

Saturn is commonly found with a more square fingertip than the rest of the fingers, and is seldom pointed. That's because Saturn is the very finger of practicality and the earth. Whether square or not, though, the fingertip of Saturn describes how you assert your skills in the material world.

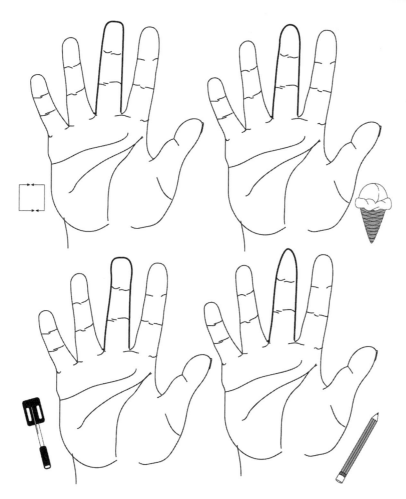

Saturn fingertips: square Saturn fingertip, conic Saturn fingertip, spatulate Saturn fingertip, pointed Saturn fingertip.

Square Saturn

Square Saturn lends itself to practical and somewhat earthy lifestyles and forms of employment: the farmer or the businessman dealing with products of the earth. The lumberyard man, the grocer, and the nurseryman tend to have square Saturn fingertips, for example. A square fingertip on Saturn indicates a traditional parenting mode as well as a reasonably strong expression of traditional gender roles. The person with a square Saturn fingertip is a pillar of society, someone who does her work consistently, with integrity, honesty, and, if not with enthusiasm, at the very least, with dogged determination.

The lawyer who actually practices law seeks to create peace, compromise, honesty, and integrity between people in society, so the lawyer who's been drawn to her profession in the guise of peacemaker and mediator—as opposed to moneymaker—may well have a square Saturn. Robin believes that if these people persevere, they will be recognized for their integrity and consistency and may rise in their ranks to achieve the rank of judge.

133

It's not impossible for the person with a square Saturn to change careers, but such changes don't come readily or easily, and he or she will frequently carry some vestige of the previous career forward into the next phase of life. The lawyer may become a writer of fiction featuring a lawyer, for example. The person with a square Saturn is a sentimentalist without being maudlin, and appreciates all things of strength, stability, and a degree of security, such as brick houses and solid core doors.

Helping Hands

The jogging octogenarian generally has a spatulate Saturn fingertip. That's because the spatulate finger of Saturn lends a certain degree of vitality, activity, and energy to its bearer.

Spatulate Saturn

The person with a spatulate Saturn tip is first and foremost a tool user, and may be a toolmaker as well. Machinists and dedicated mechanics, such as airline mechanics or specialists, tend to have spatulate Saturn fingers, for example.

The term "tool" can also be read in the sense of a manager, who seeks to place people in their most useful and worthwhile roles. If you're fortunate enough to work under a spatulate-fingered manager, you may find yourself in the surprising and pleasant circumstance where someone has "known you better than you know yourself," and given you a rewarding and productive position.

The spatulate fingertip on Saturn is drawn toward intricacies and technicalities: the patent lawyer, for example. A spatulate Saturn fingertip also indicates, at times, a rather exhaustive attention to nuance that few other-tipped individuals would have the patience or interest to follow into such levels of detail. Forensic scientists are an excellent example of these necessary but oblique pursuants of minutiae.

Robin believes that the spatulate fingertip of Saturn won't disintegrate into those elitist realms of a given profession such as insurance actuaries or bureaucrats, who generate rules or paperwork of no interest to anyone but themselves.

Conic Saturn

People with conic Saturns are everywhere, and lend themselves well to whatever roles and learning experiences they apply themselves to. Their only Saturn-related problem may be that when they achieve their goals of security and comfort, they may deteriorate into classic bureaucrats, whose efficiency is only enough to maintain the status quo. Still, a little security and comfort are not necessarily a bad thing, are they?

If the conic fingertip of Saturn is placed on a long first phalange, greater sensitivity and idealism may help to overcome this limitation. In fact, people with conic Saturn fingertips avoid overspecialization and the potentially chronic specialization that can be found in Saturnian roles. In addition, the person with a conic Saturn fingertip has a degree of compromise and flexibility that can be extremely useful in these rigid, authoritarian realms.

134

All in all, the conic Saturn fingertip may fall short of true genius, but it will almost inevitably express itself as something above mere competency, especially if given time, warning, and an opportunity to prepare for any given challenge. The conic fingertip has reserves that it can draw upon if given that time.

Pointed Saturn

A pointed Saturn is rare. Such individuals express themselves in the Saturnian realms as idealists, and seldom last long doing any one thing, although their talents may allow them high qualities of achievement in areas that aren't Saturnian. Still, a person with a pointed Saturn may have a problem with the details required for material success. Take, for example, the performer who's been cheated out of his savings by his trusted manager.

The person with a pointed Saturn has the potential to be a martyr, or an extreme example in the realm of law. There's an earmark of a fairly severe threat to the life at a relatively early age—before 30. If the person with a pointed Saturn survives past his early 30s, he'll generally have become accustomed to the material world, and may demonstrate a more moderate, less intense approach in his life. It's not an easy world for someone with a pointed Saturn to negotiate without some time to get used to it.

> **Helping Hands**
>
> Robin's seen some exceptional pointed-finger Saturn folks, who manage to live quite well with their heads in the clouds. Sometimes, others envy them for their detachment from material concerns, and with good reason. It's quite possible Einstein and Pavlova had pointed Saturn fingers.

To be fair, the person with a pointed Saturn, with his unwillingness to accept and adapt to the social, political, and physical realities of the world, is generally his own worst enemy. Even though he can see many things clearly, he doesn't always have a grounded and practical sense of the bigger picture.

Mind Your Ps and Qs: Saturn Tales

Years ago, P was a gay woman in New York City. In those days, whether she chose to live in or out of the closet affected everything in her life, from the neighborhood where she lived, to the time of day she was out, to her job itself. One night, P made the conscious decision to use her gayness to enhance her self-expression and as an opportunity to express many sides of her self, instead of treating her sexual orientation as something that stood in her way.

Today, P is a mature woman of 60+, and there's no question in her mind that from the moment she made that decision, she broadened her life considerably without losing any essence of her personal self. P, we should add, is an avid amateur palmist. So she couldn't help noticing how her right hand, the hand of activity, had developed a more and more conic Saturn tip while her left hand has remained almost pencil pointed sharp. This is a great example of someone with a pointed Saturn fingertip who learned to live in the world—her compromise shows on her right hand, and her trueness to herself on her left.

Q already had an excellent career as a veterinarian when his spatulate fingertip of Saturn led him into a second career designing specialized tools, tables, and other devices used in specific fields of veterinary medicine. He confided in Robin that the pleasure of the design and the hands-on building of the prototype was both his passion and relaxation. Though his wage as a veterinary surgeon was far more profitable, the last time Robin spoke with Q, he'd become intrigued by an aspect of applying microsurgery to the equine species. The moral: Spatulate Saturn will design new tools for his trade—no matter what.

One of the most respected and competent members of a midwestern police force, Sarge's square fingertip of Saturn had perhaps been one of the reasons he'd never advanced beyond patrol sergeant in uniform. His encyclopedic knowledge of the community and inherent understanding of human character made him extremely successful in both dealing with people and pursuing a majority of criminals. His intelligence, integrity, and acceptance from his peers was never questioned. As he once told Robin, "If you don't have competent men in the field, the less competents will have nobody to tell them what to do."

Which Saturn Are You?

Even though your Saturn's probably already reminded you, just in case it hasn't, we'd like to play the Saturn and remind you to draw your Saturn finger in your notebook and then go back through this chapter and note what we have to say about your particular Saturn.

The Least You Need to Know

➤ Your Saturn finger is your structure, boundaries, and order, as well as the karmic enforcer.

➤ The length of your Saturn finger reveals your responsible nature.

➤ The shape of your Saturn finger shows your attitude toward discipline.

➤ The Saturn phalanges reveal how you deal with authority.

➤ Your Saturn fingertips show your practicality.

Chapter 9

Your Jupiter Finger: Take Me to Your Leader

> **In This Chapter**
>
> ➤ Your Jupiter finger: your sociability, capacity for leadership, and charisma
>
> ➤ The length of your Jupiter: your leadership
>
> ➤ The shape of your Jupiter finger: your practicality
>
> ➤ The angle of your Jupiter finger: your relationships
>
> ➤ The Jupiter phalanges: your personal style
>
> ➤ The Jupiter fingertip: how you deal with others

No finger is as gregarious as your Jupiter finger, and that's because Jupiter is your social self. It's here you'll find not only your intimate relationships with those important people in your life, but your relationship with your self as well.

On this pointer finger can be found everything from your capacity for leadership to your ego and intelligence. When it comes to your social side, in fact, your Jupiter points the way.

How You Are Seen in Your Own Mirror, Spiritually, Socially, and Politically

Your *Jupiter finger* is where you'll find how you conduct your relationships with your loved ones—as opposed to Mercury, where you'll find how you conduct your social relationships. Jupiter can be the priest, the politician, or the social lion within you, the finger of both your faith and your followers. Jupiter has an aspect of intimacy that Mercury doesn't. Jupiterian people will carry any acquaintance further than those who are not Jupiterian. Jupiterian Robin, for example, knows his mail carrier's first name.

In addition, perhaps even more than your Saturn finger, your Jupiter's an expression of how you use your given tools and characteristics. More precisely, it's here you'll find your capacity to lead—and your capacity to follow.

From the tip of your Jupiter finger—where you'll discover your approach to dealing with loved ones— to the shape of the finger itself (an indication of your practicality), your Jupiter finger shows your interpersonal approach to life.

The Length of the Jupiter Finger

The length of your Jupiter finger shows how you interact with significant others and so is a natural indication of your capacity for leadership. Are you better at giving orders or receiving them? The length of your Jupiter finger reveals the answer.

When Jupiter is long, the finger rises at least past the bottom of the Saturn finger's nail, although there are exceptions when the Jupiter finger is very low set. When it is, you should be sure to use your calipers or ruler to find the proportions between the Jupiter and Saturn fingers before jumping to conclusions.

When the Jupiter finger is long, your first thought should always be some aspect of leadership. That's because people with long Jupiter fingers naturally draw other peoples' desire for guidance and direction to themselves—even though they don't seem consciously aware of it.

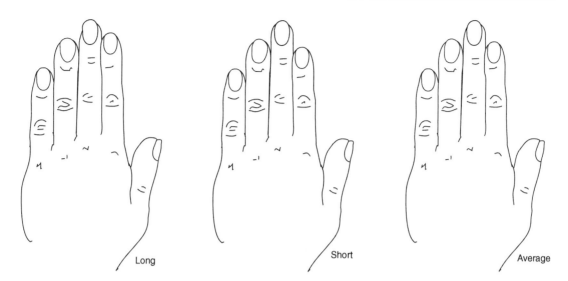

Left to right: long Jupiter finger, short Jupiter finger, average Jupiter finger.

Hand-le with Care

The long Jupiter finger isn't at its best taking direction or following orders. To give one example, film directors have found that long Jupiter-fingered actors are often difficult to direct. In fact, eventually, most long Jupiter-fingered actors become directors themselves!

The short Jupiter finger is both reasonably common and frequently unnoticed—because its bearer doesn't demand great attention. The competent right-hand woman or man, with the foresight to fulfill the boss's needs, often has a well balanced but not necessarily long Jupiter finger. The short Jupiter-fingered person may be both capable and comfortable giving orders, but only with the shadow of a greater authority who's really directing the show.

The short Jupiter finger won't be found on those persons eager to take chances involving other people—or other people's assets, resources, or money. The short Jupiter can also indicate someone who's a loner in at least one area of life. Working alone or in an isolated way is common with people who have short Jupiter fingers, for example.

Someone with a short Jupiter finger may be self-effacing—the humble backseat driver—or someone who is actively looking to serve another's needs. Often not given

More lengths of Jupiter.

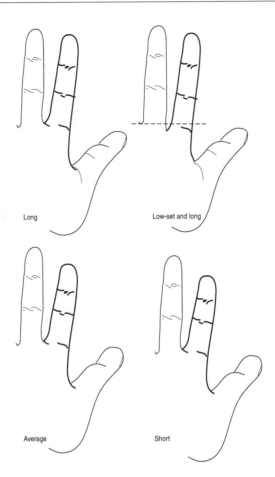

to weighty decisions of choice and philosophy, this personality is instead more comfortable accepting someone else's decisions.

The well-balanced Jupiter finger, which reaches to near the bottom of the Saturn nail, indicates someone who can both lead and follow, though the leadership usually takes a smaller role than it would with a longer Jupiter finger. In fact, the person with a moderate (well-balanced) Jupiter finger is comfortable generating and manifesting ideas, as well as criticizing, modifying—and providing the necessary (as we well know!) service of editing words or ideas.

The person with a long Jupiter finger is very willing to lead, whereas someone with a moderate Jupiter is less so. On the other extreme is the person with the short Jupiter finger who is ready to relinquish authority.

When you look at the length of the Jupiter finger, it's important to look at the Jupiter fingertip as well, because it either intensifies or minimizes the Jupiterian qualities of charisma, fairness, compassion, and rapid, if not instinctual, decision making.

The Shape of the Jupiter Finger

In the shape of the Jupiter finger you'll find your degree of practicality, attachment to established forms, and support of the status quo. When Jupiter is leaning toward the Saturn finger, the person tends to be pragmatic, willing to use the structures at hand, and unwilling to change or reorganize a thing. There's also an appreciation for the examples of history as well as the sensitivities and prejudices of society, both of which can result in a style of leadership that allows for compromise. This is not, we hasten to add, a bad thing. This person spots trends and has a finger on the pulse of what is likely or not likely to go over big with the public.

But when Jupiter leans outward, away from Saturn, you'll find a unique and different view and style. This might be, for example, someone who seeks to revolutionize or dramatically change either workplace or residence, and you shouldn't mistake this unusual person for a mere eccentric. In reality, he's the very dynamic of change—at times both the lever and the fulcrum by which a difference is created.

Helping Hands

Every successful, independent, self-employed person is expressing her Jupiter, and even more so, if she employs others or allows others to be dependent on her. In addition, it's interesting to observe that among women ministers, athletes, and *successful* entrepreneurs, the Jupiter finger is generally both long and well shaped.

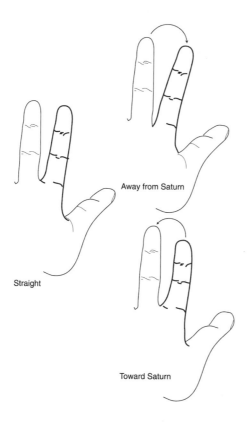

Away from Saturn

Straight

Toward Saturn

Straight Jupiter, Jupiter leaning toward Saturn, Jupiter leaning away from Saturn.

The upright Jupiter, with no particular bend or inclination, doesn't mean that you might not be either conservative or revolutionary in your approach. Other factors, such as those on the mounts of Jupiter or Mars (it's coming—in Chapter 18!), also come into play to determine whether you prefer fast and extreme action or protection of status quo.

Even more than those with upright Saturn fingers, people with upright Jupiter fingers are the conscience and opinion of society's mainstream. If you find straight and well-articulated Jupiter fingers on a majority of those within a group or organization, it's a sure thing that the group's cause has found its time, or the beginning of its time, to be heard and explored. In fact, the straight and upright Jupiter finger may be looked on as the rational balance among thinking and aware people.

The Angle of the Jupiter Finger

Palm readers look at the angle of the Jupiter finger to determine the degree of your sociability. Are you the belle of the ball or a hermit who prefers your own "cave"? The angle of your Jupiter finger tells all.

Average angle of Jupiter (top), wide angle of Jupiter (center), narrow angle of Jupiter (bottom).

An open space between the Jupiter and Saturn fingers can indicate someone with an unusually high level of independence and need for solitude. Given that the strongly Jupiter-influenced person naturally has this appetite to a high degree, especially when seeking her own spiritual clarity, this openness can indicate a quality approaching that of the hermit. Remember, though, that as a symbolic figure, or archetype, in society, hermits are seen as people who bestow wisdom, clarity, and direction. So this isn't a bad thing, either.

When the Jupiter finger shows a closer connection to the Saturn finger, the social context of the Jupiterian character is enhanced, and the person is inclined to enjoy people, appreciate their company, and network with them more readily, a role that many people appreciate due to the warmth of the Jupiterian person and her charisma. This person is great at creating and sustaining networks.

A Look at the Jupiter Phalanges

The Jupiter phalanges reveal a great deal about both your self-image and self-presentation, as well as your conscious approach to the world and your personal style. The length of the phalanges, which on a scale of 10 may be somewhere around $2^1/_2$ for the first phalange, 3 for the second, and 4 for the third, can help you determine your social strengths and weaknesses, and how to use what you have in this area to its best potential.

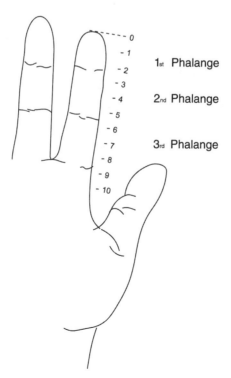

The phalanges of Jupiter.

Handy Words to Know

According to Eastern tradition, *chi* is the vital life force energy we generate and put to use on a daily basis. When the flesh at the tip of your thumb or Jupiter finger doesn't immediately spring back when you press on it, your *chi* may be low.

Helping Hands

A long first phalange of Jupiter coupled with a short second phalange can provide an excellent example of any number of popular sayings, such as "Fools rush in where angels fear to tread," or "Better to be silent and thought a fool than open your mouth and remove all doubt." If you're familiar with astrology, you may think of this as Aries energy.

The First Phalange

The first phalange of Jupiter is, in almost all hands, somewhat more pointed than the other fingers. When you come across an exception to this, be sure to give it deeper consideration in the reading of the hand than usual, just as you would with any departure from what most people show on their hands.

You can think of the first phalange of Jupiter as your self-image and self-presentation as it's motivated, practiced, and put into action. The first phalange also demonstrates, as does the thumb, the level of *chi* available to you, both in the way you express yourself and in the way you draw life force energy to you.

It's also here that you may find flesh at the tip that doesn't bounce right back when you press it, which, as you may recall from our discussion of the thumb, can indicate a lack of energy. It's nothing that an hour's rest, a light meal, or a change of environment won't cure, though. Chi is a highly transitory energy.

A long first phalange indicates a capacity of influence, again, similar to the thumb, but to a lesser degree. When the first phalange is long, it indicates a sensitivity to the environment and humankind (as well as, theoretically, other species on this planet Earth). The longer the first phalange, the more likely someone is to have an impact on the surrounding environment. A long first phalange is also a sign of a higher than usual sensitivity to other peoples' feelings.

A short first phalange of Jupiter indicates an individual who doesn't appreciate her ability to influence others and who may lack self-confidence. Someone with a short first phalange of Jupiter won't see herself as a person of uniqueness or impact at all, and will rarely overestimate her importance in a given situation. In fact, she may not include herself in the equation at all.

While Robin has seen people with short first phalanges of Jupiter who had large and complex egos, that ego was founded on some specific and generally technical expertise and gift, such as someone who knows a computer program well, and therefore considers himself an expert on the computer. At the same time, because they had short first phalanges, they weren't even aware that they had a strongly developed ego.

A long first-phalanged individual is usually quite realistic about himself and his world. If that realism fails, it's because he assumes a force greater than himself, such as divine intervention, or, at least, an act of congress, will come to bear on the goal or ideal that he's working toward!

Those with a moderate first phalange of Jupiter are sensitive souls who accept the status quo as a gift. These realistic people generally have healthy self-images and are conscientious about finding positive things about themselves and their world and she'll acknowledge and praise them as well.

While negative viewpoints aren't ignored by a person with a moderate first phalange of Jupiter, they're not dwelled on much. Even if the person's got a job others might view as difficult, such as being a prison guard, she'll still, Pollyanna-like, look for the good in everything. She may say, for example, "Sure, he's a bank robber, but he never hurt anyone—and he's expanding his literary tastes, too."

The person with a well-balanced first phalange, in other words, is both aware of her own sensitivity and willing to express it positively. Of course, emotions and sensitivity can sometimes overwhelm her just like anyone else, but she'll bounce back quickly once she sees the reality of a situation. The person with a well-balanced first phalange of Jupiter will both feel and express her grief—but she'll also pull herself together and make the necessary adjustments in her material world to compensate for her loss.

We Gotta Hand It to You

The archetypal Jupiter leader was Sir Winston Churchill. Churchill's life was marked by change after change, times of popularity and times when he was totally rejected by both his political party and his culture. It took history and perspective for people to recognize Churchill's genius, while, throughout his life, Churchill himself was torn with self-doubt and depression which he struggled deeply to overcome. Nevertheless, today we see Winston Churchill's charisma, optimism, and an intangible strength of character that we call leadership as some of the most powerful factors in World War II.

The Second Phalange

Do you mind? Who do you mind? Do you mind very much? The second phalange of Jupiter is second only to the head line, which we'll be discussing in Part 3, as a window into the great unknown—human consciousness, the mind, and intelligence. If the second phalange of your Jupiter is long, whether it's full or waisted, you're probably someone who has an unusual capacity for thought, observation, and evaluation.

If Sherlock Holmes had been real and not just a classic fictional character, he would've been sure to have both an extremely long and reasonably full second phalange of Jupiter. (He also would have been paying Watson to write those stories out of his need for recognition and attention.) In a decidedly Holmesian way, though, when the second phalange of

We Gotta Hand It to You

Did you use all of your notes when you wrote your papers in school? Did you require more research (short second phalange) or discover pages of unused potential input (long second phalange)? The person with a well-balanced second phalange of Jupiter seldom has a problem getting the peanut butter and jelly to come out right with the number of slices of bread. The person with a well-balanced second phalange doesn't write too long a speech and will seldom waste her allotted time to inform and sway an audience.

Jupiter is very long, self-consciousness, self-obsession, and, with other deteriorating aspects, self-doubt, become potentially dangerous personal pitfalls.

A short second phalange of Jupiter can indicate someone who has a hard time looking before he leaps and so may repeat the same lessons in life many times. We hasten to add that a short second phalange of Jupiter doesn't indicate an inferior mind, but one that's not necessarily inclined to reach beyond itself or expand its horizons or interests. This person is happy to go with the flow of the status quo.

The short second phalange person may be accused of having a somewhat superficial appreciation of a given book, film, or a complex real-life situation. But it's not that a person with a short second phalange can't see and appreciate great complexity, it's just that this person generally needs to be presented with a key that will unlock understanding. Great leaps of perception and insight are just not her forte.

On the other hand, a long second phalange of Jupiter may be found on someone who has more hobbies, passions, knowledge of musical instruments, or e-mail addresses than any one person can possibly use.

People with long second phalanges of Jupiter are seldom bored. Not only do they have all sorts of ways to entertain themselves, they have the resources to find new ways to do so as the need arises.

The well-designed second phalange of Jupiter isn't overly fleshy and is seldom waisted. Overfleshiness diminishes the sense of balance, while waisted-ness creates a stifled, and perhaps even selfish, attitude. Overall, someone with a well-balanced second phalange of Jupiter functions well in society, without getting too exhausted, too lazy, or too lackadaisical.

Hand-le with Care

Individuals with long second phalanges tend to collect things in the hope of someday getting around to them: that motorcycle that hasn't run in three years, for example; or that stack of unread paperbacks sitting on the shelf.

If there's a quality of obsession in the well-balanced second phalange of Jupiter, perhaps it's found in the person's pursuit of balance, or the occasional subtle quirk for symmetry in style, expression, and design. Think, for example, of a relative who feels obligated to spend an identical number of days, even approaching hours, at each family member's home when visiting for the holidays.

The Third Phalange

The importance of the third phalange of Jupiter can't be stressed enough. The length of this phalange expresses not only your personal style and appearance, but how well you use both the tools available in society, and how well you use what others can provide. The third phalange of Jupiter, in other words, describes our willingness to both use and be used in interaction with others.

Now here's a tidbit: An individual with a full third phalange of Jupiter, whether it's long or short, will have spent some special attention on the acquisition of neckwear. When the third phalange of Jupiter is both long and full, this person will wear the best example of his set's choice of neckwear: the best bandanna among the motorcycle set or only Armani for the office, for example. Would we make things like this up? Full third-phalanged Jupiter women won't miss the opportunity to wear a necklace or a silk scarf, and, if it's long as well as full, she'll be still more conscientious about both cost and appropriateness.

We Gotta Hand It to You

Show us a physically beautiful person, one of symmetry and decided attractiveness, and we'll define two things from her third phalange of Jupiter. First, how willing she is to devote time and effort to enhance and maintain her beauty (this will be found with the long and full third phalange); and second, if her personal taste is good or excellent. If it's not particularly good, there will be a short full third phalange. Check it out.

Sometimes, you'll find a clearly visible rising line on the third phalange of Jupiter on someone who wears his religion on his shirt sleeve. He may well be spiritual and sincere, but he may also be using his religion to further himself socially in some way.

If the third phalange of Jupiter is short and fairly skinny, the opposite will be true; these people aren't looking for material luxury or comfort. Such a person might drive a car without air conditioning—even though he lived in Phoenix.

With a short and unfleshed third phalange of Jupiter, you're not likely to be concerned with comfort or with appearance. If the Jupiter finger is otherwise balanced, you will have both dignity and an awareness of self-image, although you may also have excesses of style, appearance, or appetite.

The long well fleshed third phalange of Jupiter is found on someone who appreciates comfort, as well as the ability to balance his particular appetites with common sense and self-discipline. An example would be anyone with the appetite for material pleasures and the discipline to keep them as rewards rather than a constant in his or her life. Most of us can practice some form of this balance to a degree.

When the third phalange of Jupiter is of a normal and moderate length, the person is happy with his lot in life. Robin interprets the moderate Jupiter third phalange that is neither heavily fleshed nor lacking in flesh as someone who's well adjusted, satisfied, and comfortable in her particular world. This person has the ability to make the best of a situation, whether it's life in an army barracks or on the road as a salesperson. She can create a comfortable environment anywhere and display good taste and a healthily balanced demeanor while doing it—the hallmark of the moderate third phalange of Jupiter.

If the Jupiter third phalange is of moderate length but is also waisted, the person may be more rigorous, with the potential to be mildly obsessive at times. This might be someone whose desire to not waste water leads her to not have a garden at all despite her deep love for blooming tropical plants.

Jupiter Fingertips

The well-balanced Jupiter finger has a somewhat more pointed fingertip than the rest of the fingers on the hand. While you will come across the occasional spatulate or square fingertipped Jupiter, both of these are relatively rare. When you do come across spatulate or square Jupiter fingertips, you'll have found people who are remarkably humble.

Jupiter fingertips: square, conic, spatulate, pointed.

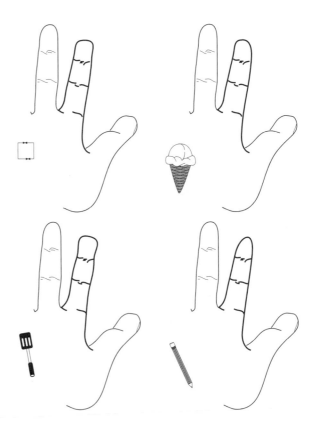

The shape of the Jupiter fingertip points to how you express yourself socially, whether in your job, speech, or religion. You'll also find your degree of comfort here, including, sometimes, the foods you like to eat. (We kid you not.)

Square Jupiter

The square Jupiter fingertip indicates someone who's both pragmatic and practical (there is a difference), with a readiness to take on the tough jobs, and lead from within the ranks. These people can be a bit slow to recognize or understand others' feelings, and may be more interested in themselves than anybody else. Still, count on square Jupiters to take on projects without complaint that others may avoid.

Spatulate Jupiter

The person with a spatulate-tip Jupiter is a doer, often specialized in some way, and this person can enjoy great success. In addition, though she is frequently private, she is still the family's well-liked loner. Such a person with a spatulate Jupiter is often an inventor, too—not just an inventor of things but of ideas as well.

Conic Jupiter

You'll see conic Jupiter fingertips everywhere—it's by far the most common shape for this particular fingertip. Someone with a conic Jupiter has a healthy and consistent expression and often a tendency to shift roles—because someone with this fingertip is so good at so many things. Conic Jupiter indicates the love of both luxury and comfort, and is also a good sign for a cleric, because it indicates both good compassion and the ability to play many roles.

Pointed Jupiter

A pointed Jupiter points to the idealist. This person is sometimes removed from society, but can also be philosophically profound. Seldom practical, someone with a pointed Jupiter finger may seem odd to more practical folks, whether it's the woman with 40 cats or the man who won't own a television. Further, a pointed Jupiter, combined with supporting evidence on the heart line (see Chapter 11), can indicate the vegetarian.

Pundits, Pulpits, and Promises: Stories About Jupiter

One woman we know rises at 4:30 a.m. and spends the time from 5:00 until 7:30 in private study, meditation, and prayer. Though she's very social, has many friends, and is extremely well liked, much of her social contact occurs over the phone rather than in person. That she works for someone who's never there, and runs a local organization whose meetings she never attends attest to her short Jupiter finger. In addition, she's a member of several spiritual esoteric orders, considered a career as a nun, and her short Jupiter finger is accentuated by a spatulate tip that points to the importance to her of usefulness and hard work. While her own humility, evidenced by the unusual shape and shortness of her Jupiter, means she doesn't recognize all that she does, she leads her office, boss, and local organization from a position in the rear and is truly the only irreplaceable individual within that organization.

Robin is also reminded of an individual whose affiliation with a well-known motorcycle club was the focus of his life. Though his distinctly pointed Jupiter first phalange created a sensitive, delicate, almost fastidious self-expression, he was respected for the polished and near show quality of his "chopper." However, his tendency to have his gang colors taken off his jacket and dry-cleaned was looked upon somewhat askance among the more earthy members (read: square, blunt first phalange Jupiter finger) of the group.

Lastly, there is the well-known television comedian, whose charm and charisma made him universally loved. His Jupiter finger revealed the subtle difference between a conic and pointed fingertip, which is somewhat difficult to appraise. Still, his Jupiter finger was longer than his Apollo, and therefore rather extreme. This resulted in a humor that is both spiritual and philosophical—his trademark—coupled with a sometimes extreme degree of sociability followed by periods of isolation.

Which Jupiter Are You?

Now it's time to find out which Jupiter you are. Take out your palmistry notebook and sketch your Jupiter finger, being sure to note the length of the phalanges, the shape of the fingertip, and the angle of the finger from Saturn. Then go back through this chapter and see what your Jupiter finger reveals about you.

The Least You Need to Know

➤ Your Jupiter finger reveals your social self, leadership, and charisma.

➤ The shape of your Jupiter finger shows your degree of practicality.

➤ The angle of your Jupiter finger reveals your approach to relationships.

➤ The Jupiter phalanges are a measure of personal style.

➤ The Jupiter fingertip shows how you deal with others.

Part 3
I've Got a Line on You

If you knew nothing else about palmistry when you began this book, chances are you did know about the lines of the hand. We like to call the lines the plots of your story, crisscrossing your hand in their meandering or straightforward paths as your story unfolds. There are more lines than life, heart, and head, too—you may have lines that rise toward any or all of your fingers, or special lines that reveal special talents.

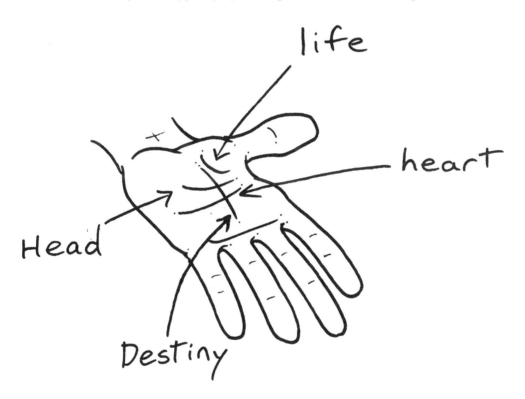

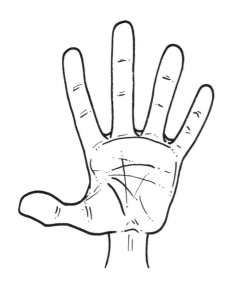

Lines, Lines, Everywhere a Line

Lines are often the first thing people think about when they consider having their palms read. Perhaps it's because the lines are so readily visible—but then, aren't fingers visible, too? It's more likely that this conception arose from the misconception of how a gypsy reads a palm. (Witness the old cartoon where the gypsy looks at a guy's life line and then asks for advance payment!)

As you'll learn in Chapter 13, though, the length of the life line has little to do with the length of the life. And, in other chapters in this section you'll learn that there are a lot more lines to look for than just the life, head, and heart.

It's as Plain as the Lines on Your Hand

If fingers are characters, *lines* might be called plots. Nowhere else in the hand are the little details of our day-to-day lives made more plain. Along the path of any line you may find small dots, channels, islands, forks, or branches, and each of these carries a significance all its own. We'll be discussing these "plot devices" in more detail at the end of this chapter—as well in each line's separate role.

Handy Words to Know

The **lines** in your hand provide the plot details that make up your life.

We Gotta Hand It to You

An old crony of Robin's once said that when the lines on the active and passive hands are identical, the person must be following a perfect life because he's following his own divine plan. Robin's response to this is, "Yeah, right. And he's never made an original decision and probably has never left town." Think about it—would you want your entire life planned before you'd lived it? We didn't think so.

Like many things in your palm, lines can and will change. This is because you're not a creature of destiny, but someone made up of your own cumulative conscious and unconscious choices. In fact, it's your choices, whether large or small, routine or dramatic, obvious or unseen, that create your future. You are a person of your own making—and this is reflected in the lines of your hands.

Remember, "your hand is a map that changes, and this includes the lines. Watch your hands for a while and you'll notice how markings come and go, how lines change, and how mounts inflate and deflate. Your unawareness of these changes is understandable and commonly shared," says Robin; however, he encourages you to photocopy your hands, date the copy, file it, and look at it again later. "Even the most uninitiated, skeptical, and nearsighted interpreter will be able to see some changes in the lines of his hand over the course of a year," adds Robin.

Just as your inner and outer lives are two different entities, the lines in your active hand will seldom be identical to the lines in your passive hand. While your active hand is busy portraying the everyday plot developments, your passive hand is busy just recording the inner you.

Both of these are reasons why a good palm reader will always read both hands—it's the only way to get a complete picture of who you are now. In addition, lines have special features unique to them that a palm reader will look at. These include a line's quality as well as its character.

Behind the Lines

The *quality* of a line is probably its most important measure. Quality is an indication of vitality and strength, and the deeper and more well cut the line, the more vital and strong that particular aspect of your life.

Throughout Part 3, we'll be using the analogy of a hand molded in clay, with lines forming water-carrying channels. The deeper the channel, the better cut it is, and the better the cut, the more "water" a line can carry.

A line's character isn't a palmistry term but one we've come up with to discuss whether a line is dominant or passive in the hand. It's simple enough to look at a palm and determine which lines are dominant. Go ahead and look at your own palm and do this now.

You probably noticed that some lines stand out more than others, while some lines are so faint you wouldn't have even seen them if we hadn't told you to always use good light when you're looking at a palm (and, good little Saturnian, you listened to us, right?). The lines that are most dominant will, not surprisingly, be more important to your story than those that are faint. But don't discount the faint lines—they play important supporting roles.

Shapes Along the Way: Dots, Triads, Squares, Channels, Islands, Forks, Branches, and Bars

Another thing a palm reader's going to look at when assessing the quality of your lines is the shapes they make along the way. Shapes along lines can take a number of aspects, each with its own particular interpretation.

➤ *Dots*, depending on their color, are spots of energy that highlight their position in some way. We like to think of these as little ships, sailing along the "river" of the particular line.

➤ You can think of *triads* as little sails, whisking the little ship on its way. Their energy is considered a boon of some kind, as they provide balance and an even keel.

➤ You can think of *squares* as locks along a canal. Squares around a break in a given line tend to "heal" the break of the line, holding its energy intact and creating a continuum.

➤ *Channels* are paths taken when the "water" of the line must find a new direction different from its original one. While they do help the "water" to keep moving, channels aren't as strong as the direct energy of the original line.

➤ *Islands* in lines cause the "water" to move around them, and divert energy in some particular way.

➤ *Forks* split the energy of the line into two directions, but this is sometimes a benefit, avoiding overspecialization or narrowness of view.

➤ *Branches* are stronger than forks, and point toward the energy of a specific mount.

Handy Words to Know

The **quality** of a line refers to its depth and clarity. The deeper and more well cut, the more strength and vitality exists in the aspect of life represented by the line.

Helping Hands

What's the difference between a fork and a branch? Look outside your window (that is, if there's a beautiful old elm, like there is outside Lisa's). Those older, thicker limbs are branches. The smaller, newer twigs are forks.

➤ *Bars*, not a single line but a pair of lines or more, act like disruptive rapids in a stream's flow. They create discordant times and a difficult period to move through. This is not a pleasurable rafting trip!

A Map of the Lines of the Hand

Like any good tour guides, we're not going to set you loose among the sites without a good map. In the following illustration, we've included some lines we'll be talking about in Part 3, including:

➤ Heart line

➤ Head line

➤ Life line

➤ Rising line to Saturn

➤ Rising line to Mercury

➤ Rising line to Apollo

➤ Rising line to Jupiter

A map of the lines of the hand.

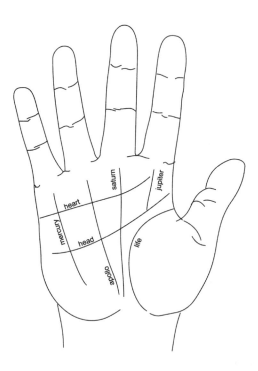

Not all of these lines will appear in your own hand—and don't worry, that's not bad news. Depending on their configurations, some of these lines are plot twists and complications. In all likelihood, you will, though, have the big three: heart, head, and life. In the unlikely event that you don't, though, you're still covered (you'll find out how when we discuss the Simian Crease in a few pages).

Heart, Head, and Life: The Three Biggies

Emotion, mind, and energy: You've gotta have all three to write the story of your life. And it is, after all, *you* who's writing that story, both as you live it and in the palm of your hand.

Whether it's the emotional nature of your heart line, the thought that goes into your head line, or the fortitude it takes to live your life, the lines in your hand tell the story of how you can live to the best of your potential.

The Heart Line: How Do You Feel About This?

What's your emotional makeup? Do you cry at the drop of a hat or do you take everything in stride? Your heart line, the most important line on your hand, is a map of your emotional nature. Some of the questions your heart line can answer include:

➤ Whom do you love?

➤ How do you love?

➤ How do you show your love?

➤ Are you emotional?

➤ Are you an idealist?

➤ Where are your passions found?

The heart line, the uppermost of the three most prominent lines on your hand, portrays your emotional inclinations and longings. Palm readers look at everything from its quality to its length to determine the answers to the above questions, as well as many others. We'll be taking an in-depth look at the heart line in Chapter 11.

The Head Line: Are You Ruled by the Mind?

What's the nature of your thinking? Are you practical or the absent-minded professor? And what's the best way for you to use your particular intelligence? Your head line, which runs across the center of the palm, reveals how you think. Your head line can answer questions such as:

➤ How independent is your thought?

➤ How do you make decisions?

➤ How fast do you evaluate information?

➤ Are you good at details?

➤ Are you direct or subtle in your dealings with others?

➤ How vivid is your imagination?

➤ Are you inventive?

Palm readers look at your head line to determine all kinds of things you may have never anticipated about how you think. Not only will your head line reveal the answers to the previous questions, it will answer many more you may have never expected to find there. We'll take a closer look at the head line in Chapter 12.

The Life Line: What's in a Line?

Palm readers equate your life line to your *chi*, or vital breath, and that's because nowhere is your energy (or lack of it) more clearly drawn than on this line of your vitality. Running from somewhere between your thumb and Jupiter finger around the thumb toward the base of your hand, your life line reveals your life and its impact on the world. Some of the questions your life line can answer include:

➤ How healthy will you be?

➤ Will you travel? When? How often? Is your travel out of control?

➤ How many jobs or careers will you have?

➤ Will you make a lasting impact on others?

➤ Will your life be easy or challenging?

➤ How adventurous are you?

➤ What kind of help can you expect in your life?

You can also use your life line to measure where you are now on the map of your palm. In Chapter 13, we'll reveal Robin's surefire method for finding your age on your life line. We'll also share with you a lot of other interesting things to be found along the line of life.

Handy Words to Know

The **Simian Crease** appears in the hand as a combined heart and head line. It can indicate single-mindedness and tenacity of purpose because feelings and thoughts are undifferentiated.

The Simian Crease: 2 for 1

Occasionally, you'll come across a hand that doesn't seem to have either a heart line or a head line. Actually, neither line is absent; instead they're paired in a line called the *Simian Crease*. This single line is more often found on one hand or the other, but seldom completely on both.

The Simian Crease is so-called because it's believed to be a characteristic of the hands of apes. You may think of apes as creatures who jump up and down, shriek, and mash their bananas, but there's far more to the Simian Crease.

The Simian Crease.

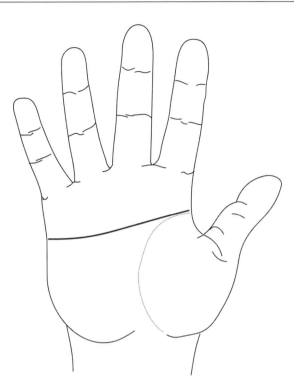

Some palm readers say that the Simian Crease can indicate stubbornness and a tendency to lose your temper if you don't get your way. But this marking is just as often associated with intense drive and focus, although there may be a tendency to be set in one's ways.

This mark is often found on those with Down's Syndrome, but it's found on people with high intelligence, too, so it's not a mark of the I.Q.

Hand-le with Care

Because the very name "Simian Crease" may not be "politically correct," you should take care when discussing this aspect with someone who has it. This is one of those cases where the name has held on despite what some might feel are negative connotations. But, as you'll note, there's nothing negative about the Simian Crease at all.

Helping Hands

Occasionally, there will be a short line above the Simian Crease that may be read as a vestigial heart line. It indicates a deep affection for and maudlin attachment to some given emotional connection.

Helping Hands

There's nothing wrong with a Simian Crease on the passive hand. In fact, this line creates the skills we all need for survival.

Those with a Simian Crease are strongly attached to nature, and you'll often find them working with animals. In addition, there's a strong appetite for a home (that is, a house), and they are loyal and expect loyalty in return. These people are survivors in its original sense, which means they're pragmatic—and just a little suspicious of others.

Still, Simian Crease people are the "salt of the earth," and many have wonderful senses of humor. They're also often handy with tools and methodical in their approach to things. They value their privacy and are fiercely protective—sometimes too protective—parents.

When there's a branching line off the Simian Crease, it should be read as a head line, and will balance the tendency to equate feeling with thinking and vice versa. Similarly, a short unattached falling line can also be read as a head line when it comes to the Simian Crease.

When reading Simian Crease people, bear in mind that they prefer to see things in stark contrasts and are most comfortable when their potentials and choices are portrayed in such a fashion.

More than anything, the Simian Crease is about feelings and thinking being synonymous—because the head line and heart line are one.

Rising Lines: Is Your Karma Weak or Strong?

Rising lines begin in the lower or center portion of the palm and point toward specific fingers. These lines can show your inclinations and tendencies that will be expressed in some degree, but it's difficult to define the specific way a rising line will manifest. Will an Apollo line, for example, point to a talent in art or music, or the charismatic athlete? Is the rising line to Saturn a social eccentric who belongs to a paramilitary organization or the career police officer?

Where a line rises, whether to the mount of Mercury, Apollo, Saturn, or Jupiter, shows inclinations toward the energies of that particular mount. Let's review those energies now.

Mount	Energy
Mercury	Communication, commerce, medicine
Apollo	Creative talent, the performer, whether artistic or in sports, the gambler
Saturn	The social structure, the business structure, the Rules (with that capital "R")
Jupiter	Leadership, spirituality, idealism, charisma

Few people have rising lines to all of the mounts, and quite a few people have none at all. This isn't necessarily a bad thing, and, in the case of some rising lines, less may in fact be more. After all, you can't serve too many masters. We'll discuss each rising line in more detail in Chapters 14 and 15.

Handy Words to Know

Rising lines are lines that begin in the lower or center portion of the palm and rise toward one of the four mounts below each finger. These lines show your inclinations and tendencies in certain areas.

Where Your Paths May Lead

We've said it before but we'll say it again: It takes both your hands to reveal the story of your life. Each decision you make along the path of your life is written in one of your hands.

When you look at the lines on your hand, you can think of them as paths that you may choose to take or not to take. Like everything in your hand, the lines draw your opportunities. But where your paths may lead is up to you.

Other Significant Lines

Other lines to look for can reveal your special talents and passions. These include:

➤ Camera's Eye, a mark of visual talent

➤ Girdle of Venus, a mark of arts appreciation

➤ Via Lascivia, a mark of a sensual nature

➤ Mark of the Teacher, a mark of the natural, dedicated, and gifted teacher

In addition, there are lines that are specific to certain mounts, such as the lines of children and marriage. We've saved these to talk about in Part 4, when we talk about the mounts in more detail.

The Camera's Eye, the Girdle of Venus, the Via Lascivia, the Mark of the Teacher.

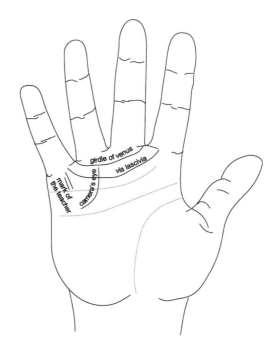

There's Always a Silver Lining

What you do with the lines in your hand is up to you. In fact, when Robin sees a cold coming in Lisa's life line (and her thumb), he'll alert her in advance so she can stock up on her herbal remedies. Knowing in advance what the lines are saying can help you decide if that's the path you really want to follow or if it's time to tinker with the plot.

What will you put your best effort into? Where do you want to focus, define, and specialize? The more you look at your hand, the more you'll notice how (and how often) the lines in your hand change to reflect your life. And now, it's time to look to your lines, and find the silver lining we all possess.

The Least You Need to Know

➤ You can think of the lines in your hand as your story's plot.

➤ The three biggies in the hand are the heart, head, and life lines.

➤ The Simian Crease appears as a combined head and heart line, but is not common.

➤ Rising lines can show your inclinations and tendencies.

➤ Other lines to look for can reveal your special talents.

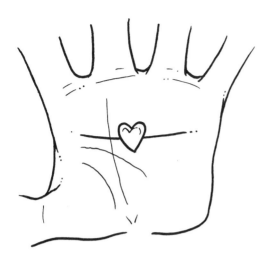

Chapter 11

The Heart Line: How Do You Love?

In This Chapter

➤ Your heart line: a map of your love

➤ How you express emotion: the end of your heart line

➤ The depth of your heart and your emotions

➤ The curve of your heart line and your emotional style

➤ Peaks on the heart line: emotional inclinations

➤ Dips on the heart line: pragmatism or tolerance

Are you generous or stingy with your love? And do you seek lovers who are giving or withholding, or people who can live up to some impossible ideal? All this can be found along the line of your heart.

Quite simply, the heart line is the most important line. The uppermost of the three most prominent lines on your hand, it reveals not only who you love, but the way you show that love. It's also here you'll find your emotional nature, the degree of your emotional idealism, and your passion.

Finding the Heart Line

The *heart line* is the horizontal line that's uppermost on your hand, underneath the fingers. You can think of it as a portrayal of your emotional inclinations and longings. Along your heart line, you'll see everything from the type of ideal you pursue emotionally to your potential for complications (and self-sabotage) in your love life. Above all, the heart line portrays who you love—and how you love them.

Handy Words to Know

The **heart line** is the uppermost of the three most prominent lines on your hand, and can be found beneath the fingers on the palm. You can think of the heart line as a portrayal of your emotional inclinations and longings.

Where It Begins

The heart line begins at the *percussion* of the hand and travels across the top of the hand toward the mounts of Saturn, Jupiter, or somewhere between them. In most cases, the heart line extends to at least a position underneath the Saturn finger, and it will frequently extend all the way up to between the Saturn and Jupiter fingers. In addition, the heart line is often branched, and the evaluation of the strength of those various branches is an important consideration in the heart line interpretation, too.

The heart line begins at the percussion of the hand.

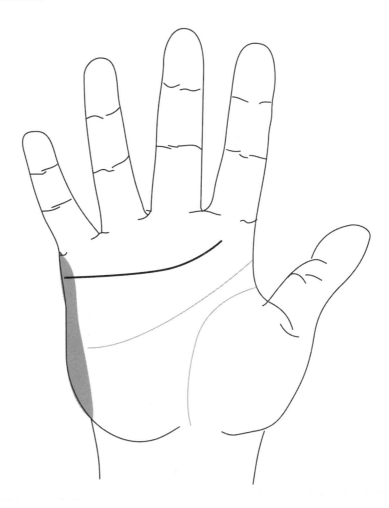

Where It Ends

Where the heart line ends is an indication of how you love, and you'll see heart lines ending in as many different places as the various ways each of us loves. Most often, the heart line ends either somewhere below the Jupiter or Saturn fingers, or somewhere between them.

When the **dominant rising line from the heart line branches to Saturn** (A in the following illustration), it indicates a powerful material perspective in romantic affairs. Whether about money, appearance, or an effort to duplicate the dominant disciplining parent figure in one's life by replacing him or her with a similarly dominating or disciplined love object, this fairly common Saturnian perspective isn't necessarily as negative as the word "material" might sound: Remember, "material" means "grounded," too.

Handy Words to Know

The **percussion** is the part of hand on the Mercury-finger side, that runs from underneath the mount of Mercury toward the wrist.

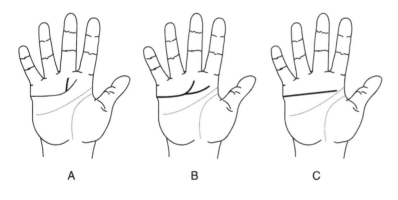

A   B   C

Branchings of the heart line: (a) rising line to Saturn, (b) branch to Jupiter/Saturn split, (c) flat with a termination under Jupiter, (d) rising up into Jupiter, (e) connecting to head line and life line, (f) terminating under Saturn.

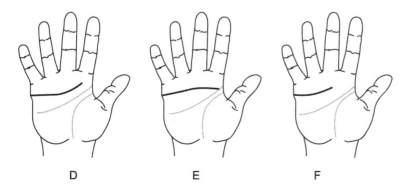

D   E   F

Hand-le with Care

Among the thousands of questions people have asked Robin about potential lovers and partners, few questions address whether or not the potential lover could live within his or her means, or whether he or she was already deeply in debt. Few also have acknowledged the need for "a hard-headed woman," or pragmatic and grounded man, to give themselves some discipline or structure. The fact is, though (as we all know), we often seek in a partner what we ourselves lack.

A heart line **branching toward the Jupiter/Saturn split** (B in the illustration) is extremely common in us baby boomers—and even some of you who aren't. Robin suspects this subtle marking may be bound up with our generation's difficulties finding lasting love and happiness. That's because a Jupiter/Saturn split on the heart line involves an extremely idealistic perspective, which, translated to love object, would mean a perfect and faithful lover who manifests both idealism and self-containment along with an abundance of patience and compassion for others. Hey—where can we sign up for one?

Helping Hands

Robin has seen the unusual heart line rising to the mount of Jupiter on people who have sacrificed themselves for a greater cause. In fact, even the servant of someone important and powerful would have this aspect of the heart line only if he loved either his superior or the superior's work. In other words, this heart line indicates a supporting role.

Still, as a baby boomer himself, Robin appreciates this ideal, but he also feels that these people may be just a trifle picky in their search for the perfect partner.

When the heart line **runs essentially flat and terminates under Jupiter** (C in the illustration), without rising up into the Jupiter mount, it indicates an extremely loving and generous heart, but one which may not be well-equipped to pair-bond with others. This "lover of all the world without specific attachment" heart line is often found on nuns, or anyone who has many dear and fast friends, but would be hard-pressed to define any one person as specifically most dear to her heart. This is also found in people who are very warm, open, and receptive to love, but who aren't always selective or consistent in their choice of partners.

When the heart line **rises up into the mount of Jupiter** (D in the illustration), you'll find the loving, supportive, power behind the throne. Any partner of a successful career politician will have some aspect of this heart line. Whether or not it's one of many branches or the only branch, this heart line indicates both devotion and sacrifice to the beloved's Jupiter-oriented endeavors.

When the heart line has a branching that **drops down underneath Jupiter and connects with the head line and the life line** (E in the illustration), it indicates an emotional need for a best friend of one's own gender. When this is the dominant branching of the heart line, it can be an indication that the *strongest* emotional bonds will be with members of one's own gender.

When the heart line **terminates under Saturn without necessarily having a rising branch to Saturn** (F in the illustration), it indicates a somewhat blunt and direct emotional approach. These are the people who seek a "package," whether it's hand-some, blonde, and blue-eyed, or brunette with great legs and a sultry voice. It's not that the flat Saturn heart line is unloving at all, but these people may have a narrow perspective and a lengthy learning process before they can move beyond the pictures in their heads. In fact, they know the language of sex—not of romance, and the love terms don't really compute at all.

The Length of the Heart

Sometimes, you'll find a heart line that doesn't spring from the percussion but instead seems to "float" in the center of the hand without being "anchored" at either end. When you come across this, you should first check the heart line in both hands. Generally, the passive hand will show a "typical" heart line that begins on the percussion and ends in one of the places we discussed earlier. You can then read the active hand with the floating heart line as an *overlay* on that typical structure. But what is the interpretation of a floating heart line?

A floating heart line can indicate a person who is especially attached to Saturnian or Apollonian ideals, but this all takes place within the family—attachment to individuals who aren't part of the immediate kith and kin just isn't part of this picture. Further, if the dominant termination of this heart line is a flat line under Jupiter, those emotional attachments are with members of the animal kingdom rather than with other humans. (Love me, love my dogs.)

Helping Hands

A heart line that starts mid-hand can indicate someone whose capacity for emotional attachment and feeling can be dated from where this line begins. Such people are often late bloomers in their emotional lives.

Handy Words to Know

In palmistry, an **overlay** is any pattern that seems to override a more typical one. More often found in the active hand, overlays can change rapidly and are therefore not read on their own, but in conjunction with the passive hand pattern.

The floating heart line.

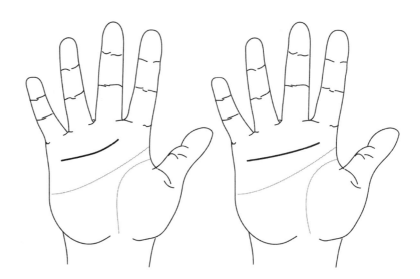

Helping Hands

The floating heart line can mean that there is a unique emotional challenge or a strong attachment in a somewhat unusual way. An Apollonian floating heart line (under the Apollo finger), for example, might be dedicated to the theater.

Someone with a floating heart line may have more passion and dedication than self-preservation when it comes to his emotions. It's also important to recognize the difference between an animal lover and someone who loves *only* animals. The latter person often lacks emotional grounding or connection with her own species—that is, humans!

People possessing floating heart lines have strong connections with nature and, if they live in an urban environment, try to create nature in microcosm. Of course, it's more likely they don't live in the big city in the first place, a further aspect of their isolationist natures. At the very least, the person with a floating heart line takes long hikes—either alone or with his faithful nonhuman companion.

The Depth of the Heart

Before you can really understand the many different depths possible on a heart line, you'll need to look at quite a few. To help you analyze them as you look, we'd like you to consider an analogy.

Imagine a reproduction of the heart line blown up a hundred times and then sculpted in clay. Now, think of the heart line as a tiny stream cut into the clay, and the volume of water that it carries an indication of its depth. To continue the analogy, other characteristics, such as chaining (see the following illustration), islands, and branching lines, are modeled here as well—helping or hindering the flow of water.

Now remember, water is the element of emotion. Are you embarrassed when your date cries or screams at movies? Chances are, if you're silent and unmoved, his heart line has a greater depth than yours. That's because the depth of the heart line indicates the depth of the emotions as well.

The **well-channeled, deeply scribed** heart line indicates that these emotions run very deep indeed, and if you seek someone whose love is demonstrated and practiced in broad and tangible ways, you should expect these emotions to spill out in other places and spaces as well. In other words, carry a handkerchief for your beloved—or for yourself, if this deep heart line describes you.

The **chained, broken, or shallow** heart line may frustrate the bearer, the bearer's beloved—and the palmist seeking to be tactful. In a young person—under 24, let's say—a chained or shallow heart line may indicate a flighty nature, someone who's not ready for lasting attachment. This will change as the person ages, though, as many of us already know.

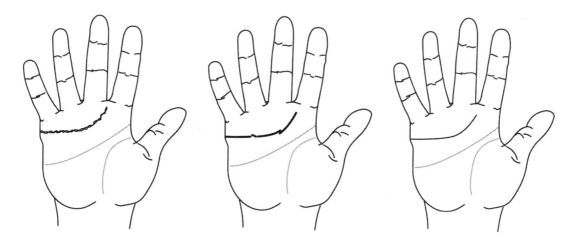

Left to right: chained heart line, broken heart line, shallow heart line.

Let's once again use our earlier analogy of the lines enlarged and modeled in clay carrying water to look at the heart line's steadfastness and reliability. Remember, fickleness is not infidelity, and a heart with many attractions and interests may be found on the most faithful of partners—whose curiosity and appetite for social and emotional variety leads them to many friends and interests.

169

Hand-le with Care

It requires patience and lots of comparison before the palmist can learn to see a continuum through the chain of broken lines, or a consistent perspective in the shallow line.
Unfortunately, a truly broken heart line usually indicates loss or some other equally
dramatic emotional change. Still, this marking is relatively rare: Divorce won't create it, for
example. A much deeper loss of faith, passion, or belief is necessary for this type of heart
line to appear—and it generally appears rapidly as well.

The Curve of the Heart

The heart line is very seldom straight. When you find a straight heart line, you've
probably also found an unusually direct (and perhaps, inappropriately blunt) person,
both in style and in whom they love. The straight heart line doesn't speak well for
people who deal in shades of grey, but rather those who will be either your fastest
friend or your worst enemy. In other words, no wishy-washies need apply here.

In addition, a heart line without a curve indicates someone whose emotional affections
and intentions are expressed succinctly and directly. There may not be much poetry or
fancy ribbons, but to use a computer term, WYSIWYG: "What you see is what you
get." To state it still more directly, these people are not very demonstrative.

Inevitably, right angles, or, for that matter, any sharp angle along the heart line, call
for a certain amount of flexibility in interpretation. The majority of heart lines you'll
see will look like gentle curves, with branches up or down along the way. More dramatic angles from the heart line can indicate a more dramatic emotional makeup. It
follows that if you need a lover with nuance, ambience, and subtlety, it's these smooth
curves you're after, rather than sharp angles.

Going Up

As it crosses the hand, the heart line may show small peaks (quite literally, little
upside-down Vs in the heart line) under various fingers. Frequently, these peaks are
under the finger of Apollo, while they're less commonly found under the finger of
Saturn, or even, on rare occasions, under Mercury or Jupiter.

When the heart line shows a peak under Apollo, it indicates a pattern of emotional
bonds with musicians, actors, and occasionally, artists; an attraction, in other words,
specifically to the Apollonian fields of endeavors. Robin has seen this many times even

when the marriage was between a secretary and an insurance salesman: The secretary soon confessed that it was his role as a drummer in a weekend dance band that had originally attracted her to him.

Conversely, when the heart line peaks under Saturn, the attraction may be to policemen, servicemen, or other people in uniform. This aspect of the heart line may again fool you, though, as the role of responsibility and authority can be worn in many guises. Hey—remember the Village People?

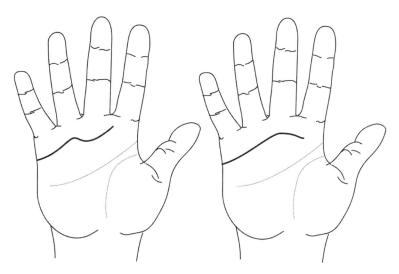

Heart line peaking: left, under Apollo; right, under Saturn.

Peaks under Mercury are rare and difficult to define. However, you may sometimes find this inclination in those with careers in the media, and it can also indicate a tendency to associate more often with members of one's own profession. Robin has found that someone with a Mercury peak on the heart line won't be as fixated or obsessive as those with Saturn or Apollo peaks. This may be why Tom Brokaw has fewer groupies than Sting or Colin Powell.

The heart line will either reach to Jupiter, fall short of Jupiter, or terminate under Jupiter. However, when the heart line terminates with a *small* peak or rise under Jupiter as well, we may find a passionate follower or a dedicated servant of the particular cause or office, although not necessarily the individual representing the cause or office. Here's where Bill Clinton's groupies are—but they were George Bush's before they were his.

Helping Hands

It's been Robin's experience that a peak (note that we mean a peak and not a rising line) under Jupiter is a relatively benign and comfortable situation. Look for this aspect on a reasonably intelligent but solitary idealist; for example, the faithful Catholic with a deep appreciation of the papal office and its history.

Going Down

A dip on the heart line has a positive interpretation because it brings a grounding, a pragmatism, and a seriousness to a given area. However, it's also frequently a sign of an intensity that can be overbearing, dramatic, and uncomfortable for the bearer. A classic example would be seen as a recessed spot on the heart line, frequently darker colored than the rest of the line. The first story this person tells might be, "I would have been a dancer, if not for that broken ankle," even though the story's 20 years old.

Dips in the heart line: left, under Saturn; right, under Mercury.

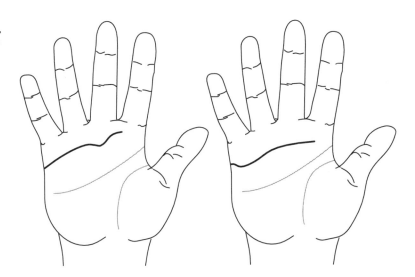

When the dip on the heart line occurs under the Saturn finger, one assumption may be that the person had an absent father, a truly abusive father, or an abusive grandfather. This can also be a sign of mental illness or incapacity in the father; for example, "My father was a loving and kind man, but he was often sick when I was a boy."

Other interpretations here, depending on the intensity of the dip and the color, may have to do with a chronic mistrust of authority or the legal system. "Let's kill all the lawyers!" might be found here, as well as the unresolved Vietnam War veteran or protestor.

If the heart line has a dip under Mercury, it's a safe assumption that its bearer doesn't appreciate commerce and the capitalistic system. Or it's possible he may have a grave distrust of modern medicine, with the appropriate horror stories to explain his distrust.

But how can you tell the difference between these varieties of Mercurial aspects? In fact, as the Wizard of Oz said, the information to make this appraisal has to a large degree been made available to you already. It can be found in the bend of the Mercury finger, which we discussed in Chapter 6, and other qualities of the heart line, such as the idealism indicated by one that's clear and well-cut, or the strong materialism indicated by a chained, floating one.

Hand-le with Care

Occasionally, when there's a heart line dip under Mercury, you'll find someone who is dishonest in some way. Whether she lies consciously or believes the lie of the moment, you might want to think twice before you loan her your money or your car.

It's pretty unusual to find a heart line with a dominant downward curve across the hand. When it's there, this curve is at the end of the heart line, curving into the head line and life line. This heart line indicates someone who is *very* serious, with deep emotions and deep loyalties, and whose strongest emotional bonds are with people of his own gender. Exceptions may be found with a Saturnian bend, where the strongest ties are with members of the bearer's family of origin.

Heart Line Extremes

It must be written somewhere (and if not, it is now, here) that one individual's passions are another's poisons, and it's on the heart line that you'll find such indications of behavior, sure to frustrate all concerned. Extremes can run the gamut from a double heart line to a triad at the end of the heart line, or one where all segments are equally strong, which lends itself to very high expectations in love.

A double heart line, defined as "railroad tracks," parallel, symmetrical, and very close together, doesn't inevitably indicate "my girlfriend, my lover, and my wife." There are individuals, the military pilot or professional athlete, for example, whose dualistic loves may be their work and their partner. This configuration can also be found on married couples who are not able to share a high profile of time or space together. For example, Lisa's husband Bob is working in Guam right now, and this configuration appears on her left (passive) hand.

However, it's also possible to read a doubled heart line as a dualism of emotional attraction. This may be entirely innocent, such as the happily married woman who was also her father's paid secretary. Her husband and family received plenty of attention and love, but her chosen role of profession was founded in an equally deep emotional bond.

Occasionally, you'll find a heart line that's clear and strong to Saturn, with a strong branch up into the mount of Saturn, and then after Saturn continues to Jupiter, chained or broken. This indicates a stubborn love of land and property, and might be found on someone who simply won't sell his family home—even though the rest of the block has long been razed to make room for a freeway.

*Railroad tracks: a double
heart line that's parallel
and symmetrical.*

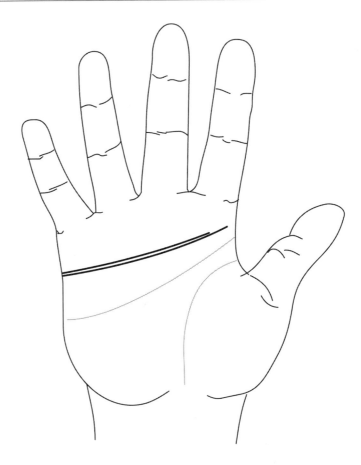

Lines from the Heart

A line from the heart, as opposed to a branching, indicates an emotional tendency, with the degree determined by the strength of the branching or line. If the line goes all the way into one of the mounts, for example, the tendency toward that mount is strongly stated, but if it's short and doesn't enter a mount, it's more likely a minor emotional quirk—or perhaps even a character affectation.

Lines are not branches, as the following illustration makes clear. While branches are clear inclinations, lines are mere tendencies.

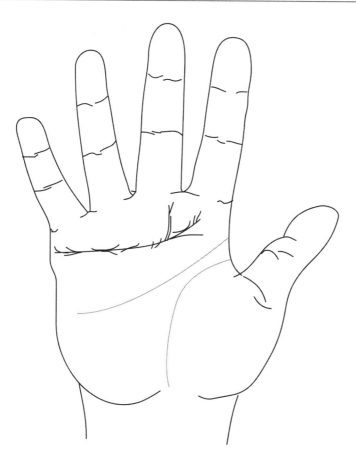

Lines from the heart line don't look the same as branchings of the heart line.

Inclinations

Inclinations can indicate such a wide variety of heart directions that it's best to let each speak for itself:

➤ People with short heart lines will not be overly emotional.

➤ A break in the heart line can indicate severe emotional trauma.

➤ Many branches of equal strength can indicate very broad taste, and perhaps a lack of selectivity.

➤ Small rising lines from the heart line can indicate an optimistic tendency, or a mild interest in a given area.

➤ Small dropping lines are seen as a tendency for a sense of failing, a negative interest, or even a prejudice against the given area. You might see dropping lines under Mercury in those with a socialistic tendency, for example.

➤ Blue dots or black dots on the heart line can be read as emotional loss and very likely, a loss of equilibrium. Many times these dots will fade away with a passage of time. Occasionally, they don't. But unless the palm reader is carrying a clean handkerchief and is prepared to spend a certain amount of time listening with compassion and sympathy, it might be wise to overlook or understate the intensity of these areas. Sometimes, such a dot must be explored as a limitation or blockage for other heart-oriented expressions. Finally, a blue dot indicates less of an emotional loss than a black dot.

➤ A red dot can be interpreted as an area of passion, though that passion may be for a friend as well as a lover, or simply a personal expression where one has deep feelings.

➤ The configuration of a red dot on the heart line, coupled with a star, can indicate a rapid and overwhelming release of pent-up energy. Ultimately, though, the emotionally involved observer may not be surprised to hear of the action or result, and state that he knew something was coming, because so-and-so had been under a great deal of pressure.

Hand-le with Care

There are palmists who interpret a red dot on the heart line as having a pulmonary or coronary impact (read: heart attack). Robin disagrees. He concedes that a red dot with a distinctive multipointed star on the heart line could possibly be read as a life challenge. But, he feels this configuration can also indicate a violent fight between family members, in which there's a good chance of both emotional and physical injury and trauma. Heart attacks, in other words, can assume many guises.

➤ In the material world, gunshot, explosion, physical danger from fire (as opposed to material loss), and other violent activities are also indicated by the red dot and the star on the heart line. Be very careful when you discuss these things with someone who has them. But also know that when you do use caution when discussing them, you may have the extremely satisfying experience of feeling you've circumvented a potential tragedy.

➤ A white dot on the heart line has several potentials. One of them is the emergence of a spiritual lesson. This can be seen as the realm of acceptance, and it may not be inevitably without tears or pain. The release of a child to adulthood, to her own life, or her own career is sometimes indicated by this white dot in the hand of an exceptionally intense and devoted parent.

➤ A white dot may also be read as the immediate predecessor or the discovery of a true and lasting friend. There are no negative interpretations for a white dot on the hand in the larger sense. However, a white dot can sometimes be read as an aspect of emotional detachment, such as the acceptance of a loved one learning a lesson.

Affectations

Affectations that can be found on the heart line are indications of your particular passions, whether it's vegetarianism, social idealism, or gambling. The degree and area of passion can be found in the strength and area of the heart line inclination, as well as some other areas of the hand, which we'll discuss individually in a moment.

First, if your heart line extends into the mount of Jupiter, you have aspects on the lunar mount (which we'll be discussing in Chapter 18), and you have a pointed Jupiter finger, you have the potential for vegetarianism. But there's also another sort of vegetarian who shows a scattering of faint lines from the heart line under Jupiter. This person might be a vegetarian because she has been persuaded by a teacher, the media, or a partner, without being truly convinced that it's inappropriate to take life for food (the belief of the first, more passionate vegetarian). This second type might even be a vegetarian who owns a lucrative string of steak houses!

In any event, tiny scattered lines from the heart line under Jupiter indicate someone who both follows and expresses a socially appropriate demeanor—which is, of course, entirely dependent on his particular society. In a society that's decidedly vegetarian, Hindu India, for example, the Jupiterian-oriented vegetarian, while expressing a subtle kind of socially confirming lifestyle, would also make sure everyone knew that he was doing so.

Another affectation is the doubled heart line that isn't expressed as paralleling lines. This can be found on those who may have dramatic and decidedly different emotional venues and directions, such as a priest with a passion for horse racing. Such an individual would have a primary heart line that was relatively low and perhaps chained on the hand, with an Apollonian peak or short rising line. A stronger continuation from Saturn into Jupiter might be clearer and better cut, with its only specific note its extension into Jupiter without much rise or fall.

An affectation of a second heart line is damaging to the subject's path only if the primary heart line is badly chained, broken, or feeds into the limitations of the second heart line. In other words, someone with a material Saturn-oriented heart line, and the establishment of a heart line indicating a passion for some form of gambling in the form of Apollo markings, might be tempted to risk stability for material gain—especially if that long shot's sure to come in.

The doubled heart line.

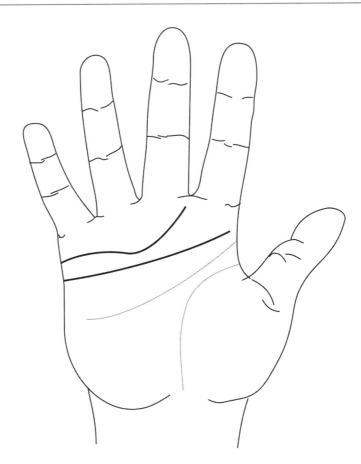

One other heart line affectation would be the assumption that there *is* no heart line! While this is possible, it's very uncommon, as we discussed in Chapter 10 when we talked about the Simian Crease.

Bad Choices

"He's a wonderful man, but..."

"I know she's tired of that life and ready to make a change..."

"I'm sure with the support of a good loving partner, he can overcome his addiction..."

The heart line alone is only part of the story of the good Samaritan who seeks to nurture and heal one more three-legged dog. In fact, when emotional bad choice seems a fact of life for someone, chances are you'll find that person has an extreme angle of the thumb and a powerful and well-accentuated lunar mount in addition to difficulties along the heart line.

When the heart line shows a great deal of breadth (such as a wide if not necessarily deep channel), has a rising line into the mount of Apollo, and carries throughout its course a consistent red color, you'll find someone with the potential to repeatedly recruit the same sort of broken individual to attempt to heal them. Whether it's the woman who seems to go from abusive husband to abusive lover, or the man who repeatedly selects emotionally remote partners, the pattern of bad choice is evident in the hand.

At another level, however, it's entirely likely that everyone has approached or flirted with this phenomena at some point. What makes it *chronic* may be that Apollonian rising line; this creates a fixation to repeat the pattern, over and over and over. Many times, the person to whom one is attracted has physical attributes that are also repeated from relationship to relationship.

Finally, the healing potential of a well-developed and utilized medical stigmata on the mount of Mercury (we'll talk more about these in Chapter 16) may relieve and redirect this potential into one of rescuing individuals with the concept that they can be repaired into the ideal lover.

When you find an impassioned (that is, a consistently bright red) heart line and a dominant broad and intense (possibly even more intense than the heart line itself) branching of the heart line up to Saturn, you may be looking at the hand of a young woman who seeks to bond with an authoritarian, dogmatic "alpha" male older than herself.

> **Helping Hands**
>
> Note that the Apollo rising line is about the appearance of the individual: same face, different person; or same voice, same body, but different person. These people are fixated on type, in other words, not specific people.

> **Hand-le with Care**
>
> The attraction to authority figures is indicated by an intense connect toward Saturn off the heart line. However, a series of small vertical lines to Saturn shouldn't be read as a lasting attachment to and fascination with authority, but rather, as an appreciation for some of the more accessible *trappings* of authority. In this case, the right briefcase may be enough.

When the person's passive Mars (more on passive Mars, the area of your ability to hold your own, in Chapter 17) isn't strong but has a strong Saturn connection, and there are accentuating marks on passive Mars as well, it may indicate someone who is seeking a mate to control him and tell him what to do. Of course, the extremes of these behaviors are better left to the psychologist—they aren't necessarily a tasteful or wise place for the palmist to go.

Still, what about the dominant partner in such a relationship? That person may show a secondary heart line branching toward Saturn, and it's unlikely that the main branch of the heart line will reach to Jupiter; control, after all, is not leadership. Lastly, it's unlikely that such an individual will show the clear curving and well-scribed heart line of emotional depth.

You Gotta Have Heart: A Story

When it came to their heart lines, Joe and Clara couldn't have been more different. Clara was sensitive, emotional, verbal, and expressive. Joe was a humorist, and a wry and dry (in fact, often sarcastic) observer of humanity.

Live theater, weddings, and funerals were situations that tried their otherwise peaceful and loving cohabitation deeply because Clara's emotions were generally open and easily expressed, and Joe's turned into gentle sarcasm. Though Clara had a slender, petite, and delicate hand, her broad and generous heart line would have carried two of Joe's within it. Still, these two had the heart to live with their differences—and Joe had long ago learned to carry tissues for Clara.

Remember, the heart line is the most important line in the hand. Even on those rare and courageous people whose life and head lines are mere sketches of cobwebs, the heart line is strong, clear, and gently curved. Just as the master of calligraphy or the *sumi* brush speaks of a line that has no beginning and no ending, the truly articulated and well-designed line in the hand, be it heart, head, or life, speaks of strength and beauty.

Heart is the indispensable energy we all must have to successfully move through this dimension we call life. While there are other ways to focus, they seem secondary to that overwhelming and all-conquering heart *chakra* energy. If you're fortunate enough to meet someone who has survived purely from the strength and empowerment of her heart, stop and recognize her unique and almost unworldly energy. There's something there for the rest of us to appreciate and emulate as best we can.

Mapping Your Heart Line

Now that we've given you a quick tour of the heart line, it's time to take a tour of your own. Get out your palmistry notebook and sketch your heart line as it appears on your hand. Be sure to approximate where it begins and ends, its depth and width, and any branching lines, as well as channels, breaks, or islands. Then, go back through this chapter and see what we have to say about your heart line—and the nature of your emotions.

The Least You Need to Know

➤ Your heart line is a map of your love life.

➤ Where your heart line ends is an indication of how you love.

➤ The depth of your heart line is a barometer of how emotional you are.

➤ The curve of your heart line reveals your emotional expression.

➤ Peaks toward particular mounts indicate inclinations toward those areas.

➤ Dips on the heart line show pragmatism in the given area or potential places to get "stuck."

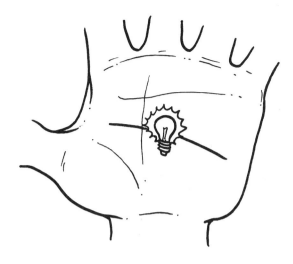

Chapter 12

The Head Line: How Do You Think?

In This Chapter

➤ Your head line is a measure of your thinking

➤ The length of your head line indicates your capacity for detail

➤ The intensity of your head line equals the intensity of your thought

➤ The curve of your head line maps your imagination and practicality

➤ Branching lines from the head line can point to your mental interests

What's the nature of your thinking? Does your imagination tend to run away when you haven't heard from your kids in the last 10 minutes? Are you practical or detail oriented? And what's the best way for you to use your intelligence?

Your head line, which runs horizontally across the center of your palm, reveals how you think, the way you think, and the things you think about. It's here you'll find not only your intelligence, but how you use your mind—and how you could be using it.

Finding the Head Line

The *head line* almost always starts between the thumb and the Jupiter finger and travels across the hand toward the percussion. (Note that the head line very seldom reaches all the way across to the percussion, or Mercury edge of the hand.) It's here that you'll find the nature of your thinking and the way you use your mind.

The head line.

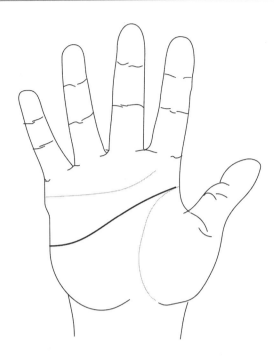

Handy Words to Know

The **head line**, the central of the three major lines on the hand, usually begins between the thumb and the Jupiter finger and travels in a gentle curve across the hand toward the percussion. Your head line reveals the nature of your thinking.

Where It Begins

There's a lot of room between the thumb and the Jupiter finger, and head lines can begin anywhere in that area. The head line may begin joined with the life line (which we'll discuss in the next chapter), above the life line, and, occasionally, from the mount of Jupiter below the Jupiter finger. The head line extends across the hand, and generally has some sort of curve rather than being ruler-straight. It rarely starts literally on the inside of the life line—more on that in just a few pages.

Sometimes a head line starts under or even inside the mount of Jupiter, which indicates a level of self-awareness separate from the family's or the parents', and hence a more independent nature. The greater the gap between the head line and the life line, in fact, the more this love of independence tends toward foolhardiness rather than merely the ability to think for one self. When these people see "wet paint" signs, they always have to touch for themselves.

184

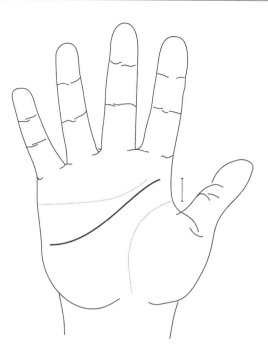

The independent head line.

The head line may also begin joined to the life line at the edge of the hand between the thumb and Jupiter (as shown in the following photo). This indicates that one's mental perspectives and attitudes were very much formed by the family's. In fact, where the head line can be distinctly separated from the life line is when independent thought and interaction, separate from the family, began.

A life line connected to the head line at its start is common. In fact, the head line and life line are quite often found together at their beginning, and the place where they separate is where the mental influence of the family values separates as well.

In the photo, this woman's head line and life line are joined at their start; her relationship with her family to this day remains complex, though she lives 2,000 miles away from them. The head line that literally starts inside the life line can indicate very physical—even elemental—people, who are challenged in some way when the head line crosses the life line. Similarly, head lines are also found that begin below the life line rather than above it,

We Gotta Hand It to You

One variation of the head line connected with the life line at the start can be found in those who've left home at a young age, but continue to have strong family attachments. This head line will remain joined with the life line throughout adolescence in the same way as someone who stayed at home. One client of Robin's, for example, left home at 17 and joined the service. Still, he continued to send money home until he was 24, and didn't make any attempt to define himself outside either his family or the military until his younger siblings had also left home.

This woman's head line and life line are joined at their start.

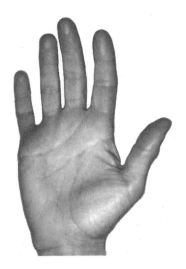

Helping Hands

A person with a head line that doesn't reach near Mercury won't enjoy crossword puzzles from Mercurian precision, accuracy of spelling, or nuance of vocabulary. Rather, she'll do them from the Apollo characteristics of winning, finishing, or getting it right.

and then cross the life line. When you find this configuration, it means that in childhood, the individual had some degree of physical challenge where the juncture of the head and life lines occurs.

This configuration can also indicate a very strong karmic bond or attachment with the family. In fact, these people may show strength of character and maturity beyond their years when young, but this isn't necessarily a particularly comfortable or easy challenge to meet.

When the head line crosses the life line, there's a strong chance of a life-threatening situation, illness, accident, or a degree of self-obsession or challenge at that point. For example, a childhood illness brought about by a poorly thought out risk might be found. "I told you to wear your jacket, dear."

Similarly, if the head line crosses back over the life line in later years, there may once again be too great a demand on the self. This is frequently seen in those who are the objects of others' ridicule, or as an aspect of mental breakdown. In fact, these are those breakdowns that occur later in life that one often thinks he "should have seen coming."

When the head line rises out of the mount of Jupiter, or there's a direct connecting rising line between the independent head line (see (A) in the following illustration) and the rising line into the mount of Jupiter, we have both the independent mindset *and* the Jupiter qualities of independence, idealism, and attachment to leadership.

A separation of the life and head lines indicates the degree of separation from the family mindset.

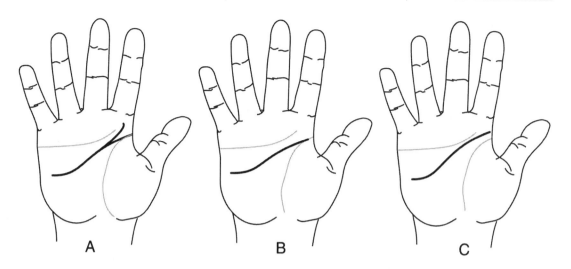

A) Head line rising out of Jupiter; (B) head line beginning below the life line and crossing it; (C) head line and life line clearly separated from the start.

Where It Ends

Just as the head line can begin in a variety of places between the thumb and Jupiter, it may end at any point across the palm, almost always short of the percussion itself. Where the head line ends isn't an indication of intelligence or lack of it, but rather of a number of things, including:

➤ Impact of the person's education

➤ Speed in evaluating information

➤ Decision making ability

➤ Attention to and appreciation of detail

Helping Hands

Robin says he can generally appraise a person's most recent IQ test score within three points by looking at her head line. He told Lisa hers—but she can't remember her last test score. An indication that its number was correct?

The head line may end abruptly under Saturn, giving the mind a strong focus on the material (real) world. It may extend across the hand until it reaches Apollo indicating Apollonian creativity and creative thinking. Or it may extend across the hand to Mercury, which indicates a Mercurial nature with a focus (or lack of focus) on communication, commerce, and healing.

The head line is also frequently found that curves down the hand toward or into the mount of the Moon low in the palm under Mercury (we'll be discussing the lunar mount more in Chapter 18). This is the area of your imagination, and we'll talk about the lunar head line in more detail when we discuss the imaginative head line in a few pages.

(A) Head line ending under Saturn; (B) extending across hand to Apollo; (C) extending across hand to Mercury; (D) curving down to lunar mount.

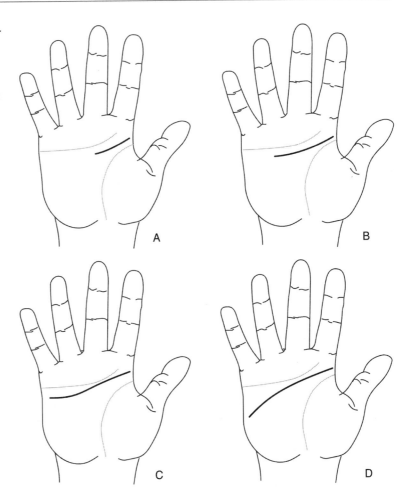

Helping Hands

The length of your head line is not just about your intelligence or a lack thereof. What its length does reveal is your detail orientation and the degree of your material orientation. But short does not equal stupid. Period.

The Length of the Head Line

Let's make one thing perfectly clear: The length of the head line is not the measure of intelligence alone. Sure, a longer head line can indicate a fondness for detail, but we know plenty of smart folks who just can't be bothered with such pesky little things.

Just as a long head line doesn't mean brilliance, a short head line doesn't mean a lack of intelligence. The short head line often ends under Saturn, which, as we mentioned earlier, indicates a strong material focus. This can indicate the business-person, entrepreneur, or farmer—someone with a dedication to economic success. You won't find this often on a lawyer or doctor, or anyone else whose career requires pragmatic essentials. That's because this head line's career is *all* about money, not just partly. There's also generally a no-nonsense approach, especially relating to land and anything concrete. You always know where you stand with these guys.

A very long head line will approach the percussion of the hand. When you find a head line like this, it's an indication of an intense involvement with detail. In fact, you'll often find this configuration on the insomniac—the person who's consumed by those details, in other words.

We Gotta Hand It to You

When the head line approaches or reaches the percussion of the hand, an "off switch" should be developed. Choice and decision may not be these people's forte unless they consciously make themselves stop whatever they're doing. This is because the percussion is a danger zone that says, "Stop! You've gone too far! You're thinking too much!" and you should respond with, "Okay! Shut off the computer! Take the dogs for a walk! Now!" These people just can't keep processing the material when there's no fresh input, so they must force themselves to take breaks to avoid making errors.

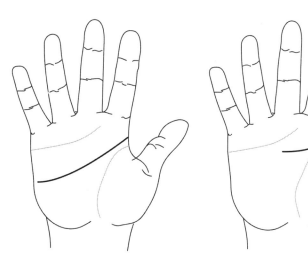

A head line traveling the width of the hand (left), a short head line (right).

Intensity of the Head Line

Like all lines in the hand, the head line's interpretation is based largely on an evaluation of its clarity and how well it's been formed. In addition, the more hands you look at, the more clearly you'll notice how much head lines vary from hand to hand.

When you look at the intensity of the head line, you should evaluate its curve as well, because this will show you the style of the intensity. The intensity of the head line is directly related to the intensity of thought, and a deep, clearly cut head line that's at least as well-cut as the heart line shows a thought process that's both organized and clever. This head line will look like a river that's cut in sandstone.

Hand-le with Care

If the heart line's stronger and clearer than the head line, decisions may be made in the heart instead of the head.

A head line that's less clear, or is chained or broken, will indicate more difficulty with the thinking process—but this again isn't an indication of intelligence or its lack. Rather, these difficulties are manifested in a number of ways, depending on their location.

The depth of the head line is an indication of a person's clarity and intensity of thought. Left: clear and strong; right: chained at the start, broken in the middle.

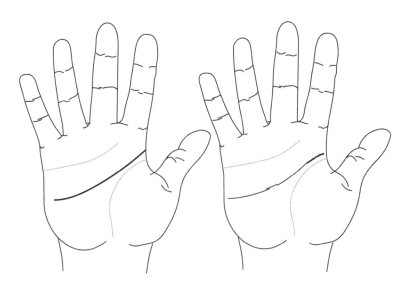

A head line that is chained at its start denotes an individual who as a child wasn't encouraged to believe that his mental capacities were strong. Perhaps his childhood lacked a solid foundation of education or discipline. A chained head line at the start can also indicate someone whose youthful environment was disruptive in some way.

A head line that has a break indicates a dramatic change in the mental energy and attitude at the place the break occurs. This may be read as tragic, life threatening—or, on a positive note, life expanding. What it is for certain, though, is a separate and distinct shift of consciousness. And in the long run, with time to process it, it's also generally a positive change as well. So maybe you won't become a doctor, but being a teacher can help people, too.

It's more difficult to interpret a head line that is chained or broken its entire length. At its best, it indicates very broad interests and many potentials. But this can also translate to a Jack or Jill of all trades—who's a master of none. A chained head line may indicate a lack of discipline or lasting focus on anything; there's not long-term dedicated mental energy found with this configuration, although it does allow for the energy of the moment.

The Curve of the Head Line (or Lack Thereof)

While a straight head line isn't common, it does have some merit in terms of goal, direction, and consistency. The straight head line's problems arise from its severity, rigidity, and lack of compromise, and people with straight head lines don't often adjust to new formats—or change jobs or managers—well.

We Gotta Hand It to You

Many New Age practitioners interpret a break on their head lines as a sign that they were called to their practice at that point in their lives. The New Age term for these practitioners is "walk-ins"—people who were "invited," so to speak. A break certainly is an indication of a new level of awareness or a marked shift in values, and will be found on the hand *before* the actual change in lifestyle or new direction is even thought of. Walk-ins consider the break on their head line the point of their walk-in.

Helping Hands

When the straight head line is also long, you've got everything you need for an accountant. This configuration indicates a need for everything to come out precisely and to the penny. If there's also a rising line to Mercury, you've got the researcher or the librarian.

What this means is that people with straight head lines are set in their ways, and when the line is additionally short, there might also be too little attention to details, or a tendency to never finish anything. Hey—come back here! We're not finished yet!

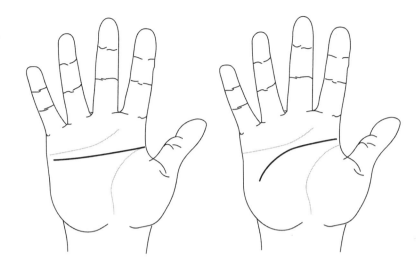

Straight head line (left), head line curving toward lunar mount (right).

When the head line curves sharply to the mount of the Moon, a deep imagination is readily apparent, and its use determined by a closer study of that mount, as we'll do in Chapter 18. But we'll also take a closer look at the imaginative head line in the next section of this chapter.

The head line is frequently branched, and some limited degree of branching is desirable, because it brings variety and openness to the mind of the bearer. In fact, short branchings on the head line are common and provide a much-needed widening of perspective.

To cite just one example, one branch may continue its journey across the hand to handle the details, while another branches down to the lunar mount to handle the imagination. You can again look at the photo earlier in this chapter for an example of this.

The head line rarely curves upward, although you'll find rising peaks along it as you did with the heart line. These peaks indicate a mental emphasis in the area of the peak:

Peak Toward	Mental Emphasis
Jupiter	Leadership
Saturn	Material world
Apollo	The arts
Mercury	Communication, commerce, medicine

The Imaginative Head Line

A head line that actually reaches the mount of the Moon indicates a truly unique soul. These people have such profound imaginations that other aspects in the hand, such as a strong Saturn for discipline or Apollo to direct the creativity, must complement it in order for their potential to come to anything.

Hand-le with Care

Sure, your husband's a half hour late. Maybe he got tied up in traffic, or his boss asked him to stay late. Are you imagining his car in a ditch or over a bridge, or that he was treed by vicious brown tree snakes (we are not making this up)? This vivid and often visual imagination is found with the head line that dips toward the mount of the Moon. Channel it into fiction and you'll save yourself a lot of stress—just ask Lisa.

When the head line approaches the mount of the Moon but doesn't actually enter it, the imagination is still strong, but the person is blessed with the ability to use her talent rather than be consumed by it, especially if creativity (found on the finger and mount of Apollo) and discipline (found on the finger and mount of Saturn) are also present.

When it's not balanced in other ways, the head line that enters the lunar mount can be extremely challenging. Yes, this is the configuration of everyone from the healer to the psychic to the artist to the magician. But if they're practicing their art, they've got something, whether it's a rising line to Mercury or a practical Apollo finger, that helps them to go down to the lunar mount to collect the goods and then to *get out of there again* to dispense them. The lunar mount is the land of the dreamy dreams, and, unregulated by other areas of the hands, it's the stuff of chaos unbound. It is both true creativity and madness.

We Gotta Hand It to You

What's your sense of time? If your head line is both long and curving, you may not have a sense of time in the same way that others do. In fact, people who travel to the beat of a different drummer often appear nearly ageless, and this tendency is strongest when the person is creative in some way as well. Just ask a writer, musician, or artist what it's like when she's on a roll, and she'll tell you that she loses all sense of time.

The Practical Head Line

When it comes to being practical, the head line is defined by some flatness along with a lack of dramatic curves. A flat spot in an otherwise curving head line brings some practicality, and practicality is also augmented by small branches from the head line.

Lines from the Head Line

Some head line branching is always a good thing to have: It provides balance between the branch and the main stem of the head line. But how do you know which branch is the main one and which is the branch? Look for the strongest line in terms of intensity, continuity, and completion. You can once again refer to the earlier photo to help you with this. The dominant branch of that head line is the one that continues across the hand.

Lines from the head line can be divided into where they're located and where they're directed. Some are located at the beginning of the head line, branching toward either Jupiter or active Mars (between the head line and the thumb), and others can be found toward the end of the head line, and deal with Mercurian aspects or the lunar aspects we discussed earlier.

A fork at the end of the head line shows a greater degree of balance and lack of prejudice than a wide branching would indicate. Balance is determined by both the angle and the length of the branching, as you can see from the following illustration. There's still the potential for rigidity with a forked head line, but this configuration limits the narrow-minded aspects of the bearer.

A triad at the end of the head line is generally quite favorable. It indicates an ability to see all sides of a situation.

When there are breaks along the head line, there may have been overload or a prohibited interest or passion, which led to burnout in that particular area.

Hand-le with Care

Spirituality is generally a good thing—although it can be trying for your friends and family if coupled with a tendency to proselytize. Ultimately, remember, spirituality *is* personal.

There are many aspects to reading spirituality in the hand (such as the sister lines to the life line, which we'll discuss in the next chapter). But a *severe* angle of the head line indicates a defined and loudly expressed conversion to a given faith. This is generally dramatic, and though in time the intensity and the need to share one's newfound spirituality may fade, the conversion is generally lasting and real. Don't forget to look at the location of any pronounced angle; it can show when the spiritual conversion will take place. We'll be discussing timing in the hand in the next chapter, too.

When you look at any line from the head line, you should also look at the angle it forms, which is an indication of its degree of spirituality. Angles of as much as 90° are possible, although 60° is quite enough to define a severe case of spiritual interest coming up strongly. A distinct and dramatic turn of the head line means somebody's getting religion.

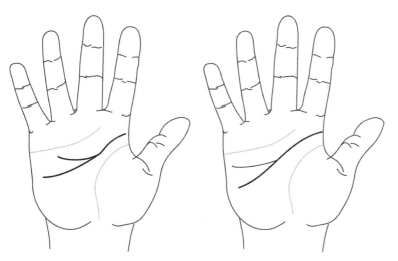

A branching head line (left), a forking head line (right).

The Inventor

While we've already explored many aspects of the inventor in our discussions of the spatulate hand and various spatulate fingertips, this type is enhanced still more when the head line branches into the mount of Neptune, the mount of Uranus—or both. Both of these mounts are in the same neighborhood as the lunar mount, and we'll discuss them each in detail in Chapter 18. At the same time, a less practical inventor may have the imaginative branching to the lunar mount that we discussed earlier.

Any inventor, though, in addition to these branchings, also will exhibit strong Mercury energies to generate activity, and some strong Saturnian aspects for discipline. In addition, there's a certain strength to the head line, including multifaceted branches. Add this strength to whichever fingertip is spatulate to find where the inventive nature lies:

Spatulate Fingertip	Area of Invention
Saturn	Tools
Apollo	Creativity
Thumb	Activity

Lucky for almost all inventors (and for the rest of us), that *all* of these fingertips aren't spatulate!

The Refiner

The refiner's head line is similar to the inventor's, with overall strength and multifaceted branches. Also, like the inventor, the refiner's potential for specialization is found in the fingertips, in this case, which fingertips are conic. When the conic fingertip also has a large third phalange, the refiner is looking for comfort as well, and this will be reflected in what she chooses to refine.

The refiner has a greater sense of overview and less detail orientation than the inventor, and this shows up in the head line as a smoother curve, shorter length, less severe angles, and fewer shifts in direction.

Read Past the Headline: A Story

Once there was a successful businessman, who, in his country of origin, was known as both a poet and a man of God. This was also readily apparent from his long, high head line, which rose from Jupiter, crossed his hand with the subtlest degree of curve, and ended with a slight rise directed toward Mercury. Because it was nearly too long and too rigid, though, Robin wondered if this man's head line allowed for *any* degree of flexibility or sense of humor.

But it was his *second* head line, which broke down and away under Saturn and reached into the mount of Uranus, that depicted this shrewd Internet-oriented businessman. He bought used electronic equipment and shipped it out of the country to be rebuilt at a very reasonable cost. Honest and moral, he used his business acuity and unrelenting pursuit of a profit to put his first son into Harvard Business School.

Nevertheless, he was always torn between two divergent roles and didn't see himself as truly successful. A doubled head line, in fact, is great for quantity of work, but while focus, true genius, and quality aren't a given here, personal satisfaction is.

Mapping Your Head Line

Now that we've shown you some of the head line's possible paths, it's time to draw a map to determine the path of your own head line. Be sure to include any branchings, forks, or lines from the head line, as well as whether it's broken or channeled in any way. Then go back through this chapter and learn the story of your head line.

The Least You Need to Know

➤ Your head line reveals the nature of your thinking and the nature of your mind.

➤ The length of your head line shows your capacity for detail.

➤ The intensity of your head line shows the intensity of your thought.

➤ The curve of your head line shows your imagination and practicality.

➤ Branching lines from the head line indicate areas of interest and balance.

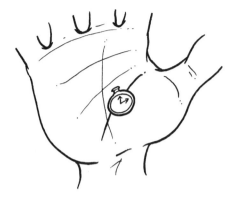

Chapter 13

The Life Line: How (and Where, and Why) Do You Do What You Do?

You may not have known much about palmistry when you began reading this book, but chances are, you did know where to find your life line. Everybody's interested in the game of life.

The life line is fundamental to the palm reader, too, but not to the extent that you might think. Still, palmists think of the life line as the defining leg of the tripod between the head, heart, and life lines, and it's here you'll find the sacred breath of your life, your *chi*.

Finding the Life Line

Now that you know where your heart line and head line lie, it's easy to find your *life line*. The third of the three dominant lines in your hand, it forms an arc that begins between your thumb and Jupiter finger and then heads around the thumb toward your wrist. The life line also defines the mount of Venus, which, as you may recall, is also the third phalange of the thumb.

The life line.

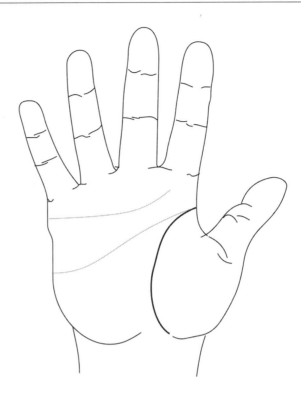

How It Begins

The life line *always* begins between the thumb and Jupiter finger, and it almost always curves around the mount of Venus toward the base of the thumb. It's the easiest line to find on your hand—but you probably know that already.

Some life lines start on the mount of Jupiter, which indicates enhanced Jupiterian qualities like leadership and independence. Others rise from active Mars and then make a wrist-ward sweep. This configuration seems to form a wedge in the hand, and an active Mars (which we'll discuss in Chapter 17) accent here indicates an energetic, even competitive, nature.

Handy Words to Know

The **life line** begins between the thumb and Jupiter finger and forms an arc to the base of the thumb. Your life line reveals your life and its impact on the world.

Where It Ends?

Repeat after us: *The length of the life line has nothing to do with the length of the life*. That's a common misconception. So if your life line seems short, you can relax!

Many healthy people have relatively short life lines. But just as a film may be shot page by page, without a finished script, a short life line may indicate that one's path, karma, or destiny isn't yet "written." In fact, there are those with short life lines who've lived past what appears to be their "defined" time according to the life line. A look at both hands to compare the life lines confirms that's this isn't very important. The life line will almost always look different on the passive hand than the active hand.

In general, the life line will terminate somewhere around the base of the thumb, or sometimes below the base of the thumb. But, as you'll find out, when a palmist looks at the life line, he'll be far more concerned with its quality than its length.

Helping Hands

It's possible, though not exactly in good taste, to find someone's opportunities and choices for "leaving this plane of existence" (dying). But Robin believes this decision is a choice because we always have choices, and so when we choose to release our grasp of this earthly plane can't be written precisely in the hand—because it's up to us. Most people are not ready.

The Length of the Life

As we've already stated, the length of the life line has nothing to do with the length of the life. In fact, Robin has found that life line length seems to be genetic, and that people of certain ethnic groups share certain life line attributes.

Those of Welsh and Irish descent, for example, are often square-handed people—whose life lines don't always get even halfway around their thumbs. This configuration, rather than indicating a brief life, points to both a resilient character and a boisterous sense of humor, and its bearers seem to live, if not forever, pretty darned close. Often "out of time," these people seldom look their age: They enter puberty young and age quite slowly thereafter.

Interestingly, extremely long life lines can be found on those of African-American descent: Robin has seen some that actually seem to go off the hand. Despite their many challenges in the United States, African-Americans often live long, long lives.

The length of the life line appears to be genetic: the life line of an Irish person (left), the life line of an African-American (right).

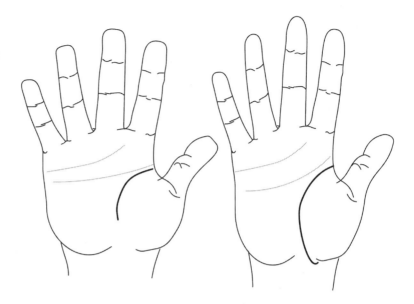

Many life lines exhibit deterioration, branching, or fraying about three-fourths of the way along their length. This may be read as a reference to the bearer's early to mid-60s, when the energy begins to wane. We'll be talking about telling time on the life line in just a few pages.

Hand-le with Care

Just as the length of the life line doesn't indicate the length of the life, you're more likely to find geographical or health changes along the life line, or ones relating your overall condition of well-being, than anything else. These are found as dots or lines, which we'll be discussing in a few pages.

The Depth of the Life Line

Everybody wants to live, and nobody wants to die, but what your life line's really about is not your death, but your life; that is, your vitality, activity, and how you occupy your life. In fact, the depth of your life line can be read as your *chi*, the vital breath that you bring to everything you do.

Think of the depth of the life line as a channel cut in the hand: Some are mere trickles; others look like the Grand Canyon.

The amount of *chi* a person has can determine whether or not you'll remember her name or face the next time you see her, and, in a similar way, the depth of the life line reveals the impact of her self-expression on the world.

When the life line is shallow and narrow, its bearer isn't likely to show much attachment to or impact on the world. While these people aren't much influenced by their environments, they don't influence the environment either, and a thin, weak life line can also mean that they're ships without rudders, blown every which way by the shifting winds.

Helping Hands

When the life line is both deep and narrow, you probably won't find someone who'll be subtle—maybe he's just too intense. In fact, while he could be known to many, he'll be intimate with few.

If, on the other hand, the life line is both deep and broad, it can compensate for many other flaws and limitations within the hand. This is a strong and solid indication of inner strength, as well as of a person whom others won't soon forget.

Quality Is Everything

Abrupt shifts and changes are as common in the life line as they are in life itself. In fact, the only danger with change is too much, when you might find yourself the beneficiary of that Chinese curse and challenge: "May you live in interesting times."

Still, abrupt change is seldom easy on your psyche, strength, or finances, whether because it's unexpected or simply jarring in some way. On the life line, these changes will be clearly marked. For example, we both know a man who finally kicked his drug habit, and his life line literally jumped into another channel.

We Gotta Hand It to You

Of course, there are those who thrive on change, who change their geographic locations, their jobs— even their spouses—frequently. Interestingly, these people may not show branching lines of relocation or travel on the life line, even though they do plenty of both. Instead, their particular status quo can be read in the smooth curving arc of their life lines, while their mobility is found in the life line's various flat places or dips rather than as more disruptive lines.

Smooth and gentle curves on the life line, of course, indicate a smoother and more comfortable progression of events, and so are much more desirable (unless, of course, the person is locked into a lifestyle of dissatisfaction). Similarly, branching lines that carry a curve similar to the life line's, or even lines that come in at a subtle angle, are always more desirable than abrupt (for example, those approaching a right angle) projections on the life line.

When you're analyzing the life line's depth, remember the analogy of clay and running water we used to discuss the heart line in Chapter 11. The deeper channel is stiller, after all—and still waters run deep.

The arc of the life line indicates the degree by which we embrace life; the depth of the life line indicates how deeply felt that embrace is; and its breadth and narrowness indicate how selective or undiscriminating we may be along the way.

It Takes Two Hands

While there may be many things you can do one-handed, when it comes to reading the life line, it takes two hands. That's because the energy of the life line reflects your own dual energy, the inner life of your passive hand, and the outer life of your active hand:

Inner Life	Outer Life
Introspective	Expressed
Internal dialogue	External dialogue
Unspoken feelings	Spoken words

Robin feels that any palm reader who fails to evaluate the passive-hand life line as having a full 45 percent voting stock in the equation is doing herself as well as her client a supreme disservice. Contradiction between the active and passive life lines is not only common, it's expected. Like your own inner and outer lives, the dichotomy of your life lines reveals the balance (and struggle) between your active and passive selves.

If the passive-hand life line has a greater quality, deeper depth, and stronger *chi* than the active hand's life line, its influences may be more defined and expressed as well. This may be the weekend gardener, for example. Of course, if the passive-hand life line is not as strong as the active hand's, its influence will have less effect.

The Curve of the Life Line

The curve of the life line indicates the grace with which one deals with incongruities, changes, and shifts in emotional, geographical, or philosophical arenas over time.

Those with graceful, smooth curves have an urbane appreciation for this sphere of existence. Robin reads them as "old souls," who have a quality of adaptability and are able to maintain high levels of integrity as life goes through its inevitable and frequently uncomfortable shifts and changes.

Sometimes, though, you'll find a life line that looks like a series of straight lines, set in obtuse angles. These peoples' attachments and courses of action are so changeable, they can be difficult to chart with any accuracy. "Erratic" describes their life courses well.

Helping Hands

Some palm readers like to call the active hand the *yang* hand, reflecting lifestyles in the survival-conquest modes of life, and the passive hand the *yin* hand, reflecting the actual lifestyle in the home-sheltered-emotional environment.

Hand-le with Care

If a salesman becomes a hermit, the life line would show an angle rather than a curve at that moment. The shift from the social mores and demands of human interaction to a solitary life is a radical one, and will show up radically on the life line as well.

Does Your Life Line Hug Your Thumb?

Have you ever left the country? Have you ever left the county? The degree to which your life line hugs or arcs away from your thumb indicates your geographical conservatism or expansion.

When the life line tightly hugs the thumb, you've probably found someone who stays close to home. Further, it's likely she usually orders vanilla, always gets "the special," and habitually buys the same make of car. You can set your watch by people with tightly hugging life lines, and, in the unlikely event that you're traveling with them, they'll always look like fish out of water.

The tightly hugging life line is a good indication of someone who'll have few jobs and will live in relatively few places during her lifetime. It can also indicate someone who's intensely focused. These people can be great chess players, for example, but forget anything more exotic like backgammon.

Left to right: a life line that hugs the thumb, an average life line, a widely arcing life line.

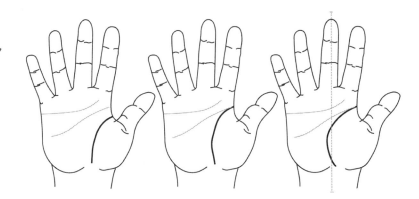

A Widely Arcing Life Line

Hey! Who left town? Chances are it was the widely arcing life line, the person with an unending appetite for geographical and environmental change. Just as the tightly hugging life line prefers the familiar, the widely arcing one hungers for the unfamiliar.

While the person with a tightly hugging life line might consider a walk to the corner store a major trip, the person with the widely arcing life line will be found trekking Everest, diving off Palau, or snowshoeing Antarctica. 'Nuff said. Wanderlust is the passion for an always new horizon, and people with wanderlust often love movies filmed in exotic places—including any National Geographic special.

You can differentiate the widely arcing life line from the gently arcing one by drawing an imaginary line (or, if you're Robin, a real one) down from the middle of your Saturn finger. A widely arcing life line will go *past* this point at about age 30 (we'll be talking about how to find age 30—and the other ages along your life line—in just a few pages).

Helping Hands

If you know a soldier or sailor who seeks to create a microcosm of his own particular environment everywhere he goes—setting out the same pictures next to his bed in the same order, for example—you've probably found a tightly hugging life line, whose changes and nuances of environment are seldom found in the active hand.

Some Life Lines Have Sisters

A *sister line* is any line that parallels the life line and is found *inside* the life line (that is, toward the thumb). This line is always good news, and is considered to have a strengthening capacity.

The sister line defines a degree of spiritual protection in the sense of physical strength and stamina. Sure, people with sister lines get sick—whether from accident, illness, or exhaustion—but they also recover quickly. A sister line may be broken or more or less consistent from its origin, but, like money in the bank, a sister line is always useful and welcome.

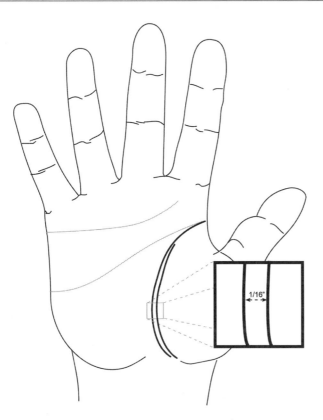

A life line with a sister line.

While those with sister lines may not be consciously religious, they're always aware of a moral imperative or rule that dictates what they try to achieve. These are people with a conscience, or, to put it less simply (though if you've got a sister line, it's simple to see), a consciousness of conscience.

When the sister line is as strong or nearly as strong as the life line itself, it can indicate a moral character that's "worn on the sleeve." This is one more aspect that may be used to define the vegetarian who is concerned for your spiritual well-being, though it can't, as some other aspects we've discussed can, define this in and of itself.

Handy Words to Know

A **sister line** is any line that runs parallel to the life line and is located on the thumb-side. These lines are always good news, and are considered to have a strengthening capacity.

When the sister line is less than $^1/_{16}$" away from the life line (and that's pretty darned close), you may have found the complex character who lives in two places at once, whether literally or figuratively (as in the distant lover). This sister line configuration may be found, for example, on someone who owns a home in town, but who lives during weekends at the lake.

Telling Time on the Life Line

Sure, there are rough formulae, but telling time on the hand is both complex and challenging. Just take a look at more than one palmistry book to see the wide variety of approaches that various authors take to this concept.

Well, here are two more authors jumping into the fray. Robin believes you *can* tell time on the hand—and that the life line's the place to do it. He illustrated this concept one afternoon at yet another Albuquerque bookstore with his trusty ballpoint on Lisa's hand. Now, she's a believer.

For Robin's method, you'll be finding three ages on the life line (of course, a fourth, age 0, is its beginning):

1. To find age 21, draw a line directly down from the Jupiter-Saturn juncture to where it bisects the life line.

2. To find age 35, draw a line beginning from the where the Mercury finger joins the hand on the percussion side diagonally to the life line.

3. To find age 65, draw a line from the base of the thumb across to the life line.

Telling time on the life line: 1. Draw a line down from the Jupiter-Saturn split to find age 21. 2. Draw a line diagonally from the Mercury finger to find age 35. 3. Draw a line from the base of the thumb to find age 65.

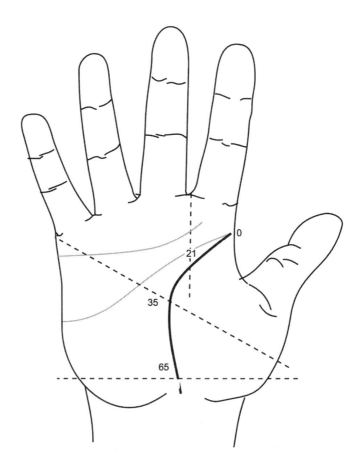

Another technique is to ask the subject her age, and then (if she'll tell you!), to look for a corresponding spot of energy on the life line. This spot is usually a warmer color than the rest of the life line, though it will take some practice before you can easily find it.

Asking when the person's next birthday is can also help determine where she is along her life line. Similar to an astrologer rectifying a birth chart in astrology, a palm reader can use the events on the life line to find the point where the subject is now.

Hand-le with Care

If things aren't going well in the subject's life (if, for example, she's depressed, in poor health, or living in a less-than-comfortable environment), the current moment on the life line may appear as a blue or black dot.

A thumb-hugging life line will never cross a line drawn down from the Saturn finger's midsection. If this is the life line configuration, you can work backward from age 35 to find the subject's earlier years.

Tightly hugging life line or not, it's important to talk to the subject so that events noted on the life line can be assigned times. You might ask when the person left home, for example, because this is indicated when the life line clearly separates from the head line. Of course, people who just moved down the block, and still go home to Mom's for both nightly dinners and laundry day, won't show this separation at all.

Hand-le with Care

Sometimes, you'll see people whose life lines and head lines stay together long after the people have left home. The explanation often turns out to be that they continue to depend on their family's opinions—as well as the opinions of those in their new environment—for all of their important decisions. In other words, they haven't yet developed independent mental self-confidence, even though they *have* left home.

You can, with practice, read time accurately in almost any hand. Exceptions can be found in people who lack grounding, are "out of time," who are creative eccentrics—or who are spending a little bit too much time with the drug of their choice.

Lines from the Life Line

Lines branching off the life line indicate travel, relocation, journeys, or any active searching on your part. If you're seeking a new career, for example, this might show on the life line as an angle between 30° and 45°. Or, if you're actively pursuing a new relationship in some new and unusual way, it can also show up as such an angle.

We like to call lines from the life line "lines of choice." That's because, whether you're pondering a move, a change of job, or new wallpaper for the bathroom, it will show up as a line from the life line—even if the change never takes place!

Travel, Journeys, and Relocations

Travel will show up in different ways, depending on your nature. If you're one of those sensitive souls who's affected by any difference in environment, travel will appear as some scattering lines in the vicinity of the life line that don't necessarily touch it.

If, on the other hand, you're a habitual traveler, such as a salesman or someone who takes the Concorde to Paris every weekend, travel lines may not appear on your life line at all. Remember, the hand reflects change—not business as usual.

Similarly, relocation makes different marks depending on how you feel about it. In fact, for relocation to appear at all, you've got to feel an emotional attachment to where you are now. If it's "just a place" to you, you can probably drop it without your life line making much note at all.

Helping Hands

A move of 100 miles may have appeared as a major line in Grandma's hand, but times have changed, and distance is relative. How relocation appears in the hand is relative to whose hand it's found in.

Sometimes relocation lines will appear when you first begin looking for a new place. These lines will be clearly defined, branching lines, which are attached to the life line.

The angle of the relocation line will depend on the degree of change the relocation means in your life. Moving from, say, San Antonio to Austin, might not show up as strongly as a move from Omaha to Timbuktu. Of course, these are extreme examples, but you get the point, right?

When you're merely changing neighborhoods—or even making a move to another place in the same neighborhood—the relocation is likely to appear as a short but defined tag on the life line. These little tags may be as short as $1/8$" long, again depending on the effect of the move.

Sometimes lines branch off the life line to connect with the rising line of Saturn (which has the whole next chapter to itself). This line indicates a job relocation.

Like all lines in your hand, relocations are choices. Sometimes, they show up as a series of lines, which you can think of as options and opportunities that you may or may not take. In addition, it's Robin's experience that the arc of the life line is directly related to your acceptance of change in the first place. But you be the judge.

Other Lines to Look At

Some lines turn inside the life line and some turn out, and you may note these especially on the lower portion of the life line. Whether turning in or out, these branches low in the hand will happen later in your life. Will you want privacy or companionship in your later years? The lines will tell. At the same time, which direction the line is turning is an indication of what you will need—or won't need—from others in your twilight years.

For example, if there are branches that go back inside the life line on its lower portion, you'll probably have a greater appetite for privacy, quiet, and solitude as you get older. People with this marking may move from the city to the country when they retire, although, again, the degree of solitude required depends on your perception of it. If you're from Manhattan, Long Island might be "the country" to you (hard as it is for us New Mexicans to imagine). In any event, inside branches do mean a move away from pressure, competition, and fellow humans to some degree.

When these lower life line branches turn outward, the opposite will be true. This configuration indicates a need for family support, or the help of others, including being near the kids, a convenience store, or the nearest Barnes & Noble.

Throw Out a Lifeline: A Story

Once there was a woman who had clear lines of relocation on her life line—so clear, that Robin could tell her exactly when the changes would occur. Happy where she was, the woman insisted Robin was wrong, and did everything she could to prove it—the first time.

When the time for that move on her life line was approaching, the woman tore out the kitchen, living room, and dining room, recarpeted the whole house, added a pantry and sunroom, and put in an attached workshop. She did admit afterwards that a move probably would have been cheaper and simpler.

The second time a relocation line indicated that a move was approaching, the woman and her husband had, through a combination of circumstances, become long-distance truck drivers. The house was left in the care of a relative while the couple drove the interstates in their big rig. That line of relocation, we should note, was even clearer than the first had been.

211

Today, the couple's retired, and Robin knows better than to say the word "move" in the woman's presence—no matter what he sees in her life line—though something nearer water might be coming up.

Mapping Your Life Line

Are you ready to draw a map of your own life line? It's time to get out your palmistry notebook and sketch how your life line looks on your hand. Be sure to note where it begins and ends, as well as where it separates from the head line, if they begin together. When you've finished your sketch, go back through this chapter and discover what your life line is saying about the way you live *your* life.

The Least You Need to Know

➤ Your life line reveals your life and its impact on the world.

➤ The depth of your life line indicates the level of your *chi*.

➤ Read the life lines on both hands to assess both your active and passive lives and the impact of each.

➤ Sister lines give you strength and spiritual assistance.

➤ You can tell time from the life line in a variety of ways.

➤ Lines from the life line can reveal much about your travel plans.

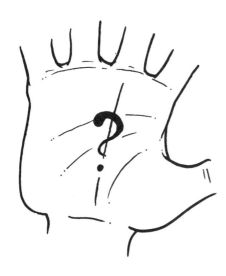

The Destiny Line: How Will You Do?

There's this great line in the movie *Back to the Future* where Michael J. Fox's dad is trying to court his mother. "Tell her she's your destiny," Michael J. tells his dad, in a scenario too complicated to explain if you haven't seen the film. The father gathers up his nerve and walks over to the girl of dreams. "Hello," he says. "You are my, you are my—*density*."

Density, destiny—they're not so far apart, really. If there's one line on your hand that can say anything about the wealth of your future, though, it's the rising line of Saturn, called by some your destiny line.

The Rising Line of Saturn: Is It Fate?

Don't think of it as fate; think of it as a barometer. The *rising line of Saturn* (or *destiny line*) is precisely what it sounds like—a line that begins in the lower portion of your palm and rises toward the mount of Saturn. This line is considered to be a measure of your standard of living and potential for material wealth, as well as your relationship with authority or your opportunities to hold authority yourself.

The rising line of Saturn.

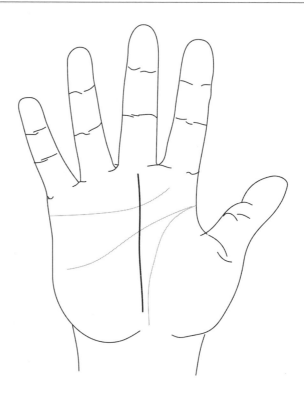

Handy Words to Know

The **rising line of Saturn**, or **destiny line**, is a line that begins in the lower portion of your hand and rises toward your Saturn mount. It's considered a barometer of your standard of living and potential for wealth, as well as your relationship with authority.

Where It Begins

If you've got a rising line of Saturn at all, it's going to begin somewhere in the lower portion of your palm. Rising Saturn lines are rarely found in the neighborhood of the life line or the mount of Venus, and, in fact, if the Saturn line does seem to begin in one of those areas, chances are that line is actually a connector to the Saturn line rather than its beginning. That connector will give the particular energy (a job location in the case of the life line, or a change in love life, in the case of Venus) to the Saturn line, but it's not the Saturn line's origin.

It's more common to find the Saturn line rising from the mount of the Moon (low in the palm under Mercury—see Chapter 18), and this isn't as much of a contradiction as it might initially seem (the lunar mount is the area of female energy, while Saturn is the area of male energy). This beginning simply indicates that there may be a partnership or connection with some emotional basis rather than an intellectual one, when it comes to the material world.

Many Saturn lines start and then stop, only to start again. We'll talk about the various possibilities for this occurrence next.

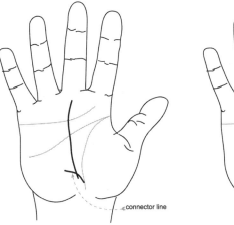
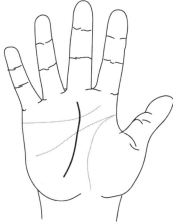

Some Saturn line beginnings.

connector line

Where It Ends

The Saturn line doesn't always cross the head line or the heart line and enter into the mount of Saturn. In fact, in the case of the rising line of Saturn, less is often better. At its best, in fact, a Saturn line that doesn't quite make it to the head line indicates someone who's eclectic in his thinking, and unafraid to try something new.

Hand-le with Care

At its worst, a Saturn line that doesn't reach the head line can indicate a lack of maturity or discipline. If Saturn crosses the head line, some form of discipline makes itself felt—for example, someone who is continually gracious to her in-laws, despite their lack of tact. A remarkable display of restraint!

With a rising line of Saturn that rises all the way through the head and heart lines to the mount of Saturn, you may find someone who's "too responsible." These are the people who have lived up to their family's expectations, or who are overly concerned with appearance—but at what cost? Did he stay in Buffalo instead of seeking his fortune? Did she miss the party because she couldn't decide what to wear for the hostess's approval? Do you hold onto your job from a false sense of security?

215

We Gotta Hand It to You

In the days when marriages were arranged, when a rising line of Saturn began in the lunar mount and rose definitively up through the head and heart lines to end in the mount of Saturn, it was considered a mark of the "good marriage." Robin believes that today this mark contains a similar meaning (bearing in mind what those folks meant by a "good marriage"). He says that material considerations and economic strength and security have played some important role in the subject's choice of spouse when this Saturn line configuration is present.

When the Saturn line breaks through the head line and reaches the heart line, but doesn't get all the way to the mount of Saturn, there's still an element of self-sacrifice for appearances or family, but the choices are less severe in their origin.

When the line of Saturn is strong and unbroken in the hand, it can actually indicate a bad back, or other musculoskeletal issues. At the same time, though, a fraying rising line of Saturn can indicate neck problems (as can lines in the mount of Saturn itself). In these instances, it's particularly important to check both hands—as the passive hand may reveal a strength that the active hand doesn't, or vice versa.

The Saturn Line Goes Off in Another Direction

Sometimes, the destiny line has a branch leading off toward Mercury. This is an indication that the person would like to be more communicative. It could also show that one's work may draw greater communication skills from him. No matter what, though, this Mercury branch is equal to communication, sales, or dealing with the public more than the current job allows.

You may also find rising lines of Saturn that branch off toward the life line under Jupiter, although these lines don't connect to the life line. Lines toward Jupiter from the rising line of Saturn show an ambition to raise oneself up in the world. But you know what? This line is getting rarer every day. Maybe we've all arrived?

What If You Don't Have a Destiny Line?

Not having a destiny line isn't such a bad thing, as you may have figured out already. After all, a lack of destiny line can mean a freedom from karmic influences or some of Saturn's more oppressive demands.

Not having a rising line of Saturn doesn't mean you can't acquire wealth, land, or property, work in the law or for a large corporation, either. However, if you're *strongly attached* to any of those things, you probably *do* have a rising line of Saturn. See the difference?

The presence of a Saturn line relates to the impact of authority on your life, so its absence may mean either that you don't have authority issues or that you aren't overly concerned with them. Either way, we (both with rising lines of Saturn) wouldn't worry, if we were you.

Who Controls Your Destiny?

Robin believes that not one person in a thousand has such intense karma that it creates an ongoing influence of destiny, and Lisa believes—in a slightly different direction—that even if there is karmic destiny, it's still in your hands. Sure, there's karmic pivots and inevitable karmic choices. But sometimes, karmic choices are found in seemingly small events that precede a "karmic abyss" one tumbles into. You know, you bought a dog, you moved to Texas, your dog ran out in the road, the neighbor's dog ran after it and got run over. According to the laws of karma, it was the neighbor's dog's time to die, and your choice seemed only to precipitate it. Here's what's important, though: If that dog hadn't run into the road after your dog, it would have run into it for some other reason. Yes, dogs have karma, too.

Does that mean that when it's time for you to run into the road, you won't have a choice? No. Precisely the opposite. Think of each choice you make as a fork in the road (we've said this before and we're saying it again). Every fork leads to still more forks. In the end, your capacity to make choices is stronger than the power of destiny over your life. It's as simple as that.

Robin says it again: Not one person in a thousand is truly a pawn of destiny. And Lisa, too: Your life is in your hands.

Changing Destiny Lines

It may seem incongruous when we tell you that the rising line of Saturn is one of the more changeable, flexible, and rapidly evolving lines in the hand. Isn't Saturn all about rules and regulations, inflexibility, and old sticks in the mud?

Yes, that's precisely the case. If you don't "honor thy mother and father," you may find it showing up on your Saturn line as a fraying or breaking, which strengthens once you apologize and tell them the error of your ways. Similarly, any time you buck the system, break the rules, or do anything against your own better instincts, it's going to show on your rising line of Saturn, possibly even shortening it! Fix the problem, though, and Saturn moves right up again.

Sometimes, quite low on the Saturn line, you may find what's called a St. Andrew's cross. This traditionally means saving a life, although there's a trend among modern palmists to read this as "service to humanity." However, if your St. Andrew's cross is drifting toward your lunar mount, we do suggest that you brush up on your lifesaving and CPR skills.

A St. Andrew's cross on the rising line of Saturn.

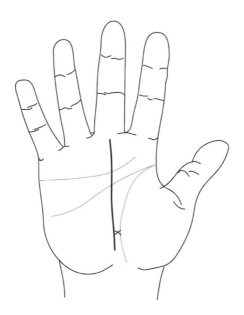

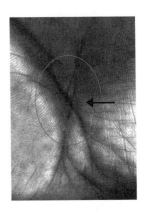

Helping Hands

Let's say you're a corporate loyalist and you've got a break on your Saturn line below the head line. Does that mean you're gonna quit before you get your gold watch? No. But it does mean you may be moving from sales to management, or from the field to the main office. Severe breaks on the Saturn line, corporate loyalist or not, mean a more major job shift is on the horizon.

Broken Destiny Lines

If the Saturn line breaks before it reaches the head line, you may be in for a change of job. It's especially important to see where the rising line of Saturn is parallel to the life line, as that's a good place to figure out exactly when the job change will occur.

Karma and Free Will

Okay, so what's *karma* anyway? Is it, as ancient Hindu tradition suggests, the actions of your past lives coming to revisit you in this one? Or is it something more tangible, like "As ye reap, so ye shall sow." The truth is, karma is both.

But it's *free will* that determines how your karma plays out. Think that doesn't make any sense? Think again. Let's say your karma is to be surrounded by children— but you have no interest in marriage or procreation. Your karma might then play itself out in your career as kindergarten teacher.

Here's another example. Let's say your karmic energy to give to children is more than your own kids can handle (or need). We'll bet you're the cub scout leader, the den mother, or the weekend soccer coach—helping other kids be all they can be.

So what we're saying is, sure you've got karma. But how you express it is your choice—and no one else's.

We Seldom Know When God Is Good to Us

Frieda's rising line of Saturn rose out of her lunar mount, but her connection to her first husband had long since run its course. Frieda felt he had achieved what he had because of her, and resented that he'd come into his own only after their divorce. Robin continued to assure her that leaving him was best for her, but it was hard for Frieda; she and her ex-husband and his new wife all lived in the same small town, and there was no avoiding his newfound seeming happiness, sobriety, and success. Only when a drunk driving accident resulted in a loss of driving privileges and considerable social embarrassment (for him) did she realize she was happy to let someone else have him after all.

Handy Words to Know

Karma is a Hindu and Buddhist concept embracing the notion that your actions, in this life or even a previous one, have consequences (for good or bad) that impact upon your situation in this life or even the next one. Your karma follows you and informs the quality of your current experience. **Free will** postulates that, as Linda Hamilton's character says in *Terminator 2:* "Fate is what YOU make it."

We Are More Empowered Than We Ever Care to Notice

Lisa's always believed that we all touch each other, however briefly, in ways that long outlast the brief contact. So when Robin told her the following story, it was one more link in the chain.

Years ago, Robin taught a palmistry class in a small, conservative midwestern town. In the back of the classroom sat a physically disabled and shy young man. He never asked questions, but it was clear he was paying attention. Some time after the class was over, he began to call Robin with further questions about palmistry, and then to send him palm prints with notations of his own and further questions for Robin to answer.

Robin realized that this young man had a clear gift for reading palms, and yet he never would have discovered it if Robin hadn't chanced to be in that rural community and the young man hadn't chanced to take that class. Or was it chance? Perhaps the young man would have come to palmistry anyway, but it would certainly have taken longer. And for Robin, the opportunity to empower this young man's life has had lasting effect on his own as well.

War Stories

A Saturn line can assume a variety of roles. A career police officer, judge, or banker will most likely have a Saturn line, for example, and you can evaluate a person's long-term connection to such work by the presence of the line. Another function of the Saturn line is concerning our Saturn karma and choices, and still another concerns male energies, including your father, and even your husband. Still, a lack of a Saturn line doesn't mean you won't be a successful father or boss.

Witness Steve, who had no rising line of Saturn. Steve was a good provider, wonderful father, and loving husband—and yet his own father had been largely absent in his life (which could begin to explain his lack of Saturn line). Steve told Robin that it was his own father's distance that led him to be the man that he was—one without expectations but nonetheless hoping for the best for both himself and those around him without making any undue demands. Steve's lack of a rising line of Saturn made him a realist—and a man who was able to pursue several different careers over the course of his life, from Realtor to hairdresser. Steve also, we should note, achieved great wealth during his lifetime.

Mapping Your Rising Line of Saturn

Have you got a destiny line? If you do, it's time to add its makeup to your palmistry notebook. Note the line's beginning and end, as well as any lines that come into it or branch away from it. In addition, be sure to clearly mark any breaks or fraying along the line. Then go back through this chapter and see what we've got to say about your rising line of Saturn.

The Least You Need to Know

➤ The rising line of Saturn is a barometer of your standard of living and potential for material wealth, as well as your relationship with authority.

➤ If you haven't got a destiny line, your future's still very much in your hands.

➤ Your destiny line may change when you're not living up to your own moral expectations.

➤ You control your karma through your own free will.

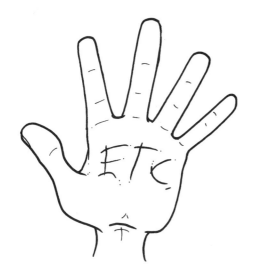

Other Lines:
Supporting Roles

If the astronauts of *2001: A Space Odyssey* had encountered a palm instead of a mysterious black cube near Europa, they might have cried, "My God—it's full of lines!" Many hands you encounter will seem to be full of lines, and this chapter is devoted to some of those lines that you may not see as often.

But how do you know which line is which? Is that a rising line to Saturn or a branching off the head line? It turns out that sometimes, your guess is as good as ours. But with Robin's handy guide to which line is which, your guess can be as educated as ours.

Handy Words to Know

The **rising line to Mercury**, found along the percussion of the hand, rises from the center of the palm or the lunar mount up to the mount of Mercury. Your rising line to Mercury points to your communication skills.

The Rising Line to Mercury

The *rising line to Mercury* can be found along the percussion of the hand, rising from the center of the palm or the lunar mount up to the mount of Mercury. Not surprisingly, this line is all about communication.

You'll find Mercury lines that are broken, that intersect the head line, and that cross the head line and the heart line. Sometimes, you won't find one at all because some people don't have a Mercury line. You'll also find Mercury lines that are doubled as well as those that are supported by other connections. Interpretations of the rising line to Mercury are as common as, well, Mercury lines themselves, but remember, Mercury is the area of versatility, too.

The rising line to Mercury.

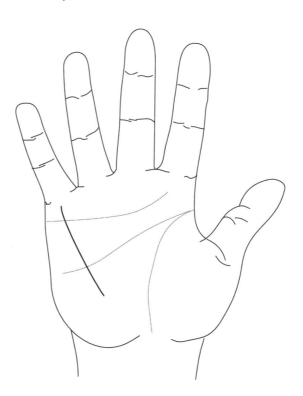

The Role of the Mercury Line

Mercury represents communication in all its many guises, and the presence of a Mercury line naturally involves some strength in that area. A rising line to Mercury can indicate, for example, the career salesman, the professional or amateur speaker, or the speechwriter.

The rising Mercury line can also be found on the physician because medicine and care giving are both found on the Mercury line—and you'll also find it on the accounts secretary in the hospital. Lastly, you'll find both the student and the teacher—whose mark we'll be talking about at the end of this chapter.

When the rising line to Mercury is both strong and clear, coming either from the rising line to Saturn or from the bottom center of the hand, it indicates a strong Mercury avocation. Whether the weekend novelist or the telethon spokesperson, the Mercury talent will be with her for her entire life.

When the Mercury line rises out of the mount of the Moon (see Chapter 18), and there are also medical stigmata on the mount of Mercury (which we'll be discussing in Chapter 16, when we look at the mount of Mercury in more detail), you've got the makings of the therapist or counselor—someone, in other words, who heals the spirit or the mind or who heals with words.

Writing by committee or partnership (who? us?) is found with a Mercury line connection to the mount of Uranus, whose impersonal energies (which we'll be exploring in Chapter 18) then come into the communication equation. But the nuances between Mercury, the head line, and the mount of Uranus take time and practice to learn—like everything else, the more you see, the more you know.

We Gotta Hand It to You

Robin once knew a man who from the age of eight knew he wanted a career in television. Although he held nearly every job possible in that field, he was happiest as a cameraman or producer. While his rising line to Mercury began with a small scattering of lines below the head line, its continuation through the heart line was both clear and well-defined. But perhaps the best sign of that passion was the fact that he was born with six fingers—in Robin's experience, this is always a signal of attraction to the media in all its manifestations.

Helping Hands

Here's an interesting tidbit: Robin's found that if the Mercury line breaks before reaching the head line and then is reformed beneath the heart line or on the mount of Mercury, the person will have a need for a pseudonym. Perhaps that's because this indicates a need for anonymity in communication.

How the Mercury's line manifests itself in communication takes time and patience to understand and read well. Lyric or limerick? Rock or libretto? Comic book author or comic? Poet or editor? Remember that Mercury is the master of malleability, and will both influence and be influenced by everything else in the rest of the hand.

What If You Don't Have a Mercury Line?

You don't need to have a Mercury line to have Mercury aspects—you may have a strong Mercury finger or Mercury mount. But if you haven't got a Mercury line, you won't likely have the same appetite for communication that someone with a Mercury line will.

Face it, though, there are those who just don't like or appreciate words or language the way some do. There are those who couldn't care less about the media, and those with no curiosity about human health or the human condition. Interest in all these things is found on the Mercury line, so if you haven't got one, you may be wondering why we're even bothering to mention them at all.

Without a Mercury line, though, a person may be honest to a fault—or, with a crooked Mercury finger, dishonest. The problem then is that, though dishonest, he's a lousy liar. That's because lying is communication—and it's not exactly his forte.

If the Mercury finger is nothing to write home about, there's no Mercury line (or very little of one), plus rising lines from the head line to Mercury or a triangle on the head line toward Mercury, it can indicate you've got a karmic lesson to learn with communication or commerce. Robin often advises people with these markings to take a part-time job in sales. It's a great place to learn these lessons, although the person may not always like them. Still, a karmic lesson's a karmic lesson.

A lack of a Mercury line can also indicate:

➤ Lack of the self-esteem to charge what one deserves for one's services or goods (this is very important)

➤ Different approach to commerce, such as barter

➤ Lack of appreciation for money (and its trappings)

The bottom line of everything Mercurial: If you're gonna like and interact with other people, you gotta have some Mercury, whether it's on the line, the finger, or the mount.

The Mercury Line and Multilingualism

We thought you'd like to have the formula for multilingualism in the hand. You'll find the line of Mercury under the mount of Apollo, with a clear-cut cross or star on the Mercury line. In addition, the Mercury line is clear and uninvolved with other lines. Sometimes a person can no longer remember her mother tongue, but the cross or star still remains clear. Then there are those who haven't yet learned another language—such as a child. This mark is still there—even before they've learned the language.

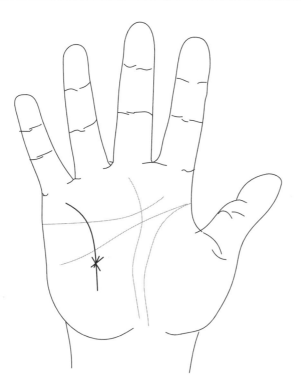

Multilingualism in the hand.

The Rising Line to Apollo

The successful singer, actor, dancer, or lion tamer. What have they got in common? A *rising line to Apollo*. This line represents success in the arts, including fame and fortune. The rising line to Apollo begins low in the hand (at least below the upper junction of the thumb) and rises clearly and distinctly, breaking through the head line to the heart line, and into the mount of Apollo.

The end of the line of Apollo is very much a part of the mount of Apollo, and we'll discuss those implications in detail in Chapter 16. No matter what, though, for an Apollo line to achieve fame, there must be a clear-cut, reasonably continuous, and distinctly defined strong definition throughout the line.

Handy Words to Know

The **rising line to Apollo** is a sign of success in the arts. It's found low in the hand and rises up into the mount of Apollo under the Apollo finger.

The rising line to Apollo.

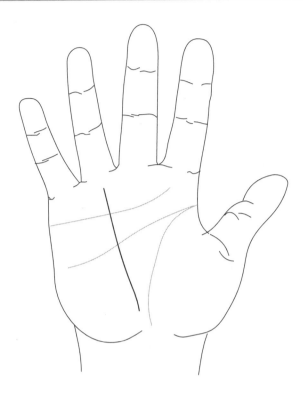

We Gotta Hand It to You

Robin has a client who supports both his wife and family selling the watercolors he works on five days a week. He's nationally known, but Robin doesn't consider him extremely gifted. Instead, he uses a broad set of skills: application, necessity, and, Robin reluctantly adds, some talent. In other words, while Apollo's not the strength here, there is Mercury for commerce and Saturn for discipline.

The Role of the Apollo Line

Let's say you're a famous writer. Let's say you are Ernest Hemingway. Let's write like Ernest Hemingway: The Apollo line is present and sturdy. The Mercury line is also present and sturdy. These are not necessarily good things.

Thanks, Ernest. But what do you mean these are not necessarily good things?

The fact is, when the Apollo line is strong, you may find its concurrent fame and fortune a burden. Look at J. D. Salinger (if you can find him). Look at Ernest Hemingway, for that matter. Especially when the fame and fortune arrive quickly or when you're young, they can be hard to deal with. For one, you can kiss your privacy good-bye.

So in the case of the Apollo line, less may be more. With a less prominent, broken, or secondary rising line to Apollo, you may find the actor who's well respected by his peers, but isn't necessarily a household name. This configuration can also be found on professional photographers, makeup artists, designers, and painters (see also the Camera's Eye, later in this

226

chapter). And don't forget that any talent is best balanced by some Saturn discipline in the hand as well.

A patron of the arts has some Apollo tendencies, whether it's a strong Apollo finger or markings on the mount of Apollo, but any artistic inclination or artistic activity that continues throughout your life means you're gonna have an Apollo line. And hey—that means the athlete, too.

Apollo is, quite simply, your appetite for attention and your desire for applause, and it just keeps on ticking—whether or not you've got any remarkably brilliant talent.

What If You Don't Have an Apollo Line?

There's nothing wrong with being anonymous. Even Tony Bennett still needs I.D. if he doesn't have his Visa check card along. A lack of a rising line to Apollo doesn't mean you're not gifted or good at what you do. It doesn't even mean your peers don't appreciate what you do and how well you do it. It does mean you probably won't be listed in *Who's Who*—but you know what? That's just one less mailing list you're on.

A lack of an Apollo line is a fine statement of being creative without expectations. A person with an Apollo line can be humble, yes, but he won't be inclined to keep it under wraps. As for the taste in clothes, if there's no Apollo line, sweats may be the fashion statement.

A Star on the Apollo Line

> * = a breakthrough

That's what it says in Lisa's notes, and she kind of likes the way it's expressed. A star on Apollo indicates a rapid release of energy resulting in some sort of recognition. But, that said, let's talk about the inherent challenges of rapid success:

➤ Too much change at once

➤ Challenge to the health

➤ Loss of equilibrium (or, quite literally, "drunk with success")

Sure, there are people who handle a star on the Apollo line well, but even they admit it was a challenge when it happened. Sometimes, in fact, their behavior wasn't something they were exactly proud of.

A star on the Apollo line isn't exactly the same as a star on the mount of Apollo. But either way, there's never a loss of the talent that propelled the person there in the first place. There is, though, behavior that may change the public perception of the bearer *after* the star's happened.

When there's a star on the line of Apollo, decorum, humility, and reserves of strength should be called on. Remember, according to Andy Warhol everyone has 15 minutes—make the most of it.

Handy Words to Know

The **rising line to Jupiter**, found next to the life line and rising toward Jupiter, is the mark of the social critic and leader.

The Rising Line to Jupiter

The *rising line to Jupiter* is very unusual, and it's often confused with an extension of the life line. The rising line to Jupiter can be found on the poet, the priest, and the politician—because it's a mark of social consciousness, leadership, and social bondings that may come saddled with ridicule. This line is found on those who are, in other words, social critics.

People with rising lines to Jupiter define themselves in some way as confessors, consciences, spiritual advisors, or spiritual critics—whether to society or to individuals. In fact, people with rising Jupiter lines may live two lives, one private and one public.

The rising line to Jupiter.

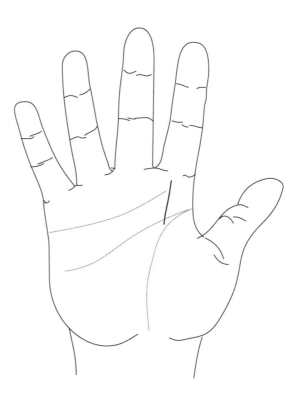

Sometimes, the rising Jupiter line may rise out of the Saturn line, and, in this case, the leadership is expressed in a grassroots way. The president of the local chapter of Mothers Against Drunk Driving (MADD) may well have a Jupiter line rising out of her Saturn line, for example.

People with rising lines to Jupiter usually define themselves in terms of spiritual ordainment, whether as minister or cleric, or as an elected official with a genuine desire to manifest change. Their efforts to right what they see as social wrongs come straight from their consciences—and often, they do make a difference, whether it's in the lives of homeless people or homeless cats.

The rising line of Jupiter won't necessarily cross the head line to manifest in the mount of Jupiter, but if it does, the impact of—and recognition from— the work the person does will be greater. Someone with a rising line of Jupiter may like the attention, but she will choose her field of work based on her convictions, not for the recognition it may bring.

The Jupiter line, if it exists, is usually clearly defined, and so a branching Jupiter line is rare. If there are branches at the lower end, they indicate a torch may be passed from a mentor. If the branches are at the upper end, you'll have a choice about which cause to champion.

We Gotta Hand It to You

There once was a woman who feared her potential for spiritual leadership—though her rising line to Jupiter was clear and strong. The first time she came to Robin, she asked him how to serve. He told her he wasn't clear on that himself, but she might consider ordainment. She left, crying. The second time she came, she told him that she didn't need ordainment, that service would bring peace. Robin agreed. The third time, she came with a gift and a beatific smile. She'd been offered an honorary degree in divinity for her charitable work with a bible college, and she'd accepted—with trepidation. Still, she said, "It was as if a great sense of discretion and clarity was opened up in me. A compass was uncovered—and now I know my direction."

The influence of a Jupiter line shouldn't be taken lightly. This line gives the bearer an opportunity to bring about change. If, in addition to a Jupiter line, you've also got a strong Jupiter finger, it may be easier for you than if you don't. Still, Robin's seen many people who've approached their Jupiter-line manifestations with fear, doubt, and trepidation. It's not always easy to tread where no one's trod before, and self-doubt can be the Jupiter's plague.

A Few Other Lines to Look For

Beyond the heart, head, and life lines, and the various rising lines, you may have noticed some other lines in your hand we've yet to discuss. Some of those lines appear on specific mounts, such as the medical stigmata that are sometimes found on the mount of Mercury. When this happens, their interpretation is closely associated with their mounts, and so we'll be discussing them in Part 4, when we look at all the mounts in detail.

Still, there are a few other lines we've yet to discuss: the Camera's Eye, the Girdle of Venus, the Via Lascivia, and the Mark of the Teacher. Much like the rising lines we've discussed in this chapter, these lines can reveal a great deal about your career choices.

The Camera's Eye: A Knack for the Visual

If you've got a line from the mount of Apollo that curves between the head and heart lines into a junction with the head line, chances are you're looking at what's called the *Camera's Eye*. When it's clear and distinct, this line is considered the mark of the photographer—or anyone whose career requires a vision for balance, color, and appearance.

Handy Words to Know

The **Camera's Eye** is a line that can be found curving down from the mount of Apollo to between the head and heart lines to a junction with the head line. This line shows a talent for visual balance and coordination that's often found in the photographer, hence its name.

As much as any line, this formation indicates a natural instinct for the visual, and while it's most often found in the professional photographer, you'll also come across it in visual fields as diverse as window dressers, floral arrangers, hairdressers, interior decorators, set or costume designers, and make-up artists. What all these careers have in common is a knack for turning a mental picture into a stunning reality.

Two examples of the Camera's Eye.

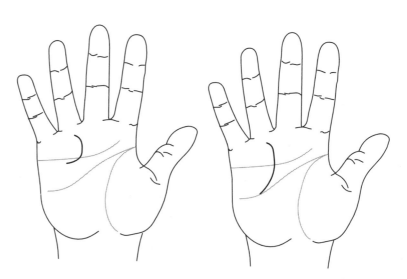

Still, for the Camera's Eye to be the career focus (as opposed to a hobby), other aspects in the hand come into play. These may include the conical or pointed fingers of the artistically inclined, as well as a long head line for details, and a reasonably high set thumb for specialization.

This line is actually fairly common, but, while you may find it on people who are brusque or direct in their manner, they'll also be neat and tidy, with their colors coordinated, and their garage neatly swept. In fact, this line may be one of the unsung manifestations of being "civilized"—if "civilized" means tidy and organized.

The Girdle of Venus (Patron of the Arts) and the Via Lascivia (the World According to Freud)

While they live in the same neighborhood, the *Girdle of Venus* and the *Via Lascivia* are easily told apart once you know which is which. In addition, there's a subtle difference in the meanings of these two lines. The Girdle of Venus, a curving line across the mounts from Jupiter to Mercury (or from the Jupiter-Saturn split to Mercury) is the longer of these two lines, and shows someone with an appreciation for the finer things in life.

The Girdle of Venus, unlike the Via Lascivia, embraces at least part of Jupiter or Mercury, and it is this difference that also accounts for what's different about these two lines.

Handy Words to Know

The **Girdle of Venus**, which curves from either Jupiter or the Jupiter-Saturn split to Mercury, shows an appreciation for the finer things in life. The **Via Lascivia**, which curves from the Jupiter-Saturn split no farther than the Apollo-Mercury split, is an indication of sensuality.

When there's a Girdle of Venus, chances are you've found someone who's strongly attracted to the arts in some way, and this will include displaying and collecting things of beauty. These people may also be "clothes horses" to some degree.

The person with a Girdle of Venus constantly seeks the new and different, expanding the breadth of how she experiences creativity. This is a mark of appreciation of the creative, someone who attends every gallery opening, is at the forefront of every arts organization fund drive, or is chair for every invitational dinner.

Someone with a Via Lascivia is far more likely to express his or her fondness for silk or fur, luxuriate in a bubble bath (candlelit, we should add), or lean back in the hot tub under the stars. The masseuse whose touch comes straight from the soul has a strong Via Lascivia, too—and is worth his or her weight in gold.

Note the difference between the Via Lascivia (left) and the Girdle of Venus (right): the Girdle of Venus is wider, encircling more fingers than the Via Lascivia. Their meanings are subtly different as well.

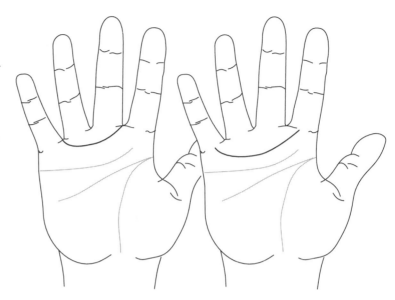

Helping Hands

When the Via Lascivia drops to touch the heart line, you've got the fortuitous circumstance of intense sexuality—with love included. This is a joy not only to the bearer—but to his or her partner as well.

What if you find a hand with both a Girdle of Venus and a Via Lascivia? This isn't exactly desirable, although the Girdle of Venus can modify the Via Lascivia. The problem is that, without some controls, a Via Lascivia may tend to make a person, well, too self-indulgent. Coupled with a Girdle of Venus, her love of the erotic may spill into what some people might consider pornographic. Of course, there's always the possibility one can channel such a configuration, as did the wholesome mother of three who designed costumes for exotic dancers on the side. (Of course, she had a spatulate Apollo—she couldn't help but use her creativity practically.)

Mark of the Teacher: Showing Others the Way

All of us, to some degree or another, are teachers, whether it's showing a child how to tie a shoe or pointing a lost motorist toward his destination. The *Mark of the Teacher* indicates something more, a marking that indicates not only teaching as a vocation, but a profound impact as a teacher.

The first marking of the Mark of the Teacher is a distinct diagonal line on the mount of Mercury, and the second is a diagonal line that lies between the head and heart lines below the mount of Mercury that's roughly parallel to the first.

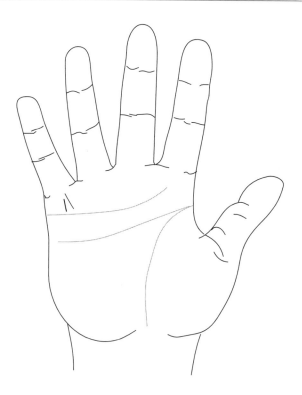

The Mark of the Teacher is comprised of two lines, roughly parallel, under the mount of the Mercury.

The first line is common. We all teach, after all, and this line is found on the student as well as the teacher—anyone, in other words, who's actively involved in communicating information and ideas. This line represents a decision to help define and create choices for others, and when it occurs alone, the person has the capacity to:

➤ Create examples

➤ Construct lessons

➤ Empower individuals by encouraging them to test their boundaries and limits

But it's the second line, which Robin calls a "God-given gift that empowers the intellect and encourages decision to help define life choices," that empowers the second to become unique. Think of this line as the teacher with a capital "T"— that teacher who made a lasting difference in your life. If you've ever had the pleasure of having one, you know what we mean.

Handy Words to Know

The **Mark of the Teacher**, which shows profound skill in that arena, is comprised of two separate markings on the hand: a diagonal line on the mount of Mercury, and another that lies between the head and heart line under the mount of Mercury, that's roughly parallel to the first.

As a representation of that teacher, this line can be thought of as a one-two punch. That's because this line indicates someone who can motivate both the head and the heart, and so instill a lesson in such a way that it's indelibly printed on the learner. In fact, lessons from these teachers become "imprinted on the soul," and remain with you forever.

Because it's a Mercury-influenced line, the Mark of the Teacher rises and falls with the blowing of Mercurial winds. When it diminishes, the opportunities to use it may diminish as well, and when it rises, new or more teaching opportunities may be on the way. Like all Mercury-influenced lines, the Mark of the Teacher has its ups and downs—but, if you've ever been a teacher, you already know about that.

Which Line Is Which?

By now we've talked about so many lines, you're probably wondering how to tell them apart. How do you tell the difference between a rising line to Apollo and a branching off the heart line? The following illustration may help.

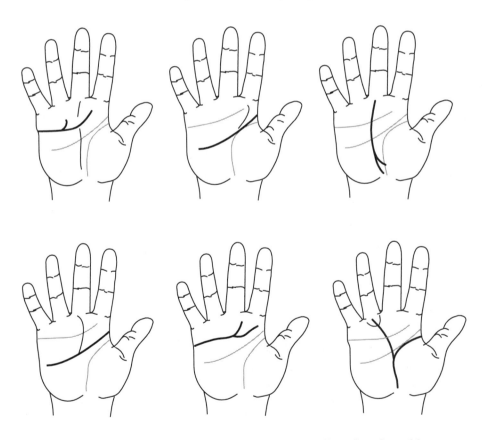

Here we've exaggerated some lines to show you how to tell rising lines from branching ones.

It may help if you visualize how lines connect to each other as intersections between roads. A deceleration lane off the freeway, for example, isn't very likely to cut in at an obtuse angle. Instead, it's going to create a smooth gradual flow into the other line. When you find this configuration, the line is most likely a branching line rather than a rising one.

Rising lines, however, create their own energy, and, as such, have both direction and purpose. In the previous illustration, for example, we've exaggerated the starting point of a rising line to Saturn to show you how it narrows as it rises. You can in fact see these subtle differences yourself, the more hands you look at and study. Good luck!

Looking for Lines in All the Right Places

Your own hands are as good a point of study as any, especially because they're so convenient. Now that we've pointed out all the major lines on the hand, you can complete the map of your hands' lines that you began in Chapter 10. Look carefully to see if you have rising lines to Mercury, Apollo, or Jupiter, or any of the other distinguishing lines we've noted in this chapter. If you do, add your thoughts about what we have to say to your ever-growing palmistry notebook. Because now, it's time to move on to the mounts.

The Least You Need to Know

➤ The rising line to Mercury indicates special communications talent or a readiness to deal with people.

➤ The rising line to Apollo shows special success in the arts.

➤ The person with a rising line to Jupiter may be a minister or cleric, politician, or poet.

➤ The Camera's Eye reveals a knack for visual appraisal.

➤ The person with a Girdle of Venus can be a patron of the arts, while someone with a Via Lascivia shows a mark of his sensual nature.

➤ The Mark of the Teacher combines talent and empathy with a gift for impressing others.

➤ It takes time and study to learn which line is which.

Part 4
Ain't No Mount High Enough

Mounts are the names we give to the different areas of your hands, and you can think of these as the places where your story unfolds. From the mounts of the fingers, which share the fingers' names, to the mounts of the palm—where you'll find everything from your love to your anger—the mounts of the hand are areas where you can more fully explore your story.

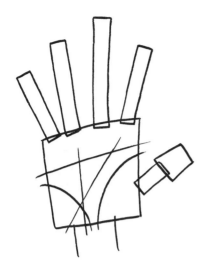

Chapter 16

The Geometry of the Palm: Squares, Islands, Triangles, and Other Shapes

---

In This Chapter

➤ Dermatoglypics: look to the whorls

➤ Circles, ovals, and squares enclose energy

➤ Thank your lucky triangle

➤ Supporting tridents

➤ Warning signs: the cross, the star, and the grid

As you've studied your fingers and the lines in your hands, you've probably noticed that there are also geometric shapes and doodles that we haven't yet discussed in detail, except for some brief references in Chapter 10. Well, wonder no more. Before we move on to the mounts, we're devoting an entire chapter to the geometry of the palm.

As long as we're here, we're going to take a look at dermatoglyphics as well. This study of fingerprint patterns and patterns in the hand has possibly as many interpretations as there are palmists. But how significant are these patterns? Let's find out.

All About Dermatoglyphics

Dermatoglyphics is the study of fingerprint patterns, both on the finger and on the skin of the hand. Depending on which palm reader you consult, these patterns can be assigned primary significance or completely ignored. Many palm readers don't give them too much credence, including Robin, but we wanted to satisfy your curiosity.

Handy Words to Know

Dermatoglyphics is the study of fingerprint patterns, both on the finger and on the skin of the hand.

As you know, each person's fingerprint pattern is as unique as her palm, and for this reason, Robin feels that dermatoglyphics are well worth a glance. He believes that these patterns are signs of karmically won attributes—but they don't always come to bear in any given situation. In other words, just because you've learned to karmically play the game well, doesn't mean you'll win every time. As you may recall reading in Chapter 14, karma is a principle that suggests you "do unto others" or it will be done unto you. Robin's personal belief is that karma also operates together with reincarnation, which could help explain why "bad things happen to good people."

For this chapter, you may want to keep the annotated palm on the tear-out Reference Card handy to locate the mounts we'll be discussing in the following pages.

Your Karma in Your Fingertips

The dermatoglyphic patterns in your hand will appear as *whorls*, and these whorls will in turn be either loops, ovals, tents, or bull's-eyes. Here's what each looks like:

Left to right: a bull's-eye, an oval, a loop, and a tent on the fingertip.

You can see these patterns on your palm in one of several ways:

➤ Make a print of your hand and fingers.

➤ Use a magnifying glass, and, as always, good light.

➤ If your eyes are good, you can see these without a magnifying glass if the light is good as well.

Handy Words to Know

Whorls, which may appear in the form of bull's-eyes, ovals, loops, or tents, are dermatoglyphic patterns on the fingertip or hand.

Robin prefers to view these patterns as "details" that provide karmic assistance or cross-purpose in the areas in which they appear. For example, a bull's-eye on a fingertip can indicate that you've done a lot of karmic work in that area (don't forget to check both hands). Further, when at least eight of the fingers have bull's-eyes, you've achieved an exceptionally healthy karmic balance. While this doesn't mean you'll always have easy sailing in that area, it *will* be easier than others.

Let's take a look at what some of these different patterns indicate:

➤ **Bull's-eyes** can help you see which areas are weaker and require more attention. In other words, if your karma isn't strong in a particular area, you'll probably have work to do there.

➤ **Ovals** carry less karmic strength than bull's-eyes, and people with these markings will be more flexible in those particular areas.

➤ **Loops,** which often look like multilayered tents, are quite common. They indicate that your karmic lessons will be evolving at your own pace.

➤ **Tents** are quite common and indicate that you have an average level of growth in the area where they appear.

A more unusual dermatoglyphic configuration you may find is a *yin/yang* on the fingertip. Most often found on the Jupiter finger or the thumb, this indicates a karmic connection to or fascination with all things Oriental—and the potential to marry an Asian.

A yin/yang whorl on the thumb.

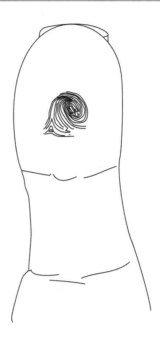

What's in Those Whorls?

The best way to understand what's in a whorl is to look at a few specific ones more closely (and that means with a magnifying glass—examining whorls is far beyond 20/20 vision). A whorl on the mount of active Mars (see illustration on the following page), for example, indicates karmic assistance in the area of active Mars, which translates to "courage in battle." This means that people with this marking will be strong when faced with tears, or even the surgery of a loved one. This courage, in other words, will always come in handy during any confrontation, whether literal or figurative.

Then there's the mark of nobility, indicated by loops at the juncture between the Apollo and Saturn fingers. These loops indicate karmic assistance in bringing humanitarian energy to speak in defense of the defenseless. In other words, people with these loops will stand up for the underdogs.

Another mark is sometimes called "the mark of royalty" (Robin likes to call it "the mark of inbreeding"). This marking, which consists of whorls at the Saturn-Jupiter juncture, does seem to indicate refinement and strong family responsibility. People with a whorl here, in fact, often don't pursue their own interests but concentrate on fulfilling the family needs instead.

The last finger juncture whorl can be found between Apollo and Mercury. Traditionally called the mark of humor, this mark can actually indicate an almost cruel wit. Robin feels it's best to let this sleeping dog lie when you see it in someone's palm to avoid being bitten!

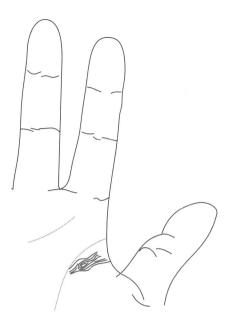

A whorl on the mount of active Mars.

It's also worth noting whorls that appear lower in the hand. Whorls between the mounts of Venus and the Moon are common, for example, and indicate a powerful bond between siblings. Sometimes this bond is based on a challenge the siblings must face together, although it's not, as you might immediately think, necessarily the mark of twins.

When whorls are found in the mount of Uranus, this area's inventive and sometimes eccentric energy is emphasized in some way, not always to the good of the bearer. On the positive side, though, there is a drive to form and build. Sometimes this mark is seen on those who are building their own homes.

A whorl in the mount of Neptune can be too much: Neptune's dominion is water, after all, and a whorl creates a whirlpool, emblematic of self-destruction. We'll be talking more about all of these mounts themselves in Chapters 18 and 19.

Geometric Designs

You can find any design you want in the hand, and there are palm readers who have particular interests in finding particular shapes, such as *runes*, animal shapes, or letters of our own alphabet, and attaching their particular significance to them.

If you'd like to find your desired love's initials in your hand, you probably can, but it's probably not terribly significant. Here, we're going to stick with

Handy Words to Know

The **runes**, part of an ancient alphabet of Norse and Germanic origin, are often used for divination.

Marks on the hand: the circle, the dot, the square, the triangle, the cross, the star, the trident, the grid, the oval.

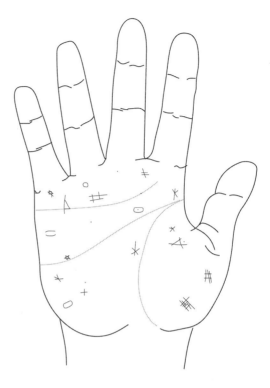

the more basic geometry: the circle, the dot, the square, the triangle, the cross, the star, the trident, the grid, and the oval.

As you take the time to locate and study each of these shapes, you should also take note of their colors. Dots are most likely to show noticeable color variances, but you may occasionally find a different color in one of the other shapes as well.

Squares Give You Strength and Enclose Energy

Squares can be either clear cut or have tails, which means they'll look like a tic-tac-toe board (grids and grilles are different, as you'll see when we discuss them shortly). Squares provide substance and foundation, and are considered, always, to give you strength and enclose energy, although, as you approach the energies they represent in the self, they may seem overwhelming.

You'll sometimes find squares enclosing other, less fortuitous, shapes. This means that the square's energy will help you face the challenge of the other marking, and perhaps will even temper or limit the otherwise negative flow.

When a square appears on a line, whether life, head, heart, or a rising line, no matter what traumas or circumstances you face there, the challenge will be survived. "This, too, shall pass," says a square. You just have to look forward.

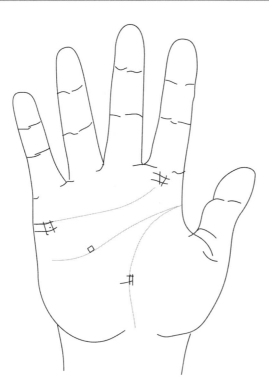

Some squares.

Ovals and Lozenges

Ovals (and lozenges) are considered to be subtle gifts, which often have to do with women or a distinctly female energy. You may find such a whorl on the manager of a women's clothing store or a cosmetics salesperson, for example. Challenges are worth meeting when an oval appears, and whether the oval is lighter or darker in color will indicate the degree of challenge one must face to reap its rewards.

One example of such a subtle challenge/gift is the girl whose sixth-grade teacher seemed more like a drill sergeant. The two were constantly at odds—but when the girl entered junior high school, she found she'd developed stronger study habits and purpose than any of her peers. On her hand, this challenge/gift appeared as grey ovals on her rising line to Mercury and on her mount of Mercury, both indicating that the conflict with the teacher had to be endured—ultimately to the girl's advantage.

Helping Hands

You may find an oval on the cattle breeder or anyone whose work is animal husbandry, especially during calving season. If the oval appears on the rising line of Saturn as well, there will also be a profit to be made!

245

Lucky Triangles

Did you have a flat tire in your own driveway on Sunday morning? Or was it on the freeway during Monday morning rush hour? Triangles indicate a continuing positive karma at work in a given place in your life. You won't avoid trials and tribulations with a triangle, but the tools to meet them will be readily available.

If you've got a lucky triangle, you've probably often thanked your "lucky star." Lisa can recall countless occasions when her lucky triangles have served her well, such as the well-placed tire changers who seem to miraculously appear whenever she gets a flat. If you've got lucky triangles, we're sure you've thanked them, too.

Hand-le with Care

The rare darker-colored triangle can indicate a difficult task, but one which you'll nonetheless be able to face. This can mean firing your own son so he can learn responsibility (a dark triangle on the rising line to Saturn), or telling your cheatin' lover goodbye (a dark triangle on the heart line). Be assured, though, that this marking is indeed rare.

Sometimes you'll find two triangles end-to-end in an hourglass formation. This shape indicates a need for reciprocal energy. Lennon and McCartney's succinct, "And in the end, the love you take is equal to the love you make" states the work of this configuration beautifully.

If you're generous to others, the hourglass says, your generosity will be rewarded—even if it doesn't feel like it now. The generosity of the hourglass is usually quite focused on an individual, organization, or specific purpose, such as, for example, team writing. Not that Robin and Lisa are Lennon and McCartney, but we're both sporting hourglasses these days.

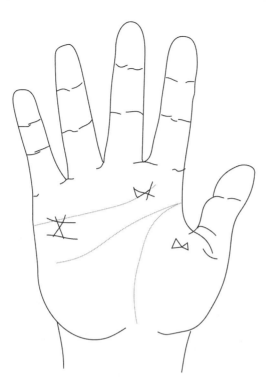

Some hourglasses.

Will the Circle Be Unbroken?

When a circle encloses a line or a large dot of a particular color, you'll have a reservoir of energy at your disposal to meet a challenge. For example, if there's a dark circle on your rising line to Saturn, you may need to attempt to discipline your child about something that's been going on for a while.

White or pink circles on the mount of Venus are fairly common, and indicate a depth of feeling in the heart *chakra* that resides there.

Circles usually draw on the energy that created the situation in the first place. For example, if you're not slowing down despite all the warning signs, a circle may "make you" slow down.

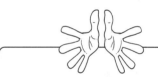

Helping Hands

Even when a circle seems to be in a threatening position or a "negative" color, you're being offered a reservoir of energy to meet the challenge positively.

Circles with dots in the center are very rare, and the circumstances they're highlighting may fade away before the worst happens. For example, your child's criminal behavior may come to an end before he's ever arrested. If you're the child's mother, this might appear on your lunar mount, while if you're the father, it's more likely found on the mount of Saturn.

247

This configuration will appear in the hand rather quickly to highlight the danger. As the situation disappears, the dot will disappear first, and then the circle will gradually fade away as well. Sometimes, when we're the last to know, it can be a blessing in disguise.

Red or white dots within circles aren't necessarily negative, although they do involve some change in the status quo. Red dots can be read quite literally as a fire or explosion—but this is a potential, not a certainty.

When Robin saw this mark in one woman's hand, he thought little of it—until he saw a red dot in a circle in her roommate's hand as well. He then suggested they check their smoke detectors, although it was the woman's discovery of a charred two-by-four in the roof (caused by a faulty new gas water heater) that ultimately avoided a fire. Now he calls the red dot an "uncontrolled expression of energy unlikely to be to your advantage."

More Than Mere Doodles

Unlike the geometric shapes that appear on the hand, stars, crosses, tridents, grids, and grilles may bring challenges that are still more difficult to face. But, as anyone knows, life is not without its ups and downs, and, when we're aware of what our particular challenges may be, we can, with work, turn the tables to our advantage.

Star Light, Star Bright…

A star on the hand can take a number of forms: a five-pointed or six-pointed asterisk, or the actual shape of a five- or six-pointed star. No matter what its form, though, a star indicates a complex situation that demands both assimilation and release of energy.

Some palm readers make a great deal of any star in the hand, and, yes, stars do indicate that you've got some work to do. The most common stars, for example, those of five or more lines, say "Clear the decks—let's get moving!" If you can't drop everything when these show up, you should at least try to have a garage sale.

When a star is more than an asterisk, you'll probably need the help of others to get the job done. This is, as always, not a bad thing: Robin recalls the man with this configuration who custom-built a car but wouldn't do the wiring, upholstery, or paint it. A star like this will bring people together—whatever the reason.

When a star is very large, its challenge may take time—even decades. If you haven't developed long-term goals when this configuration appears in your hand, it may be time to sit down and think about them.

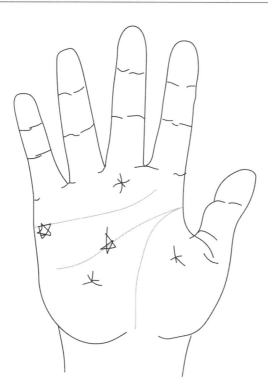

Some stars.

Crosses of Fortune

A cross is considered any intersection of lines, even if one of the lines isn't exactly perpendicular to the other. Crosses indicate opposition and acceleration, or, to put it another way, a choice where your direction, focus, or attitude will change. A cross offers some sort of compromise, so ultimately, it's probably a good thing.

Of course, sometimes, before we accelerate, we slow down to evaluate the opportunity. You can think of a cross as the time spent shaking out your shoes while you're hiking up a mountain. Sure—you'll get to the top of the mountain a little later, but you'll also have avoided getting a blister from that pesky pebble.

We all experience crosses in our hands—and our lives—many, many times. That's because we face the choices they represent every single day, and each cross will eventually lead to another. Crosses are part of what life is all about.

Some crosses.

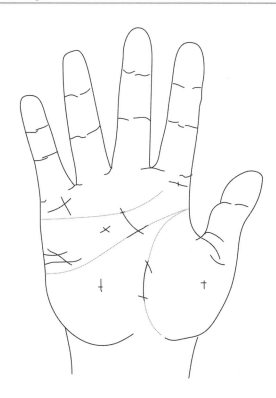

Helping Hands

A trident on the mount of Saturn indicates that you'll come through your legal problems without too much trouble. It might be worth checking your lawyer's hand, too...

Tridents: Forks in the Road?

Tridents can appear anywhere in the hand, and may face up or down. While upward-facing tridents are the better of the two, downward-facing ones are still okay—and both offer protection and strength in the area where they appear.

Tridents are a mark of security and additional protection. There will still be stress when a trident appears, but you'll come through it relatively unscathed.

When a trident is large, it can indicate that the struggle in that area is ongoing, but that you will ultimately come out on top.

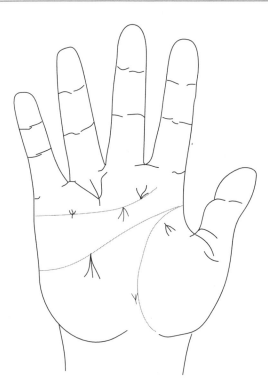

Some tridents.

Grids and Grilles: Take Warning

It's easy to differentiate a grid or grille from a square: A grid or grille will have at least one more line than that standard tic-tac-toe board we talked about earlier. If there are only two lines in either direction, go back to the square for interpretation.

Grids and grilles indicate sensitive areas, warning signs on the path of life. A grid may be saying "unstable footing" or "beware of being overwhelmed." Similar to the street signs in Sacramento that say "undulations" (it took Lisa a while to figure out this was another way of saying "speed bumps"), grids are reminders that you're not on *terra firma* anymore.

Grilles may take the form of others who don't live up to your expectations, or situations that don't seem to be going as you'd planned. If a red grille appears, conflicting opinions may deteriorate into argument, and if the grille is black, melodrama may be at hand. In fact, you may find black grilles on the hands of people convinced that a massive conspiracy is afoot.

Grilles aren't always negative: White grilles can indicate the potential for an in-depth stopping place with a personal transformation, or a time for healing. They may also manifest as a dramatic stop and rejection of the status quo.

Sometimes, if you ignore a grille's warning, circumstances may take matters in their own hands (if circumstances have hands...). A traveling salesperson who really wanted to spend more time at home ended up falling down a client's stairs, which forced a long convalescence at home—and the decision to work closer to home in the future. This person's hand featured a grille below the heart line under Mercury before the event came to pass.

We Gotta Hand It to You

Among Hindu palmists, the interpretation of a strong rising line on the third phalange of Jupiter (especially if it's full and plump) is a man who "has many cows." A search for this marking throughout the intermountain West, however, indicates that you won't often find it on the cattle barons of today—though you might find it on a man who loves his luxury cars.

What the Hindus Say: A Brief Glimpse

Hindu palmistry is a topic broad enough to have an *Idiot's Guide* of its own. But, while the Hindus have been studying palmistry far longer than Westerners, it's interesting to note that the best-selling palmistry book in India this century has been *The Benham Book of Palmistry,* by the oh-so-British William G. Benham. Of course, Hindu palmistry was largely an oral art, passed down from generation to generation, so there weren't really any Hindu books to compete with Benham's until quite recently.

But we bring up Hindu palmistry in this chapter because of Hindu interpretations of various markings in the hand. While they're not considered overly important, various marks on the hand are what we'll call "saving graces" in Hindu tradition. They also have such lovely names that we'd like to list some of them here, as if they were a poem:

➤ The arrow of Vishnu

➤ The broken tusk of Ganesha

➤ The chain of Kali

➤ The mark of the Brahman

➤ The indications of the many aspects of the cow

Vishnu, Ganesha, and Kali are Hindu deities, so it's easy to see why their marks would be considered beneficial to their bearers. Similarly, under the Indian caste system, Brahmans were considered to be of the highest social status. Lastly, the cow is considered a highly evolved karmic creature, and having its mark in the hand showed that the bearer, too, had lived many lifetimes or would achieve much merit in this one.

Hand-le with Care

Hindu palmistry is often "practiced" by less-than-accurate practitioners such as the stereo-typical "lady with a turban" or "guy with seven rings on eight fingers and a goatee." These people may interpret Hindu palmistry's set of givens as having no negatives, but Robin believes that while much is possible, it's not always going to happen today. In other words, you gotta take the bad with the good, and a good palmist will point out both.

Your Own Graphic Analysis

It's time to take a look at the geometry of your own hand, and it's particularly important to take your time here. Note what shapes appear on your hand and where they appear, as well as whether their colors differs from the rest of the hand in any way. Take your time, too, as you draw these shapes onto your hand in your palmistry journal. If you'd like to examine the dermatoglyphics on your hand as well, use one of the methods in the section "Your Karma in Your Fingertips" early in this chapter to do so. When you're ready, go back through this chapter and discover what the geometry of your hand is telling you.

The Least You Need to Know

➤ Dermatoglypics is the study of whorls in the hand that may have karmic value.

➤ Circles, ovals, and squares enclose energy and help you face challenges.

➤ Ovals deal with female energy.

➤ Triangles offer karmic assistance.

➤ The cross, star, trident, grid, and grille are both warnings and helpers.

➤ Hindu palmistry attaches karmic importance to various marks in the hand.

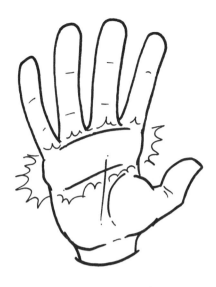

Chapter 17

The Mounts of the Fingers

In This Chapter

➤ The mounts of the fingers: where you do the things you do

➤ The mount of Jupiter: if you lead, I will follow

➤ The mount of Saturn: the karmic law enforcer

➤ The mount of Apollo: the golden youth

➤ The mount of Mercury: words and their expression

If fingers are characters and lines are plots, then the mounts are the places where the story's going to play out. You can think of the mounts of the fingers as mounts of the self because they reside in the areas accentuated by your finger's characters. Similarly, you can think of the mounts of the palm, which we'll be discussing in Chapters 17 and 18, as mounts of information.

The mounts of the fingers are closely connected to the fingers themselves, both literally and figuratively, and so naturally they share their names—Mercury, Apollo, Saturn, and Jupiter—and their particular energies. Which energy is accentuated in your hand? It's time to find out.

Mounts of the Self

The *mounts of the fingers* are the fleshy areas just below each finger and share their name with the finger. You can think of the mounts of the fingers as areas where your story will unfold: These are the mounts of yourself.

Handy Words to Know

The **mounts of the fingers**, the fleshy areas just below each finger, share a name with the respective finger. These are the mounts of yourself, the areas where your story will unfold.

All mounts, both of the finger and the palm, are considered places where you have the potential for empowerment or a lack of enthusiasm for a given area. This is because mounts are accentuated by their presence or absence, and a quick look at the hand can tell you where you've still got work to do—and where you'll shine.

Just to give you an idea of how much mounts can be accentuated, we've provided you with a photo of the hand of a woman with very strong mounts. This will also help you see just where on the hand the mounts are, even though we haven't labeled them yet.

This woman's mounts are highly accentuated. Studying this photograph will help you see where the mounts are on the palm, and what strong mounts look like.

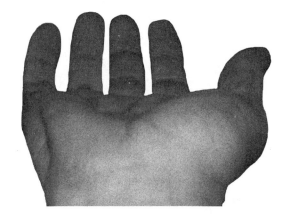

Locating the Mounts of the Fingers

In Part 2 you learned the names of each finger. That will make it easy to locate the mounts of the fingers because each mount shares the name of its respective finger. If you've got any question about a particular mount, though, use the following drawing to help you find it.

Note that the mounts can extend into the finger. Where the mount ends is determined by the joint at the bottom of the finger's third phalange. To see why this is so, bend one of your fingers from the third phalange joint. See how the joint is actually *above* the bottom of the finger? That area is considered a part of the mount rather than part of the finger.

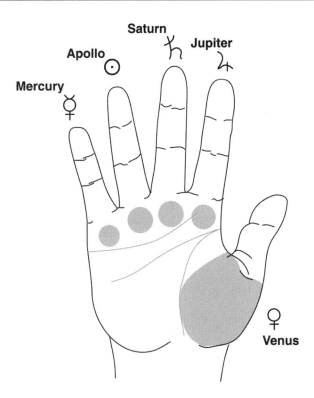

The mounts of the fingers.

Which Way Do They Go?

Mounts aren't necessarily centered under the fingers, and that's because, like the fingers, they may tend toward one direction or another. In fact, when one finger's mount leans toward another finger's mount, you can be sure that that the second mount is going to influence the first.

William G. Benham suggests that you can locate the center of each mount by determining where the whorl of the mount is centered. You'll need a magnifying glass to do this, but it's an effective method for finding a mount's center.

When the mount isn't centered under the finger, the energy is displaced, and which direction a mount is leaning is an important tool in determining what's influencing what in your life. Just as an Apollo finger leaning toward a Mercury finger can indicate that you've got a creative approach to communication, an Apollo mount pushing into the Mercury mount can indicate creative energy that can be used for communication.

At the same time, if one mount seems to overpower or overwhelm another, that area of your life may be strongly influenced by the other right now. This isn't a bad thing. For example, if your mount of Saturn is pushing into your mount of Apollo, you may have the discipline needed to complete a creative project.

257

Use a magnifying glass to look at the mount's whorl to find the mount's center.

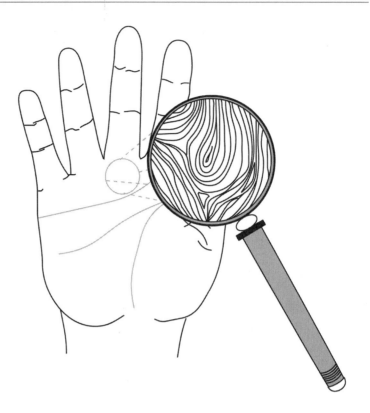

Sometimes, the mounts seem to be accentuated *between* the fingers rather than directly under them. Think of this as a melding of the energy of the areas of those two mounts, although, as always, sometimes this will be a complement and sometimes it will be a problem.

Mounts can also be placed either high or low in their respective area. Higher-set mounts have their vertical center closer to the finger itself and accent that particular area in the hand. Mounts are accentuated by their lack of inflation as well as by their strength. In addition, any marking on a mount adds to its emphasis.

Each mount represents a specific area of your life. These areas have the same names as the fingers, and so, of course, share that area of influence as well. But where the fingers are characters, the mounts are actually places where the action occurs, so let's review what each area represents.

Mount	Area of Influence
Jupiter	Image you present to the world
Saturn	Rules and regulations
Apollo	Creativity and self-expression
Mercury	Communication, commerce, and medicine

Because mounts are places, markings on them take on special meaning as well. Squares, grilles, lines, stars, and other markings on mounts concentrate their particular energy in the mount (we introduced this concept in Chapter 16). We'll look at how certain markings manifest in each mount when we look at the mounts individually.

The Mount of Jupiter

Nowhere is your strength of character more clearly visible than on the mount of Jupiter. This is the area of your ideals and enthusiasm, as well as your ambition and spirituality. Just as the Jupiter finger shows your leadership style and how you interact with others, the mount of Jupiter is the arena of your interaction. Among the areas found here are your:

➤ Ways of relating to yourself

➤ Depth of character

➤ Leadership

➤ Ambition

➤ Chutzpah

➤ Self-confidence

➤ Charisma

➤ Internal fortitude

➤ Idealism

➤ Religion

➤ Spirituality

➤ Love of animals and nature

Are You Manifesting Your Leadership?

If you've got a strong mount of Jupiter, chances are you're already manifesting your leadership—and many of the other characteristics we listed above. But, in addition to being where you'll find all of these characteristics, the mount of Jupiter relates to your head and cranium. This means that when there are possible health issues in these areas, it will show up on this mount.

When the mount of Jupiter is strong, it will be rich and inflated, and rise above the plain of the hand. A strong mount of Jupiter emphasizes the Jupiterian characteristics, and, if there are markings as well, there will be further emphasis in this area.

When the mount of Jupiter is weak, the person may be physically strong, but he won't always make decisions or give directions well. A weak mount of Jupiter can indicate a lack of self-esteem, and, while the person may have good visual acuity, he won't be terribly observant.

Note in this simulated side view, how a strong mount, in this case Jupiter, rises above the plain of the hand.

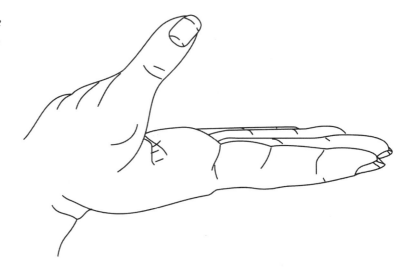

Helping Hands

Because Jupiter rules the head, an emphasis here can indicate sensitivity to bright light or other eye strain. If Jupiter's not emphasized, the vision is probably fine.

Sometimes someone with a weak mount of Jupiter may scatter her energies, such as holding down a full-time job while coaching the soccer team and directing the school play. As any Super Mom can tell you, the result is that none of these things get done as well as they might.

When the mount of Jupiter leans toward Saturn, you'll find someone who's more inclined to work within the system. This is also the person who, even when he recognizes that change is possible, will want to change the existing systems rather than try something new.

When the mount of Jupiter leans away from Saturn, the opposite is true. This person may believe that soon the Internet will replace books, that we'll all be using antigravity devices instead of cars, and that online relationships will replace any need for real human interaction. We call her the Future Shocker. Could she be right?

Marks on the Mount of Jupiter

No matter what its location, a specific mark will generally have the same meaning. As we discussed in Chapter 16, some marks strengthen and some deplete a mount's energy in a particular way. Marks on the mount of Jupiter will accentuate or diminish aspects of your leadership.

Lines that help include squares and crosses, while lines that work at cross-purposes include grilles and chaos lines. Use the following table to determine which mark is helping or hindering your Jupiter energy.

Type of Marking	Meaning
Clear rising lines	Support, if 1 or 2 lines; 3 can be too much (see chaos lines)
Cross	A supportive partner, positive luck, and assistance
Triangle	Karmic support
Star	Rapid expansion or release of energy, rapid accomplishment
Square	A partner who provides what you lack, security, lasting compatibility
Dot	Black or blue: problems with teeth or jaw; Red: headache or infection; White: inspiration, a teacher coming, tools you can use
Chaos lines	Possible astigmatism or overcommitment
Grille	Blocked energy, overuse of attribute
Birthmark	Lack of self-esteem; belief in own inappropriateness
Hourglass	Mutual benefit, a karma of giving and receiving; work on this *now*

Animals on the hand.

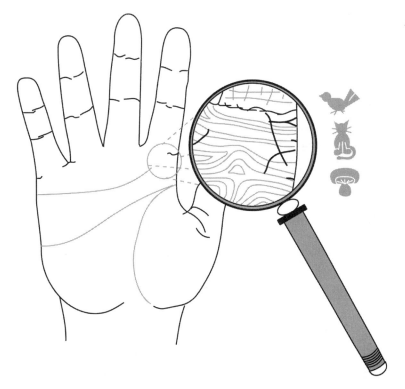

261

Helping Hands

If any animal marking is particularly long, heading off the side of the hand to the mount, it can indicate the breeder or professional. And when you've got someone who specializes in a variety of animals, such as the veterinarian or pet-shop owner, several of these lines will be strong.

It's time for the animals to have their say, and you'll find them all on the side of the hand beneath the Jupiter finger. The following drawing shows which animals appear as which lines in this area, with fungi and lower orders of life occupying the lower region and birds the uppermost. Your dogs and cats, we should add, will appear somewhere in the middle, and your horses, about three-quarters of the way up.

The Mount of Saturn

The mount of Saturn isn't called the karmic law enforcer for nothing. It's here you'll find aspects of your father and all the rules and regulations you live by. Among the areas covered by this mount, you'll find your:

➤ Nervous system and skeleton

➤ Duties

➤ Diligence

➤ Organization and organizations

➤ Systems

➤ Rules

➤ Responsibilities

The Karmic Law Enforcer

The mount of Saturn is seldom inflated, and, in fact, is usually somewhat depressed. That's a good thing for most of us, because too much Saturn can indicate an obsessive nature. Because Saturn rules the nervous system and skeleton, it's also here that you'll find the health of the upper back and shoulder blades—so markings here can indicate how well you know your chiropractor.

While it's not emphasized in terms of size, the mount of Saturn is most often marked in some way, either with lots of lines or with a single line that branches at the end. You'll seldom find a Saturn that's so overly marked that it creates confusion.

A weak mount of Saturn is not a bad thing. In the case of Saturn, less is better. In addition, markings on Saturn help as often as they hinder, as you'll see in a moment.

When the mount of Saturn leans toward Jupiter, the capacity for organization leadership are strengthened. You'll often find this on someone who's risen through the ranks to achieve the recognition of his peers.

When the mount of Saturn leans toward Apollo, you may find the entertainment manager, whether it's an agent, concert promoter, or film director. You may also find the contortionist here, of course, because an Apollo-leaning Saturn mount indicates that one's art requires discipline.

Marks on the Mount of Saturn

No matter what the marking, marks on the mount of Saturn indicate help or hindrance with land, systems, or organizations. Remember, Saturn's the land of rules and discipline, so some markings here can help you complete things, while others can stand in your way. What you do with the marks on your Saturn mount, though, is, as always, up to you.

Helping Hands

If your landlord owns a lot of property, chances are she's got a square on her Saturn mount. This marking shows success in dealing with land and property.

Type of Marking	Meaning
2 strong parallel lines or triad	Strength of purpose
Cross	Challenge that must be met but will be overcome with effort, tool, or assistance from another
Star	High on mount: legal problems; Low on mount: conflicts with physical limitations
Triangle	Can diminish difficulties
Grille	Fear of legal system
Square	Involvement with land and property (may be by profession, a probate lawyer, or surveyor)
Black dot	Loss of parental figure or material property
Fraying/deterioration	Poisons or challenge to nervous system

The Mount of Apollo

Apollo, as you already know, is the symbol of the Sun, and it's here you'll find your creativity and self-expression. Among the areas accentuated by the mount of Apollo are your:

➤ Talents

➤ Appreciation of the arts and the aesthetic

➤ Success

➤ Happiness

➤ Appreciation of beauty

➤ Creativity

➤ Self-expression

Helping Hands

People with their Apollo mount leaning toward Mercury can probably "get it for you wholesale." These agile networkers will always land on their feet—and use their creativity to be extremely successful when it comes to business deals.

The Golden Youth

When the mount of Apollo is strong and full, you can be sure you're looking at someone who's using her creativity in some way, and when it's very full, the person may be "dripping with talent"—and drive those less talented than she is crazy.

In fact, a reduced Apollo is common. That's because most of us live everyday lives, with our creativity on the back burner, so to speak. A diminished Apollo doesn't mean a lack of talent, and the markings here may accentuate this mount as much as its inflation or lack of inflation.

When the mount of Apollo leans toward Saturn, you may find the team captain, organization secretary, or spokesperson. With this leaning, the creativity is geared toward hard work and discipline.

If, on the other hand, the mount of Apollo leans toward Mercury, you may have the case of someone who's "too clever by far." These people can be too glib, too talkative, or a bit radical in their approach—but they may also be gifted caricaturists or mimics.

Marks on the Mount of Apollo

The mount of Apollo is seldom without markings, but when there are too many rising lines, approaching chaos lines, perhaps it's time to limit your activity to one particular area of creativity. Rather than paint *and* sculpt, why not concentrate on watercolor? Instead of writing *Idiot's Guides*, why not work on that novel for a while?

As on all the mounts, marks on Apollo can either help or hinder your creativity. What you make of these marks, though, is up to you.

Hand-le with Care

Don't tattoo your hand! Tattoos disrupt your hand's energy, creating short circuits. If you're waiting for your ship to come down the Rio Grande, a star on your Apollo mount won't do the trick. In fact, it will have the opposite effect and trick-wire your Apollo energy, so that that ship might never arrive.

Type of Marking	Meaning
Clear rising lines	1 or 2 give strength and support
Cross	Helpful energy from another—a teacher or tool
Triangle	A karmic tool to help, strength
Star	Creative arrival, but with a challenge to structure and health
White star	Completion of life's work
Square	Contentment with a consistent quality of expression
Black or blue dot	Stifled or destructive energy
Red dot	A creative gestation period (and probably, some touchiness)
White dot	Spiritual or temporal assistance to get the project done
Chaos lines	Too much creativity; "Jack of all arts"
Horizontal line or lines	Blockage or fear (but remember: "You have nothing to fear but fear itself.")

Hand-le with Care

All those dangers we discussed in Chapter 15 about the trappings of success associated with a star on the Apollo line can be doubly dangerous if the star appears on the mount of Apollo. Remember—fame and fortune have their price, and a star on Apollo, while promising success, can also extract more than you may wish to pay.

One other marking to note on the line of Apollo is the Mark of the Historian. When there's a diagonal slash coming out of the Apollo line on the Apollo mount, you've got the love of history. When there's a line going into the Apollo line on the Apollo mount, you've got the practice of history. If these lines meet at the Apollo line, you've got the tour guide at Gettysburg!

Of course, we should also note that Robin and Lisa both show these lines very clearly. That's because the "historian" is someone who's by nature curious—about the past, present, and future. Of course, one of Lisa's undergrad degrees is in history, and Robin can't seem to read enough books about Alexander the Great. Or Marco Polo. Or Cleopatra. Or the French Revolution. Or...

The Mark of the Historian.

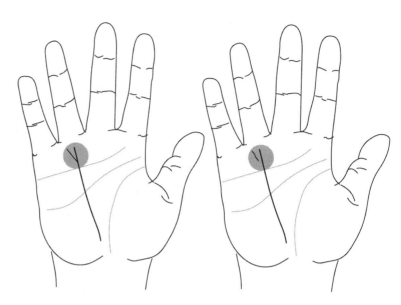

The Mount of Mercury

The last of the finger mounts is found under the Mercury finger. Not only are the Mercury areas we've already discussed—communication and commerce—found here, but a number of other areas as well. These include your:

➤ Capacity for healing

➤ Teaching abilities

➤ Impersonal relationship with society

➤ Relationships with children

➤ Learning and intelligence

Not only is Mercury the god of versatility, it's a pure element, one that changes with the temperature. No mount will manifest change more quickly because no mount's more articulate in its expression.

The Great Communicator—Are You Listening?

When the mount of Mercury is full and inflated, the person is an articulate communicator, as well as someone who's able to make a profit. That's because commerce and communication are Mercury's middle names (well, not really, but you know what we mean), and these areas will be accentuated when Mercury is strongly marked.

In addition, markings on Mercury will accentuate or diminish the Mercury energy in particular ways. We'll be talking more about those in just a few pages.

When Mercury is less than strong, you may have found someone who's quite literally a "stranger in a strange land." These people won't always "get" what other people are saying, and they may have difficulty relating to others, or figuring out who's their friend or who's their coworker. Someone with a diminished mount of Mercury probably won't be shrewd when it comes to business dealings, either.

If the mount of Mercury is leaning toward Apollo, you've got someone like Robin, who won't use one word when a paragraph or two will do. Even when Robin was six, this predilection was clear: When a neighbor asked him if he liked school, he replied, "Not much." "Why not?" the well-meaning neighbor asked. "For reasons too numerous to mention," Robin answered.

In other words, when the mount of Mercury is heading for Apollo, the expression will be creative or circuitous—or both.

Still, a mount of Mercury leaning toward an Apollo mount that is also fully inflated (as both Lisa's and Robin's are) can indicate curiosity so pronounced that we can entertain ourselves for days finding things out. This is not, needless to say, conducive to writing a book or delivering any kind of a project under deadline, but it's a whole lot of fun (and it makes for a better book).

When the mount of Mercury leans away from Apollo, you've got a Mercury for Mercury's sake. Quick-changing, quick-moving, and quick-thinking, these people won't stay in one place for long. In addition, they'll love commerce for commerce's sake, and people for people's sake.

The Medical Stigmata

When it comes to marks on Mercury, there are several distinct markings that we need to discuss first. These are the medical stigmata, and the lines of relationships and children. But let's take these one at a time.

Medical stigmata are five coherent parallel, either horizontal or vertical, lines on the mount of Mercury, and they indicate a capacity for healing. Doctors and nurses should have these markings, and when those with these markings aren't involved with medicine in some way, they'll still have a subscription to *Prevention* or *Psychology Today*, or be closet herbalists.

Handy Words to Know

Medical stigmata, five parallel lines on the mount of Mercury, indicate a capacity for healing.

Medical stigmata are the sign of the healer in all its manifestations. It's important to note that at least five clear and distinct lines must be present for this marking to be medical stigmata, however. When there are fewer lines, or they are not clear and defined, you're more likely to find the chiropractor, massage therapist, homeopath, or midwife.

Medical stigmata.

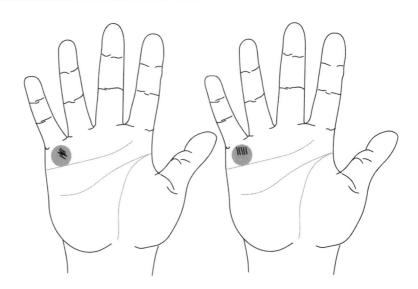

Lines of Love and Children

It's possible you've already heard about these lines: Like the life line, they're one of the better-known aspects of palmistry, and, like the life line, they're quite overrated. Yes, it is possible to find relationships and children on the mount of Mercury. But these are not necessarily an accurate reading of the number of marriages or number of children. That's because the first line is the line of relationships—and the children of the other relationship lines may not be your own.

First, though, let's look at where on the mount of Mercury these lines can be found. Pair-bonded relationships are found coming from the percussion of the hand on the mount of Mercury, parallel to the heart line, and children are lines that are perpendicular to these. Note that the lines of children don't always touch the relationship lines. We should add that other palmistry texts suggest different locations for relationship and children lines, but Robin stands by his.

Your first love, while important to your teen years, probably won't be found here—unless you married her. Even then, it takes time for a partner to make a distinctive relationship mark on the hand. In fact, your relationship with your significant other is more likely to be found on other parts of your hand, such as your life line and mount of Venus.

Instead, these lines register your potential for a true and lasting relationship—which is good news for those who are still searching—and your potential children. It's important to note, though, that someone with the Mark of the Teacher (see Chapter 15) may also have many children lines—because her students are in a very real sense her progeny.

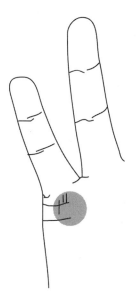

The lines of relationships and children.

Experienced palm readers like Robin can look at a mother's hand and determine the number, nature, and sometimes, gender, of her children—as well as whether another may soon be on the way. When a line is fainter, with a reversed, away from Apollo, slant, it's likely to be a girl. When it's stronger, leaning toward Apollo, you've probably got a bouncing baby boy. It's important to note that these slants show introversion and extroversion, so they aren't a definite indication of gender.

Marks on the Mount of Mercury

One other distinctive mark found on the mount of Mercury is the mark of the humorist. A diagonal line (not the Mark of the Teacher) over toward Apollo, can indicate someone whose name is tied to humor in other's minds. We'll bet Bill Murray has this mark.

Other marks on the mount of Mercury can help or hinder how you communicate and conduct business. Let's take a look at them one at a time.

Type of Marking	Meaning
Cross	Temporary business partnership
Triangle	A gift for communication
Star	Too much to do, too little time
Square	Honesty, integrity, and practicality in the Mercury endeavors

continues

continued

Type of Marking	Meaning
Black or blue dot	Upcoming surgery
Chaos lines	Problems with communication such as dyslexia or those who "don't hear" (they're not deaf—they're just not listening)

Hand-le with Care

Whether a surgery dot is black or blue doesn't indicate whether you'll come through the surgery or not. Rather, the color shows your experience with surgery. Those who've never been operated on before will probably show a much darker color dot. That's because this dot shows fear, not the relative challenge of the surgery itself.

We Gotta Hand It to You

A square on the mount of Mercury can be very helpful because it can slow down the sometimes too quick Mercury mind (just ask Mercury-minded Lisa, who'd love a little square now and then). A square may also enclose some negative condition such as a blue or black dot or a star on the mount of Mercury, which can help control or even minimize the effect of those otherwise difficult markings.

Take a Look at the Mounts of *Your* Fingers

By now it's clear that every finger's mount is very busy. When you look at the mounts of your fingers, take your time. Make sure as you draw each of your finger's mounts in your palmistry notebook that you place each marking in its appropriate location and note whether it's, say, a grille or a square. When you're sure you've got everything about the mounts of your fingers noted, go back through this chapter and see what they reveal about you.

The Least You Need to Know

➤ The mounts of the fingers are the places you express your life and times.

➤ The mount of Jupiter is where you'll find your leadership and charisma.

➤ The mount of Saturn is where you'll find your rules and discipline.

➤ The mount of Apollo is where your creativity is manifested.

➤ The mount of Mercury reveals the nature of your communication.

➤ The medical stigmata show your capacity for and interest in healing.

➤ The lines of relationships and children show important relationships in your life.

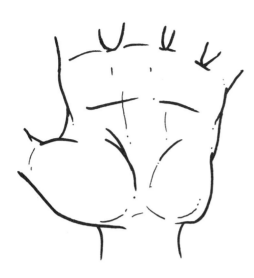

Chapter 18

The Mounts of the Palm, Part 1

> **In This Chapter**
>
> ➤ The mounts of the palm: your personality strengths
>
> ➤ The mount of Venus: a barometer of love
>
> ➤ Active Mars: aggression, temper, and self-discipline
>
> ➤ Passive Mars: holding your own
>
> ➤ The plain of Mars: your own private proving ground

The mounts of the palm are so important that they require two chapters instead of just one. Ranging from the heart *chakra* of the mount of Venus to the inventiveness of the mount of Uranus, the mounts of the palm color your personality in a way that makes you unique.

Whether it's the temperament of active Mars, the ability to hold your own of passive Mars, or the proving ground provided by the plain of Mars, the mounts of the palm reveal information that you can use to improve not only your relationship with others, but your understanding of yourself as well.

Mounts of Information

The mount of Venus, which, as you may recall, is also the third phalange of your thumb, is *chakra*-ful of information about the ways in which you give and receive love. Similarly, the three mounts of Mars—active, passive, and the plain of Mars—reveal the specifics of your temperament, including:

➤ How readily you get angry (active Mars)

➤ How you hold up under group pressure (passive Mars)

➤ What happens when you get out in the world with your own ideas (the plain of Mars)

➤ How well you deal with slights, hurts, and the potential of revenge (the plain of Mars)

Mars and Venus, of course, are our closest planetary neighbors, and so it's natural that their areas of influence are going to affect us in substantial ways. But the information provided by these mounts is subtle as well, as you'll find out when we explore the mounts of the palm.

Locating the Mounts of the Palm

Before we get into the specifics of the mounts of Venus and Mars, take a moment to locate each of these mounts on your own hand.

The mount of Venus, active Mars, passive Mars, the plain of Mars.

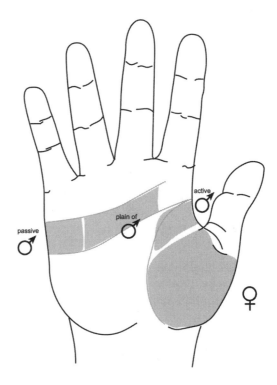

Remember that mounts can be accentuated either by their inflation or lack of inflation, as well as by the markings that appear on them, so it may help to look at them by looking across the horizon of your palm, almost as if you were about to fly over its surface, as the following drawing suggests.

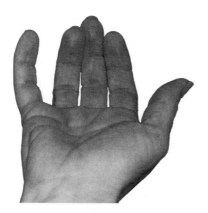

When you view your palm horizontally, as if you were about to fly over its surface, it's easy to see which mounts are inflated and which are diminished.

It's also important to remember that these mounts, like everything in your hand, can change rapidly, depending on the mood of the moment. Active Mars in particular may inflate as your anger grows, while your passive Mars may shrink away if you're drained or feeling belittled. Your hand, after all, is a mirror of yourself—nothing gets by unnoticed here.

Which Way Do They Go?

The mounts of Venus and Mars represent the extremes of your nature, where the lines and signs play out their story. Robin likes to characterize the good and bad possibilities of these mounts as the difference between instant coffee and imported, freshly ground, hand-picked beans, which is particularly apt when you think about what can happen if you drink too much of either.

Just as a builder will use only the finest lumber available to build the foundation of a house, the mounts of Venus and Mars can make the difference between someone who makes the best of her life and someone who fights it every step of the way.

Which way these mounts go determines your behavior when it comes to:

➤ Aggression

➤ Holding your own space and opinion

➤ Letting go of insult and injury

➤ The long-term expression of your heart *chakra*

➤ Your unconscious

➤ Your subconscious

➤ The collective unconscious

➤ Your need to improve things

➤ Your relationship with your siblings and other karmic connections

➤ Nurturing

Just as these areas are subtly interrelated in your life, the interaction of the mounts of Venus and Mars are subtly interrelated in your hand. While it may be oversimplification, you can think of these mounts as aspects of how you love and hate. The passionate emotion of hatred is more closely related to love than you might realize.

Handy Words to Know

The **mount of Venus**, located at the base of the thumb, is where you'll find your heart *chakra* energy. You can think of it as a barometer of your love.

Helping Hands

What do you do for yourself when you're "down in the dumps"? Do you buy yourself a new scarf or settle down with your favorite author? Do you pick up the saddest movie you can find at the video store, so you can have a good cry? Maybe you call your best friend and talk for hours. Whatever your choice of pick-me-up, *you* are the one who knows what's best for a blue mount of Venus.

The Mount of Venus

Any time a grandmother picks up her grandbaby, her mount of Venus will be pinker and more inflated than usual. Why? Because the *mount of Venus* is a mirror of the heart *chakra* energy, and when your love swells, so does your Venus mount.

Located at the base of your thumb, the mount of Venus can be thought of as a barometer of how you love. Not surprisingly, it's usually warm-colored, so paleness isn't going to be an advantage here. In fact, when the mount of Venus is approaching blue or grey, it's time to refill your emotional reservoirs. Chances are, if your mount of Venus is one of those colors, though, you already know this: It's not called "the blues" for nothing.

As you probably know, it doesn't take a drastic loss, such as lost love, or worse, the death of a loved one, to give you "the blues." What the blues really is, is a loss of enthusiasm for love and a reaching out for empathy, and the older you are, the more you begin to realize that the blues do have their purpose. (Next time you're feeling blue, check out *The Idiot's Guide to Beating the Blues*.)

When you're young (or young at heart), your Venus is young, too, and every experience will be new and exciting—and imprint itself more clearly on the Venus mount. We're not saying that life becomes less exciting as you get older, but you do become better tuned into yourself, and so better able to deal with the highs and lows of your life as well.

The Ways of Love

So what makes your heart *chakra* rise up and sing? Do certain songs have you singing along, oblivious to those around you? Whatever warms your heart and makes your heart *chakra* open up will be reflected on your mount of Venus.

Just as we each love differently, there's an astonishing variety in Venus mounts. Its fullness, quality of influence, and color all reflect the degree of your particular passion—whether it's for Beanie Babies or the girl or boy next door.

When there's true passion, it's going to be directed in some way at more than just you. Think: Can someone truly love another without being attracted to others? This is a hard question, but if we put it in less personal terms, it may become clearer. How do you feel about puppies? Or orchids? Or the aforementioned Beanie Babies? What, in other words, is your passion? Can you confine it to just one, or do you love them all?

Hand-le with Care

There is a danger with a passionate nature, and if the mount of Venus is always fully inflated, that you may have the *bon vivant*, which is French for "the good life." These are the people who love too much—and sometimes, without discrimination. They may also lack discretion and have addictive personalities. But then, there are entire books about these folks.

Like the heart line, the mount of Venus should be looked at in both hands. In this case, what's good for the goose may not be good for the gander, and a comparison of the Venus mounts in both hands will determine if the active Venus needs to be reined in.

Marks on the Venus Mount

Venus is a busy mount, so it's important to take your time when you look at the marks here. Some will come and go so quickly that you may note them and they'll be gone. That's because lots of things make your heart go pitter-patter—and the same things show up on the mount of Venus.

Most people have a prominent vein across their Venus mounts, which actually gives a bluish cast to at least a portion of it. When this becomes a dominant feature of the mount, though, you may actually prefer melancholy to happiness. In other words, a dominant blue vein can mean a severe case of the blues.

Marks on the mount of Venus.

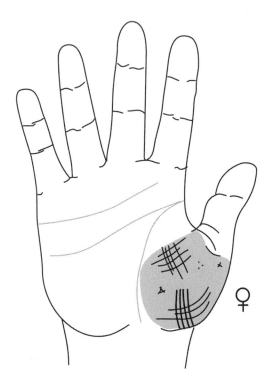

You're also likely to have a variety of lines crisscrossing the mount of Venus. Lines that come from the base of the hand up into the life line are aspects of your material desires and goals, which can be everything from a college degree to a new car. Prominent horizontal lines that come out and touch the life line can be read as the actual achievement of a goal.

Rising lines from the base of the thumb at the bottom of the hand that reach into the mount of Venus are common, but when they're extreme, and nearly cross the entire mount, they can indicate obsessive worry about something. You may find this on the hand of the mother of a teen—but these lines still won't dominate the mount of Venus, as any mother of a teen can tell you.

What about dots? As you've learned, dots, whether singular or plural, focus energy in a particular area, with the color indicating the type of energy.

Color of Dot	Type of Energy
Red	Intense, localized, sexual passion (may occur in multiples)
White	Powerful passion to connect or possess (not sexual, as red is)
Blue, Grey, Black	Break in heart *chakra* energy of hope, optimism, and faith

Cross-hatchings on the Venus mount can indicate either an overabundance of sexuality or sexual burnout, depending on their location. If this marking appears very low on the mount of Venus, near the life line, you may very well be the mother of twins, if you get our drift: Your sexual energy may well be drained.

True squares on the mount of Venus are rare. This marking indicates the acquisition of something of lasting value—the "made" person, in other words. This might be the writer with all the time in the world to pursue her craft, or the sailor who has the tools, talent, and time to build his own boat.

A triangle here is always a karmic boon of a spiritual or character-related nature. You may not always have a good time getting through this triangle energy, but rest assured the results will be worth it.

Circles or ovals are equally rare, and indicate female energy of assistance. True crosses and stars are rare as well, with the cross providing some partnership benefit, and the star, the love of something that may spill over into a passion, such as the skier who becomes a ski bum.

Active Mars

How quick are you to anger? How likely are you to pick a fight? Whether your nature is gentle or fiery can be found on your active Mars.

Look for your *active Mars* inside the life line, just above the thumb. Usually slightly inflated in some way and having some lines, too, active Mars reveals your temperament.

Anger in the Palm of Your Hand

Sometimes you'll see an active Mars that's smooth and flat, and when you do, you've found a truly gentle and kind person—although he may need a protector to see that he gets his fair share in the world.

Helping Hands

If you want to know if your new lover really loves you, look for white dots on her mount of Venus. If they're there, you can be assured it's more than mere lust.

We Gotta Hand It to You

Remember—you can't have the good times without the bad ones. If you feel as if your heart is broken, chances are there's a blue, grey, or black dot on your Venus mount. When people come to Robin asking if they'll get back together with the one they love, this dot is often on their heart *chakra* (mount of Venus). But, as anyone who's ever had his heart broken knows, time heals all wounds. Or, as the pundits have it, "wounds all heels."

Handy Words to Know

Your **active Mars**, located between the thumb and the life line, reveals your temperament—and your temper.

People with a diminished active Mars aren't disciplinarians, nor are they compromisers or self-defense aficionados. In the unlikely event that they're into fencing, they'll always have a foil on their foil (which is what the sword used by fencers is called), and if they learn any art of self-defense, it will most likely be T'ai Chi. Fencing, after all, is a far more aggressive mode of self-defense than the more gentle art of T'ai Chi.

Most people have a reasonably flat active Mars with a slight inflation, along with some markings that are neither too empowering nor powerful. This means that most of us handle confrontation when necessary, but aren't overly attached to it. We'll also be reasonably competitive, but we won't keep lists of our conquests.

Hand-le with Care

If a diminished active Mars also has a red line, star, or blue dot, you may have someone whose temper will rise and fall without warning. Markings like these can be a sign of the saboteur or passive-aggressive. Forewarned, though, is not necessarily forearmed— this person's attacks will often catch you off guard. Of course, he's not always consciously aware of the onset of his attacks, either, so he's no more forewarned than you are.

Reasonable active-Mars people are quite capable of losing their tempers, but they'll rarely hurt someone else, as might someone with negative markings on an overinflated or underinflated active Mars. When they do lose their tempers, they may get loud and gesture—but they won't take a swing at you, or throw your best dishes in your direction.

Inflated active Mars is best determined by comparing the mounts of Jupiter and Apollo. If your active Mars, viewed horizontally, is higher than either of these mounts, you're unlikely to suffer in silence, and the only reason you may turn the other cheek is to get better footing to deliver the next punch.

When active Mars is inflated, there is indeed an aggressive nature, but these people are often quite aware of it. Of course, they're not very likely to be either pacifists or vegans, but they may have developed passions, such as boxing or bumper cars, to keep their active Mars energy in check. They may also be in the military.

Still, people with inflated active Mars do have tempers, and, as these people will be the first to tell you, they are nobody's fool. As two people with inflated active Mars, though, Robin and Lisa will also assure you that this condition can be controlled with time—or by losing a few fights.

Marks on Active Mars

Marks on active Mars often accentuate a bad temper, whether your fuse is long or short. Sometimes, though, as with a back or blue dot, a marking can indicate remorse for spontaneous acts of temper, such as throwing that can opener at your husband.

Red dots on active Mars can quite literally indicate a tendency to pick things up and throw them. Good thing these markings appear and disappear quickly—and that we know how to duck.

A star on active Mars is not good news. You may want to invest in boxing, judo, or karate lessons for this person. If this marking is on your palm, we suggest that you go out and chop wood rather than head to the gun shop. It's best to use this energy in a constructive way rather than attempt to deny its existence.

Squares on active Mars can enclose and protect otherwise negative energy, and circles or ovals can mean that the protection comes from a woman who has a calming effect. This marking is often found on those whose roles of responsibility require extra control, such as a school teacher.

A cross can help you bear the load of whatever your active Mars presents, although it may not always be easy. Crosses, remember, are quite literally crossroads, places where you need to slow down and make a decision.

Passive Mars

On *passive Mars* lies your ability to hold your own against the rest of the world. Can you survive six months in Guam, far away from your spouse, family, and friends? If so, your passive Mars has helped you through—it's the mark of those we call "survivors."

Helping Hands

The difference between a long fuse and a short fuse is the difference between a diminished active Mars with negative markings (for example, the passive-aggressive) and an inflated active Mars. Sometimes, the bad temper you know is preferable to the bad temper that you never saw before.

Handy Words to Know

Passive Mars, located between the head and heart lines on the percussion of the hand below the mount of Mercury, shows your ability to hold your own against the world.

It's not always easy to tell if passive Mars is inflated or diminished, and this is another case where it's best to view the mount horizontally. You can locate your passive Mars by imagining a head line that crosses the hand, then noting the area that lies between that imaginary head line and the heart line, below the mount of Mercury.

Resistance Is Futile

How concerned are you with keeping up with the Joneses? If Robin could make one sweeping change in peoples' hands, it would be to enlarge their passive Mars, so that, like TV evangelist and author Terry Cole Whittaker, we could all say, "What you think of me is none of my business." (This is the actual title of her book, available as a Jove paperback.)

Hand-le with Care

When passive Mars is subtly accented by a collection of fine lines, resistance is indeed futile, whether you've encountered a Borg collective or the Joneses. Passive Mars is strengthened by fine lines because they mean the bearer won't be shifted or changed. This indicates that you may destroy people with these markings—but you'll never change their minds. In fact, when this appears, the possibility of martyrdom is very real.

Passive Mars is often deflated after a battle is won. If you've been agonizing over a difficult decision involving someone else, for example, when you make the decision (not necessarily act on it, but make it), your passive Mars can take a break.

You can think of passive Mars as the place where your self-image meets everyone else's. If you're reasonably self-assured, you'll hold your own here. But all too often, in all too many areas, this is where we can each, in one way or another, become doormats.

Marks on Passive Mars

Red or white dots on passive Mars can mean you're marshaling your defenses to withstand an internal demand for conformity. Facing down the majority is never an easy task—but red or white dots in this case can help you do so. Red dots can indicate the demand is more emphatic or even violent, while white dots are more spiritual challenges.

When black or blue dots appear on passive Mars, though, you may well be under attack in some way. These markings often appear when people who say they love us try to get us to do things "for our own good"—and these things can, as we all know, go on for years. Even when it's over, guilt can remain—both literally and as dark dots that just don't go away.

Squares are rarely found on passive Mars; they can indicate someone like Thoreau or Gandhi, who took a true and solitary stand against society in order to improve it.

In the also rare instance where lines come into passive Mars and stop there, or where lines rise upward out of passive Mars, you've got the dedicated social protestors. These are the folks who continue to picket despite the blizzard, or continue to shout even though the reporters have long since returned to their stations. If these lines rise toward Mercury, the protestors will be more media-oriented, and toward Apollo, the writers of social-protest songs.

Hand-le with Care

A series of fine horizontal lines on the percussive edge of passive Mars can indicate a mild hearing loss, such as that brought on by too many Led Zeppelin concerts in one's youth. Fortunately, a visit to your ear doctor or wearing a small hearing aid may be all you need to set things right again.

The Plain of Mars

The *plain of Mars* is the proving ground where your active Mars meets your passive Mars—and everybody else. This area, bounded by the head and heart lines and Mars's other plains, could be defined as your ability to deal with slights and insults, real and imagined—and bounce right back to live another day.

The plain of Mars is a testing ground where your emotional convictions and dedication to particular courses of action meet reality. For this reason, like the various rising lines cross the plain of Mars, they're often sent off in a new direction.

Handy Words to Know

You can think of the **plain of Mars** as your ability to deal with slights and insults, real and imagined—and bounce right back to live another day. It's also, more negatively, your tendency to hold a grudge or try to get even. This mount is located between the head and heart lines, and active and passive Mars.

We Gotta Hand It to You

Lisa first began keeping a vengeance notebook in her early 20s. The stories she wrote about people who'd slighted her (both real and imagined—an important territory of the plain of Mars) involved intricate plots of revenge that could never be traced to her. Soon, the fun of storytelling took over the need for revenge, and Lisa's yet to enact one of these plots. Still, it may be best not to cross her...

Vengeance Is Thine

If vengeance is your heart's desire, a dominant set of lines or dots will show on the plain of Mars. It should come as no surprise that this plain of activity is the home of vengeance in the hand, but that vengeance can take many forms.

Whether you merely plot revenge, or are spending the rest of your life in jail, it shows how well you do when you meet up with the challenges the rest of the world constantly puts before you. Remember, one of the laws of physics is that when an immovable object meets an irresistible force, something's gotta give. But there are different ways to give, without getting 40 years to life.

It's important to note here that the actual phrase in the Bible is, "Vengeance is mine, thus sayeth the Lord." That's because the Bible recognized that the human capacity for vengeance may sometimes take violent forms, which are later regretted. In fact, Robin says there are still a few guys he wouldn't mind running into on moonless nights in dark alleys. Of course, he keeps *two* lists: "Better Dead" and "Never Missed."

Marks on the Plain of Mars

Lying in the center of the palm, the plain of Mars is a natural haven of activity. Lines rise and fall here, change direction as we've noted, and all sorts of other markings can be found here as well. It's when the plain of Mars is overly marked that you'll find people who have long "better dead" lists—or overly paranoid natures.

Triangles are frequent occupants in the plain of Mars, and they indicate opportunities to use situations or tools you might not use ordinarily. Was this the road sign Lisa and Bob used as a snow shovel when their Scout got stuck in the snow? This configuration did appear in the hand of a man who lost his license and rode his bike to work—and then discovered that he preferred that method of commuting.

A forking line that's part of a line that continues on through the plain of Mars is a clear indication of a pragmatic compromise. Did you learn to type, as Lisa did, so you'd always have "something to fall back on"?

Some lines, branches, and ill-defined dots or islands may also be found on the plain of Mars. These can indicate places where there were unresolved wounds to your dignity, ego, or personal values. Robin likes to cite the young man who committed suicide in the film *Dead Poets' Society* as an unfortunate extreme of this occurrence.

The plain of Mars is also where you'll sometimes find what's called a *mystic cross* or *cross of mystery*. This marking, found under the mount of Saturn or between Saturn and

Apollo, is interpreted as someone with a taste for the occult or metaphysical studies. Robin likes to refer to this mark as an indication of a strong intuition. Whether this is the curiosity of the dabbler or the sincerely interested student will be found in other areas, such as the shape of the head line and the depth of the heart line.

Because a "taste for the occult" can run the gamut from the church-social palm reader to the true mystic, it's important to determine how well-defined this marking is. If it's unique unto itself and not a branching or forking of other lines, there is indeed a deep calling and potential for strength in these areas.

Handy Words to Know

The **mystic cross** or **cross of mystery**, found under the mount of Saturn or between Saturn and Apollo, is interpreted as someone with a strong intuition or a taste for the occult.

Because the plain of Mars is a meeting ground, it's not always easy to decide which lines here are temporary and which are more permanent. On the plain of Mars more than in any other area of the palm, it's ongoing analysis that can make the difference between possible and definite interpretation.

The mystic cross.

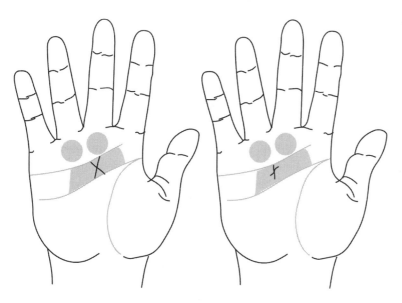

Some Mounts of Your Own

Now that we've looked at the mounts of Venus and Mars, it's time to get a look at your own. Remember that these areas can change quickly, so you'll want to look at them often and note in your palmistry notebook how these changes are manifesting in your hand. Be sure to note the relative inflation or deflation in each of these mounts, as well as how certain markings come and go, depending on your mood. You'll find that a study of these mounts is a good indicator of how you feel at any given moment, and the more you learn to look to them, the more you'll know about what's going on inside yourself.

The Least You Need to Know

➤ The mounts of the palm are the areas of your personality strengths and weaknesses.

➤ The mount of Venus is a barometer of your love and passions.

➤ Active Mars reveals your temper, aggression, and self-discipline—or your lack of these things.

➤ Passive Mars is the place where you hold your own ideas and tools.

➤ The plain of Mars represents your own private internal or external proving ground—it's you against the world here.

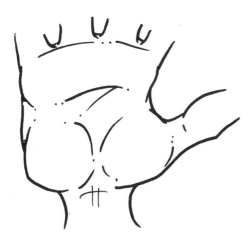

Chapter 19

The Mounts of the Palm, Part 2

In This Chapter

➤ The lunar mount: your ability to receive, your nurturing, your imagination, and your creativity

➤ The mount of Uranus: idealism and invention

➤ The mount of Neptune: the pragmatic romantic

➤ The mount of Pluto: saints and sinners

Are you imaginative? Idealistic? Inventive? Are you a builder or a dreamer? What about your possibilities for transformative experience? The last of the mounts—the Moon, Uranus, Neptune, and Pluto—are the areas where you'll find all of these life-changing potentials, and a whole lot more besides.

The mount of the Moon is the area of your nurturing and imagination, the mount of Uranus is where your imagination meets your practical side, the mount of Neptune is where dreams meet reality, and the mount of Pluto takes you to the otherworldly realm of transformative experience.

The last three mounts of the hand are far more interpersonally oriented than the other mounts, and they have the names of what astrologers consider the "transpersonal" planets: Uranus, Neptune, and Pluto. Because these mounts are more concerned with your interaction with your larger world than with yourself, they'll often point to a career that seeks to improve that world in some way. Pluto, in addition, also explores those relationships over which you have no choice, such as with your siblings and your neighbors.

Handy Words to Know

The **lunar mount** or **mount of the Moon** is the area on your hand where you'll find your imagination and subconscious. It's located on the percussion of the hand below passive Mars.

Remember, a mount's emphasis or lack of emphasis is related to how inflated or deflated it is. In addition, remember that your dominant hand's mounts will have 55 percent voting stock when it comes to emphasis. If any mount (or any aspect of the hand) appears only in your passive hand, then it will be felt rather than expressed.

The Lunar Mount

The *lunar mount* or *mount of the Moon* could be called the well of your deepest psyche. It's here, on the percussion of the hand below passive Mars, that you'll find everything from your imagination to your mother and sisters, your health to your subconscious, your ability to receive to your capacity for nurturing.

The lunar mount.

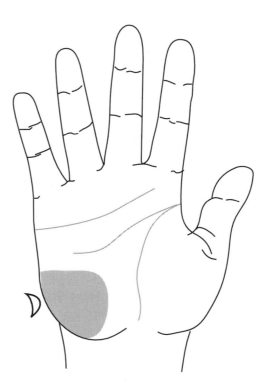

According to myth, the Moon rules the female side of each of us, which includes the imagination, romanticism, curiosity, and creation. It's important to note here that older palmistry books, in particular those written in the 19th century, cast a negative slant on feminine attributes. Imagination was called "impracticality"; romanticism, "an unfortunate tendency toward the romantic"; curiosity, "nosiness"; and creation, "female difficulties."

Even today you'll find palmistry books that toe that old line and fall into that old rut—but you won't find that here. We recognize that the feminine is not only *yin* to the masculine *yang* but the sacred arena of maternity, sensitivity, and receptivity.

Your Mother/Your Psyche

Not only is the lunar mount the mother of creation, it's where you'll find your actual mother on your hand as well. If your relationship with her is less than ideal, this may be revealed here as a red, white, or dark deep channel or rising line. Similarly, if you have sisters, they'll show up here as well, as smaller lines rising up, less developed than the mother's line.

More than anything else, your lunar mount reflects your psyche, and this deep well includes your:

Helping Hands

Did your sister or grandmother raise you? Are you still close to her? Chances are, your primary mother line will represent her rather than your biological mother. This is, after all, the line of the primary female caregiver, no matter what her actual relation to you.

➤ Subconscious

➤ Unconscious

➤ Relationship to the collective unconscious

➤ Creativity and creation

➤ Receptivity

➤ Sensitivity

➤ Capacity for nurturing

➤ Sense of balance

➤ Capacity for madness

➤ Relationship with drugs and alcohol

➤ Health issues

A healthy lunar mount will indicate that you're both intuitive and imaginative, without being overly emotional. If, in addition, your head line approaches your lunar mount but doesn't enter it, you'll have the ability to use your imagination in some concrete way.

Helping Hands

Too large a lunar mount can indicate an overemphasis on the feminine and, consequently, a fey character. A male with a large lunar mount may appear effeminate even if he's not homosexual. People with large lunar mounts may also be moody—and very Moon-sensitive.

When the mount of the Moon is overemphasized, that is, extremely inflated and pronounced, the imagination may be overactive as well. People with this configuration who in addition have a head line that enters the lunar mount will be best served if other areas of the hand, such as strong Saturnian aspects or a branching of the head line, temper the imagination with a strong dose of reality.

People with "too much Moon" may not be able to sleep during a full Moon, and also feel somewhat "flat" during the Moon's dark phase. That's because these people can be "too receptive," and so, too much in tune with the Moon's cycles.

A deficient lunar mount—low, flat, and not emphasized in any way—belongs to someone who's both calm and realistic. Of course, this person is also unimaginative if uninspired, and set in her ways. It's hard for her to receive, and it can also be hard for her to give. In fact, if this were a 19th-century palmistry book, we'd be tempted to call such a person "a man." Fortunately, in the late 20th century, we now know that "Men are from Mars" (with a little bit of Neptune thrown in), not from a lack of lunar influence.

Hand-le with Care

Can there really be such a thing as "too much Moon"? What's wrong with being creative, anyway? The problem with an overemphasized lunar mount that's not balanced by other areas of the hand is that the person may never use the creativity in any concrete way (except, perhaps, as a hypochondriac...of course, a good agent or publicist can do wonders for the less-than-businesslike artist or writer, and help to channel the creativity in a more productive direction.)

But seriously, when the lunar mount is underdeveloped, you'll find "reality" as the ruling concept. These people will have little patience for—or understanding of—their more imaginative peers. They will, however, make excellent managers for those imaginative people. Though, not only will those with underdeveloped lunar mounts not "get" science fiction, they'll think Trekkies *are* science fiction.

Health on the Mount of the Moon

The lunar mount is also the area of the kidneys and female reproductive system, and if there's a red or dark-colored grid here, it can indicate a kidney infection or other kidney weakness. Using a water filter, drinking bottled water, and cutting out caffeine and sugar can help alleviate these problems. We hasten to add that we're not doctors, and the best thing to do when this warning sign appears is to consult a licensed health professional.

A grid on a male's lunar mount may indicate a prostate problem, while a set of three or more red horizontal lines could mean a kidney problem that's a result of alcohol abuse.

If a woman's lunar mount is warm, pink, and full, a pregnancy may be in the offing—and this can appear before the actual pregnancy! Don't make this interpretation for anyone, though, until you've seen her hand several times, so you can tell if this is her regular lunar mount configuration or something new and exciting.

A lunar mount that's withered, deflated, and worn can indicate incontinence or other bladder difficulties. You may find this on older people.

The Three Realms of the Moon

Experienced palm readers divide the lunar mount into three realms: the upper realm of the imagination, the center mental realm, and the lower material realm.

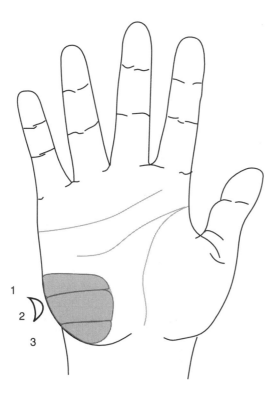

The three realms of the lunar mount.

➤ A lunar mount that is highest in its upper realm (1) indicates that the creativity may reach fruition, especially when coupled with a good passive Mars that's unconcerned with what others think. Still, these people can be as weird as they need to be!

➤ When the lunar mount is highest at its center (2), it can indicate someone for whom imagination is more important than reality. Inventive in the extreme, these people will have very good memories, but can be obsessive with a bull's-eye. With or without a bull's-eye, they may be self-conscious about their eccentricities.

➤ Unless other areas of the hand diminish its effects, the lunar mount that's emphasized in its lowest third (3) can indicate a certain mental imbalance. This can be the hypochondriac or those who never really leave their mothers. The shape of the fingertips can help here, as can a strong or branching head line.

Is There Insanity in the Hand?

Can the hand indicate insanity? Some palmists say that an extreme lunar mount into which the head line descends, coupled with pointed fingertips, a weak thumb, and no other aspects of the hand to counteract these things, is an indication of madness.

But let's look at these same ideas without denigrating the feminine. Head line into lunar mount: vivid imagination. Extreme lunar mount: receptivity. Pointed fingertips: artistic. Weak thumb: inconsistent and easily led. The only thing wrong with this picture is, perhaps, a lack of balance, which 19th-century palmistry translated into "madness."

Helping Hands

Just as the Moon controls the tides, the lunar mount is connected with the sea. A star or cross on a full lunar mount is the mark of the sailor. If there are also prominent rising lines here, he's probably far from home, while if his Neptune is strong as well, he's likely an officer (and, quite possibly, a gentleman).

We believe that creativity that's allowed to blossom gives the imagination a place to flourish, not go mad. Still, people with too much Moon may never walk on the Moon or finish their karmic tasks because they don't always have the strength for continuing past their dreams. They may become fixated on one foolish thing after another, forever unconsciously seeking their mother's approval. But creativity doesn't have to mean madness—it's in your hands.

Marks on the Mount of the Moon

As with all the mounts, marks can either assist or stand in the way of the lunar mount's energy. Markings such as triangles or squares can offer strength and karmic assistance, while grilles or dots can work at cross-purposes to the imagination or serve as warning signs. Let's look at these markings individually.

Marking on Lunar Mount	Meaning
Square	Strong family energy, strength, coherent, pragmatic
Oval	Helpful female energy, an assistant (often real person)
Circle	Energy to meet challenge
Triangle	Good family energy, karmic good fortune
Cross	A choice to be made, some alliances struck
Star	Explosion of energy (may be part of a larger phenomenon)
Grille	Warning sign, exhaustion, overuse
Red or white dot	Change in status quo, general emotional shift
Blue or black dot	Lack of energy, weakness, possible sign of poisoning, dysentery

One or two vertical lines on the lunar mount can add strength to the area, which in the case of the lunar mount means a good imagination. Horizontal lines cut off the energy here, and so can keep the imagination from finding creative outlets.

The Mount of Uranus

The *mount of Uranus* can be found where passive Mars meets the lunar mount and the plain of Mars. It's frequently found as an aspect of the head line, which, with its mental emphasis, should come as no surprise. That's because it's on the mount of Uranus that you'll find your capacity for idealism and invention, the media and the electron (that is, whatever creative energy is in the forefront at a particular time). You can think of the mount of Uranus as the area of modern styles, so it's here you'll find spin doctors and speechwriters, for example.

Not all palmists talk about the mount of Uranus, in large part because, like Neptune and Pluto, it's been discovered only in this century and so isn't even a part of the 19th-century palmistry texts. In addition, not all palmists seem to value this subtle energy— although we hope this book will make some effort to change that. (Maybe they're not very Uranian.)

> **Handy Words to Know**
>
> The **mount of Uranus**, at the conjunction of passive Mars, the lunar mount, and the plain of Mars, shows your capacity for idealism and invention, and how you use the media and the electron. It's the area of modern styles.

Like astrology, though, palmistry evolves with the times, and, as Uranus is associated with the electron, its place on the hand can be clearly seen along the head line, where inventiveness and idealism flourish or flounder. You can think of Uranus as the modern mechanic (the electron pusher), who can use the latest tools to achieve his or her inventive goals.

293

The mount of Uranus.

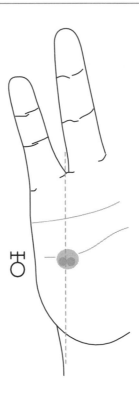

Helping Hands

Uranians are the people who are at the forefront of communication—*in their day.* In other words, in the 1950s, ham radio operators probably showed strong mounts of Uranus, while today, you'll find it on computer software innovators. The ham radio operators are still out there, but probably aren't the strong Uranians they once were. Today's ham radio operator, in fact, will likely exhibit strong Saturn mounts, or some collector markings on his Apollo mount.

The Idealistic Inventor

What are the qualities that make up the idealistic inventor? First, there's the capacity to see things not as they are, but as what they could be. You'll also find that inventors are intense, and probably positive, thinkers, seeing the possible in the future rather than the impossible: That's what idealism is all about. These people aren't always quite "of this realm," and may be very dedicated to their particular pursuit.

Next, inventors are creative in a highly mental way—that's why Uranus is located where the head line approaches the lunar mount. They'll have a knack for using tools, which will be even more pronounced if spatulate fingertips are present as well. They may also have an interest in physics or other post-modern science.

What are the possibilities for Uranian invention? If the mount is augmented by a strong Mercury, you might find the publisher or editor of a New Age magazine, science fiction, or fantasy, or the chemist who's designing potentially healing drugs. These people can actually see the possibilities, and may be doctors of the spirit or people who are raising mass consciousness in some way.

More practical Uranian applications might be found in the person with a Saturnian lean, which can indicate the innovative social critic or the criminal justice reformer. You may find a good Uranus mount on the computer "nerd" as well as the end-of-the-world conspiracy theorist.

Uranus is also the planet of androgyny, and if there's truly hope for a future where women's work will have the same societal validation as men's, you'll find it here on the Uranus mount. In addition, many strong Uranus people are gently androgynous—whether male or female.

Marks on Uranus

Because it's rather small, Uranus often isn't as well marked as some of the other mounts. If you do find any markings here, they are likely to be blue, red, or white. Uranus is normally red, although white isn't all that unusual when the person is under some imperative, pressure, or drive. Uranian souls are often driven, in fact, when they're pursuing something that they've chosen.

When a blue dot appears on the Uranus mount, there may be a need for electronic tools of some kind, as dots often indicate blockages or pressure. It may be time to check the fax or e-mail for messages!

Not surprisingly, if the mount of Uranus has a bull's-eye dermatoglyph, its energy will be strengthened.

The Mount of Neptune

The *mount of Neptune*, located where the lunar mount approaches the lower center of the palm, is where you'll find the deeper aspect or octave of Venus—perhaps Venus's male aspect. Let's think about this for a moment: What is Venus's domain? Well, there's your passion. And your possessions. In addition, Venus is how you love and how you're loved.

When we translate Venus to a male aspect, we find the mount of Neptune is concerned with foundations and dreams. Foundations, after all, are the solid base on which everything can be built, and dreams are the stuff reality is made of.

Handy Words to Know

The **mount of Neptune** is concerned with foundations and dreams. It's located where the lunar mount approaches the lower center of the palm.

The mount of Neptune.

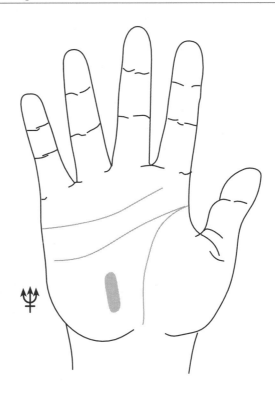

The Engineer of Dreams

We like to call the mount of Neptune "the engineer of dreams," because it's here that you'll find practicality applied to what seems impractical. Two of the careers of those with strong Neptune mounts are engineer and architect, and that's because these people can translate an idea—especially a large and unusual one—into actuality, and approach really big tasks without feeling daunted.

There's no question that the sea or water may play an important role in the Neptune career, and Neptune + the Moon = water, water, water. One man's strong Neptune and lunar mount led Robin to believe that he must be a sailor. It turned out that he was a hydraulic engineer who was the director of a city water works in the Midwest. He did admit, though, that if he could have, he would have re-enlisted in the Navy when he was younger.

Neptune's also an empire builder, and this can mean any empire. One strong Neptune person Robin recalls began with a hot dog cart, expanded to three hot dog carts, sold them to buy a "roach coach," and now owns a chain of small restaurants!

Marks on the Mount of Neptune

You'll find the usual assortment of crosses, stars, squares, and such on Neptune, but a grid on Neptune is very unkind because it can mean "broken dreams." A star, on the other hand, can be inspirational, and, while it's not more practical here than say, on Apollo, it can be more lasting.

Dots and dermatoglyphic whorls can also be found here. Bull's-eyes make their own specific demands, such as a need to work on a personal project at the expense of one's job.

The Mount of Pluto

Ah, Pluto. Out there in the cold reaches at the far end of our solar system. Pluto takes 248 years to complete a cycle around the sun, and it wasn't even "discovered" until 1930.

Are you healing physically, psychically, or morally? Is your sibling undergoing some powerful change? In Greek mythology, Pluto rules the underworld. In palmistry, the *mount of Pluto* rules saints as well as sinners because it's here you'll find your potential for transformative experiences, as well as your relationships with siblings when these situations are challenged or changed.

Handy Words to Know

The **mount of Pluto** rules your potential for transformative experiences and your karmic connections to others. Seldom unmoving, it's found at the lower center of the palm where it meets the wrist.

It may be easier to think of Pluto as a mark rather than a mount. That's because Pluto will appear somewhere in the lower center of the palm as a floating oval, and may be blue, red, grey, or white. We'll discuss the color of the Pluto mount a little later in this chapter.

Not everyone has a Pluto all the time, and if you can't find one, consider yourself lucky—for the moment. It's here you'll find your siblings, healing, lessons, and karma—and your Pluto will move, depending on what's going on here.

The mount of Pluto is constantly in motion, as we'll discuss soon, but can be found, when it's around, at the lower center of the palm, where it meets the wrist.

The mount of Pluto.

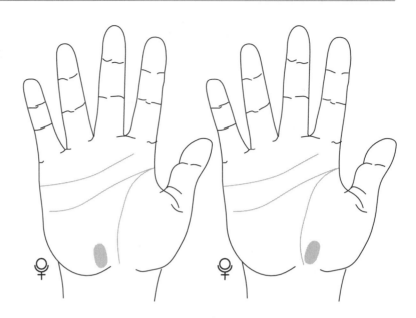

Helping Hands

So you haven't got any siblings? According to the Koran, "If you mingle your affairs with them then they are indeed your brothers." When others who affect you deeply and consistently have issues going on, you'll find it on your Pluto mount.

Saints and Sinners

Nowhere are your relationships with others more compelled than on the mount of Pluto. Enforced pairings, such as those with your siblings—or your cellmates—are the hallmark here. You'll also find your coworkers and your neighbors, all those seemingly incidental people who are important in your life whether you want them to be or not. It's also here you'll find your karmic clearings (matters that you have to deal with)—also whether you want them or not.

Pluto the god ruled the underworld, which as we all know, can be hell. But not everyone has hellish times, and if you don't, you probably don't have much of a mount of Pluto, either.

If, on the other hand, your mount of Pluto is pronounced, it's quite possible the lords of karma have picked up your cards. Pluto, by location and by design, goes to the roots of your karma, more specifically, your past lives. It also rules your feet and ankles.

Why Won't My Pluto Stay Put?

Not only does Pluto not stay put, it comes and goes with a karmic breeze. Pluto's domain is a complicated one, connected to karmic bonds about which you don't have a choice. Is your sister or brother undergoing a transformation or healing? A Pluto will show up. If it's your sister, it will appear closer to your lunar mount, and your brother, closer to Venus.

The appearance of a Pluto indicates a subtle shift of energy related to healing and responsibility. Therapists often have prominent Plutos, although doctors sometimes do not (of course, podiatrists *always* will because, remember, Pluto rules the feet and ankles). Sports medicine practitioners may sport a Pluto, as may family counselors. The strength of the Pluto mount in all these cases is directly related to the healing capabilities being practiced.

Your Pluto may also show up if you've sprained your ankle because that's one of its domains. Or, if someone with whom you've got a karmic bond is ill, your Pluto may appear as well.

It's hard to nail down Pluto, both in the hand and in definition. Pluto won't stay put because it can't; its mission is always changing.

Marks on the Mount of Pluto

As we discussed earlier, Pluto is really a mark itself, so it's not very likely you'll find additional marks on it. When Pluto appears, you'll find it in the lower center of the palm as a floating oval, and it may be blue, red, grey, or white. The color of the Pluto mount can determine the nature of the healing that's going on.

Color	Meaning
Blue	Lament, inattention, loneliness
Red	Active conflict needs attention, fresh hurt, perhaps on others' part
Grey	Old wound, not always healed or clear, unrequited caring
White	Energy to heal, opportunity to communicate

More Mounts of Your Own

Now that we've looked at the Moon, Uranus, Neptune, and Pluto, it's time to take a look at your own mounts. Draw your lunar mount in your palmistry notebook, making sure to note any markings on it. Then locate your mounts of Uranus, Neptune, and Pluto (if you've got one), and note them in your drawing as well. Once you know where these mounts are and whether they're strong or weak, you can go back through this chapter and find out what these four mounts reveal about you.

The Least You Need to Know

➤ The lunar mount is where you'll find your imagination, creativity, nurturing, and receiving.

➤ The mount of Uranus is the location of idealism and invention, the electron, and the media.

➤ The mount of Neptune reveals the pragmatic romantic empire builder.

➤ The mount of Pluto covers both saints and sinners—as well as the feet and ankles and your karma with others you haven't "chosen."

Part 5

Looking for Love, Money, and Happiness

Now that you've learned what's what and who's who in your hands, it's time to ask your palm some questions. Do you want to know about love? About money? About the pursuit of happiness? No matter what issue you want to address, your palm holds the answer—if you know how to ask and where to look for the answer.

Chapter 20

What Do *You* Want Your Palm to Answer?

In This Chapter

➤ Why do you want to know the future?

➤ How to read between the lines to find your gestalt and potential

➤ Some of the ways your hands can change

➤ Practice on some sample palms

➤ Try asking your palm a question

Now that you've learned what the various areas of your hand represent, it's time to try to use that knowledge to answer some questions. Returning to our analogy of the palm as a map of yourself, you can pinpoint certain areas on that map to address specific questions you might have about specific areas of your life.

We'd like to once again point out that, like the Wizard of Oz, your palm isn't providing information that's not already available about you. What it does do, though, is provide that information in a format that you can use this book to understand and interpret.

Is the Future in Your Hands?

Your future is in your hands as much as your past and present because *you* are the one who's drawing this particular map. We all have established patterns of behavior—even if the pattern is for the unexpected or spontaneous. Studying these patterns as they appear in the palm can help you determine what the next course of action can—or should—be.

Of course, if you don't like the way things have gone for you in the past, knowing how to read your palm can also give you the opportunity to break the patterns and venture out in new directions. You can use your knowledge of your fingers, lines, and mounts to explore how or where this can occur.

Some of the questions your palm can answer include:

➤ What's the difference between my gestalt and my potential?

➤ What is my story and can I change it?

➤ What possibilities for my future exist in my hand?

➤ How can I use what I have to make the best of my life?

We'll be addressing each of these questions in more detail throughout this chapter. But first, let's explore our urge to know the future in the first place.

Helping Hands

Your particular patterns are written in your hands for anyone who knows how to read them (including you!) to see. Similarly, you can look at a potential lover's hand to see if she's likely to be faithful, how much "heart" she's got, or how attached she is to her family. Or, you can look at a potential employer's hand to see if he'll offer you a lucrative future or has a compassionate nature.

The Urge to Know the Future

Have you ever said, "If I only knew then what I know now"? Many people think they'd like to know the future, for a variety of reasons. Some would prefer not to waste their time if a certain outcome's already a given. Others would like their paths in full view to avoid future errors. Maybe we wouldn't lend a friend money or buy that car that's going to turn out to be a lemon.

But what would life be like if we really *could* know the future? Would it be a "primrose path," paved with promises that were kept and possibilities whose outcomes were certain? And, more importantly, would that be what you really wanted?

If the future were really predetermined, we'd have little choice about it anyway. Even knowing what would happen wouldn't give us the power to change it, if it existed in some definite way.

What we *can* know about the future, though, is how we—and others—might behave. We can look at human patterns, in other words, and put together the cause and effect of particular people in particular situations and predict what might evolve.

Still, what you do with these potentials are up to you. The future, as we've said, is in your hands.

Examining Your Motives: A Quiz

Before we talk about how you can find your future in your hands, let's examine your motives for wanting to know the future in the first place. This quiz is all in fun, so grab a pencil, and see what you can make of your future.

Pick the answer that best applies to you, then check the Scoring section to assign points to each of your answers.

1. If I knew my lover was cheating on me, I'd
    a. break up with her
    b. break his neck
    c. keep the information to myself—it's probably my fault
    d. call her lover's spouse
    e. none of the above

2. If I knew I wasn't going to get the promotion, I'd
    a. quit my job
    b. sabotage my boss
    c. know it was my own stupid fault
    d. see what I could do to change it
    e. none of the above

3. If my investment decisions could be made for me, I'd
    a. sit back and relax
    b. fight tooth and nail
    c. try to figure out how to change it for the better
    d. trust others to make the right investment decisions
    e. what investment decisions?

4. If I could subtly control my loved ones' lives, I'd
    a. make sure everyone did things my way
    b. push them in one direction and then pull their strings
    c. use that power to empower their lives
    d. I already subtly control my loved ones' lives

5. My personal future fantasy is

    a. to wreak vengeance on everyone who's ever crossed me

    b. to live in a tropical paradise with all my needs taken care of

    c. a better world for all

    d. to live happily ever after

<u>Scoring</u>

1.	a. 4	2.	a. 4	3.	a. 3	4.	a. 4	5.	a. 5
	b. 5		b. 5		b. 5		b. 5		b. 3
	c. 2		c. 2		c. 2		c. 0		c. 0
	d. 3		d. 1		d. 0		d. 3		d. 2
	e. 0		e. 0		e. 4				

Now, add your total points together, and then use the following key to determine your motives.

0–5. Come on! No one's that holier-than-thou. Do you truly put the rest of the world ahead of yourself? That's quite a rising line to Jupiter you've got there.

6–14. You're interested in the future because you care about what happens to yourself and others. You wouldn't ordinarily use your knowledge to try to change things, but you do have some self-esteem issues to address.

15–20. If you knew your choices were already made for you, you wouldn't bother trying in the first place. This is not necessarily a good thing.

21–25. Take a good look at your plain of Mars. You've got some serious vengeance issues going on.

So, what are your motives for wanting to know the future? Do you want direction, encouragement, or a caveat cast in concrete? Do you really want your choices made for you? Do you really want control over someone else's life? Or do you want your personal fantasy justified in the palm of your hand?

Your palm isn't going to make—or change—your future. But it can empower you to make informed decisions. It's all about reading between the lines to find your gestalt and potential.

Reading Between the Lines: Gestalt and Potential

When you approach a palm reader, he'll most likely explain both how he reads palms and how he'll address your particular questions about the future. Robin always starts out by saying that if there's something about your reading that you don't like or are unclear about, you should take the time to discuss it right then.

Robin will go on to explain: "Understand that there are a hundred more potentials than there is one single probability. Your death is most likely a choice that's in your hands—and it's not today. Your love, marriage, work—all of these things are the result of choices, and those choices are more constant than most of us are ever willing to admit. The concept of the fortune-teller is truly antiquated and outmoded. I would prefer to be thought of as a 'choice explorer' and an 'opportunity definer,' though certainly these don't have the same ring."

"Choice explorer." "Opportunity definer." Here's where your *gestalt* and potential lie: In knowing what your choices and opportunities are, so that you can determine the best path towards your future.

Handy Words to Know

In German psychology, **Gestalt** refers to the integrated structures or patterns that make up experience. According to Gestalt theory, the whole is more than the sum of its parts—it *is* the sum of its parts.

The Story of You

We'd like to return to the concept of archetype for a moment that we first discussed in Chapter 2 because, in a very real way, archetype is closely connected to the story of you. Archetypal symbols are personal as well as universal—and when you begin to examine your personal ones, some very clear patterns will begin to emerge.

An example of a universal archetype might be a skull and crossbones—but the meaning of this symbol has changed over time. At first, this symbol appeared on the flag of pirate ships. Today, it's a universal symbol for "poison." Who knows what it might mean tomorrow? Perhaps the name of the latest rave band.

Just as there are universal archetypes that have certain meanings for everyone, personal archetypes have certain meanings for you alone. A certain corporate logo might mean "lunch" to one person and "animal murderers" to another. Or one person might see the symbol of a fish as a sign of a good Christian while another might see it as an astrological archetype for a Piscean nature.

Before we go on to examine the possibilities that exist in the patterns of your hands, we'd like you to take a moment to think about some of your personal archetypes. Who or what, for example, archetypally represents a hero in your mind? Is it John Glenn? Your Uncle Monty? Anyone who takes a risk? Who represents a villain? For us, the Wicked Witch of the West works very well. Is there a picture in your head when you think of a trickster or a mentor? Han Solo of the first *Star Wars* films is an example of a trickster, while Obi-wan Kenobi from the same series is an example of a mentor. Use the spaces below to write down your personal archetypes. They'll come in handy as you explore your potential.

Hero: _____

Heroine: _____

Best Friend: _____

Villain: _____

Trickster: _____

Wise Man: _____

Wise Woman: _____

Other: _____

Possibilities in the Patterns

Now that you've got your list of personal archetypes in hand, it's time to use them to explore the possibilities that exist in your hand. For this exercise, you'll want to get out your palmistry notebook and review what your hand has revealed about you.

Now, let's look at some areas of your palm to see how you might respond to a given situation. Let's say someone has been talking about you behind your back, and worse, that someone else feels it her duty to report everything that person is saying. How would you deal with this situation? And, perhaps more importantly, what's the best way for you to deal with this situation?

Look at:

➤ Your active Mars: Do you hit both of them, confront them, or put skunks in their cars?

➤ Your passive Mars: Do you find your own limitations, or think you might avoid facing what they are?

➤ Your plain of Mars: Do you put both of them on your "hit list?"

➤ Your lunar mount: Do you cry?

➤ Your thumb: Do you drive to their houses with an open mind or a loaded shotgun?

➤ Your Mercury finger: Is it crooked? Pointed? Spatulate? Straight? Do you slander them or talk it out peacefully?

➤ Your rising line to Mercury: How do you communicate? Is it important to you that you explain to them exactly what you're thinking?

The Mars mounts indicate how you feel about what these people are saying about you in the first place. Do you feel hurt? Threatened? Angry? Frustrated? If so, chances are your passive Mars is weak. Maybe you don't care in the first place. If that's the case, your passive Mars is probably stronger—maybe even exceptional.

Your lunar mount, the area of your imagination, may cause you to imagine countless scenarios, both about what these people think of you and about what you might say. If your lunar mount is particularly well developed, you may spend so much time imagining these scenarios that you never do anything about the situation at all. Although with a balanced head line and a bit of humor from Mercury, you might laugh at yourself as well.

Your thumb shows your will, logic, and heart *chakra*, and these three areas will determine how you approach the issue. If your will rules, you may insist they "take it back," while if you're more logical, you may realize that what they're saying isn't all that important to who you are. If your heart rules your will and logic, you may be crying about this all the time—and wondering why.

Lastly, your Mercury finger will help you assess the best way to communicate to these people what you want them to know. Whether you decide that you want them to know you think they're jerks or want to hurt them back, your Mercury will help you figure out the best way for you to deal with it. A crooked Mercury may be inclined to slander not only them but their families, while a straight one will choose more straightforward communication methods.

See how it works? Ask a question, then look to the appropriate areas of the hand for an answer. It's easy, it's simple, and it's fun. It may even take your mind off all those people talking about you!

How Your Hands Can Change

As we've said, lines and markings in your hands can and will change, some as quickly as within weeks, and the major lines within a matter of months. Your hands change with every decision (cross) you make, and so it follows that for your future decisions, you'll be consulting different hands than the ones you looked at yesterday or today.

Why is this important? First of all, because it can help you commit to a change that might not seem possible. Second, it can help you avoid near misses and self-sabotage.

Strength of Commitment

How well you can commit to things depends in large part on your thumb. If it's pretty stiff, or if it's a long thumb that can't be pulled back far, you're unlikely to back down from things once you've made up your mind. Stiff or not, if a thumb's flexible in the joints, there's still the capacity for compromise.

At the same time, a strong head line is an asset here. In particular, if your head line curves, it adds a degree of faith, which is a very important aspect of how you view your future.

Hand-le with Care

Don't forget that you'll expect others to be as committed to things as you are. If you're always on time, for example, you'll expect the same of others. But if, in addition, your passive Mars isn't strong, you'll take it personally when others are late—instead of remembering that each person's style of commitment is different.

What if your thumb is flexible and your head line is straight? Does that mean you shouldn't try to change your life until your thumb stiffens up and your head line develops a more definitive curve? Not at all. But it does mean you'll need to be aware of how others' influences may try to deter you from your path, and how your own lack of faith or consistency can stand in your way. In other words, when you understand your strengths and weaknesses, you can use them to your advantage.

Near Misses

Sometimes, you'll discover a goal quite different from the one you were originally seeking. An example might be a man who goes to Tulsa to court Jean (who doesn't want to marry him). While there, he meets Jean's cousin Betty, whom he does marry—and with whom he lives happily ever after. Now let's say Jean's prettier, but Betty's more sensible—which is just what the man needs. Are these two women going to appear in the man's hand?

The answer is "Yes." They're both going to appear as crosses. When you're looking for information about relationships, you can look in the following figure for those crosses.

Jean, who's prettier, appears as a frayed cross under Apollo. Betty, who's more practical, appears below Mercury as a stronger, more clearly defined cross.

We'll talk more about finding relationships in the hand in the next chapter. But other "near misses" can be found in the hand as well. One marking of special note is the red dot on active Mars (see Chapter 18) because this can indicate that you're about to lose your temper.

When you see this marking, *step back*. Examine your motives. Is this really important, or are you just being stubborn? Is the situation worth an angry confrontation? Even for temperamental sorts with inflated active Mars, knowing what a red dot means and remembering to check for it can make the difference between confrontation and resolution without confrontation.

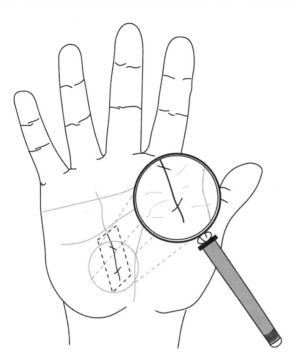

Where to look for future relationships.

Similarly, a temporary obscuring of the life line can indicate a notice to simplify. This may be as simple as "get off the freeway and find a motel room now. Why is it so important to get to Needles tonight? There are plenty of rooms in Kingman, and you're starting to see large bunnies hopping across I-40."

Once you recognize your hand's particular warning signs, you can use them to determine if your behavior is being extreme for no good reason. Then you can step back and turn your hits into near misses—and thank your lucky stars and triangles.

Some Samples for Study

Just for fun, we're going to give you three sample hands to study. We've selected these hands because it should be easy to pick out the five dominant characteristics on each of them.

What do we mean by dominant characteristics? What do you notice first about this particular hand? Are you struck by how far its Mercury leans away from the other fingers? Or does its lunar mount seem unusually well developed? Maybe it's the deep and straight head line or heart line that catches your eye.

No matter what you find in these hands, the more hands you study, the more you'll be able to pick up each hand's dominant characteristics at first glance. Here's three for you to study now. List what you think are the dominant characteristics in each hand.

Sample hand #1.

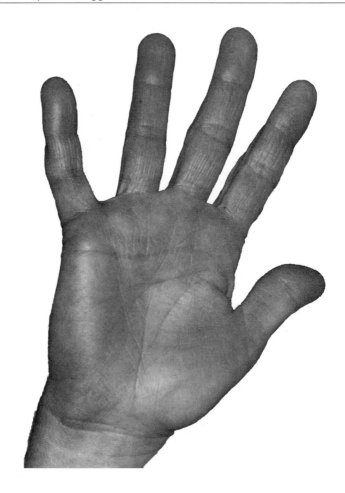

Dominant characteristics:

1. _____

2. _____

3. _____

4. _____

5. _____

Sample hand #2.

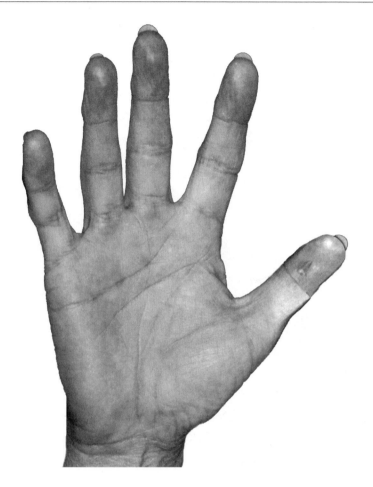

Dominant characteristics:

1. _____

2. _____

3. _____

4. _____

5. _____

Sample hand #3.

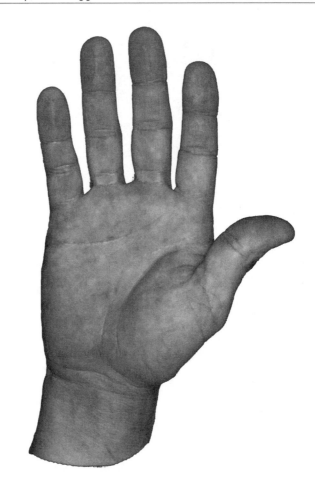

Dominant characteristics:

1. _____
2. _____
3. _____
4. _____
5. _____

Okay, let's test your knowledge. Here's what *we* found were the dominant characteristics of each of these hands.

Sample hand #1:

1. Pulled back tip of thumb: subtle manipulation; may not be in touch with real goal.

2. Long 3rd phalanges: This woman is a landscape designer and gardener, and long third phalanges indicate material world interest and strengths.

3. Girdle of Venus: sensual; high libido.

4. Forked head line: balance and good; broad judgment.

5. Apollo mount energies: performer; creative flashes.

6. Inflated lunar mount: good imagination.

7. Saturn line with Mercury branch: serious about communication.

8. Strong angle of eccentricity: a bit of a rogue.

9. Bent Mercury finger: also indicates a bit of roguishness.

10. Prominent active Mars: a bit of a temper, too.

Sample hand #2:

1. Very strong heart and head lines: strong heart and mind.

2. Rising line to Saturn goes inside Saturn: feminist tendencies; belief in women and sympathy for them.

3. Life line starts on Jupiter mount: idealism.

4. Life line has a break at about 28 years of age: major change at that age.

5. Strong, stubborn thumb: stubborn; set her in ways.

6. Eccentric Mercury finger: a bit of a rogue (like Sample hand #1).

7. Enclosed Saturn mount: skeletal or nervous system problems, or some link with those who are incarcerated.

8. Heightened first phalanges with deteriorating lines: good intuition, but possibly not using to best of ability.

Sample hand #3:

1. Strong, stubborn thumb: stubborn; set in ways (just like his wife, Sample hand #2)

2. Strong active Mars: another one with a temper.

3. Secondary life line (sister line): added strength.

4. Split head line: depth of imagination.

5. Good heart line and Venus mount: strong giver of love.

6. Branching of heart line: idealistic.

7. Long Apollo, short Jupiter: ego not involved.

8. Blotchiness on Pluto and life line: must deal with emotional issues, probably about sibling.

Ask Your Palm a Question

What do you want your palm to answer? We asked you this at the beginning of this chapter, but now it's time for you to try it yourself. Let's say you want to know if your income will increase in the next year. First, you need to rephrase the question to get to the "real" question underlying it.

What you might really want to know in this case is whether you'll learn to control your impulsive spending and generosity? To answer this question, you'd look at your Saturn line to determine your income, your Venus mount to explore your generosity, and your Mercury mount to assess your business savvy.

So go ahead, ask your palm a question. Be sure to phrase it in the form of a question—that is, a "real" question. Then, look to your palm and see what it has to say about your future.

The Least You Need to Know

➤ Most of us would like to know the future—but would it make us change the present?

➤ Reading between the lines can reveal both your gestalt and potential.

➤ Your hands can change with every decision your make.

➤ Studying sample palms can help you spot a hand's dominant characteristics.

➤ You can ask your own palm questions—if you know how to phrase them.

Chapter 21

Where to Look When You're Looking for Love

In This Chapter

➤ How to find the love in your hand

➤ Matching thumbs can mean a match made in heaven

➤ Looking beneath the Sun to find your potential relationships

➤ Heart + Head = Needs

➤ Venus is the goddess of love—*your* love

➤ Comparing your hands with your lover's

"Love makes the world go 'round."

"Might as well face it, I'm addicted to love."

"Will you still love me tomorrow?"

Love isn't simply the focus of songs, it's also at the center of almost every reading Robin does. Robin's clients won't just ask if they'll find true love—or if their love is true. Just as often, he's asked by those who already have good relationships how they can make them better.

Whether you're in love or looking for love, you can find some answers to your questions about the world's oldest story. In this chapter, we'll show you how to find the love in your hand—and in your lover's.

Finding the Love in Your Hand

Whether it's the giving of love found in your mount of Venus or the receiving of love found in your lunar mount, there's love all over your hands. While you may be inclined to look first at the heart line and Venus mount, there are many other areas to study as well, including:

➤ Curve of the heart line

➤ Fullness of the mount of Venus

➤ Head line

➤ Thumb

➤ Lunar mount

➤ Via Lascivia

➤ Rising line to Apollo

➤ Relationship lines on Mercury

➤ Phalanges of the fingers

➤ Rising line to Saturn

Finding love in your hands.

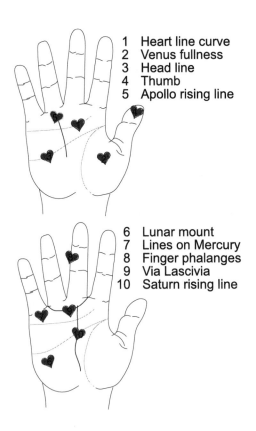

1 Heart line curve
2 Venus fullness
3 Head line
4 Thumb
5 Apollo rising line

6 Lunar mount
7 Lines on Mercury
8 Finger phalanges
9 Via Lascivia
10 Saturn rising line

Thumb Wrestling

It may surprise you to learn that the thumb is the first place to look to assess compatibility, but remember that the thumb is one of the most important aspects of the hand. Here, after all, is where you'll find your will, logic, and heart *chakra*, and if your lover's thumb isn't similar to your own, checking the rest of the hand may be a waste of time.

In long-term relationships, someone's gotta give sometimes, and what this translates to in thumbs is either two equally strong thumbs, or, if one thumb is less strong, the other's should be no more than average. The best relationships are naturally made between equal thumbs—whether strong or less emphasized—where will, logic, and heart *chakra* are evenly matched.

Helping Hands

What's important when you're looking for love in the hand is to study both peoples' hands. Sure, you may have the capacity to give and a heart as big as Kansas, but does your lover (or potential lover) have the capacity to receive and an equally big heart?

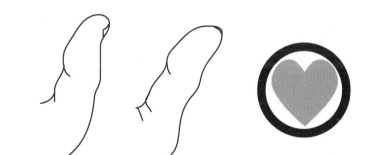

Equal thumbs make the best relationships.

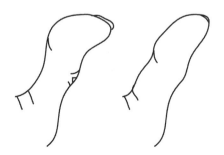 

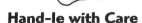

Hand-le with Care

If you've got a thumb that will bend over backwards, you may want to avoid someone with a stiff thumb. They may walk all over you—and you may let them. You'll be much better off with an equally flexible thumb, so that both of you can bend when necessary to meet each other's needs.

Looking Beneath the Sun: Where Your Search Begins and Ends

After the thumb, you should look under Apollo. It's here that your search may literally begin and end because it's here you'll find both your partnerships and your potential relationships.

Do you remember Jean and Betty from the last chapter? Remember how the prettier Jean appeared as a cross directly under Apollo, while the more practical Betty appeared as a cross closer to under Mercury? Both of these crosses appeared in what we're going to call the Plain of Potential Relationships (this is not a palmistry term, although perhaps it should be).

No crosses in this area doesn't necessarily mean a lack of relationships. You may very well be in a long-term relationship already; remember that the norm isn't always present in the palm. If you're not in a long-term relationship but are dating someone, yet there's no cross, you don't have a decision about that person coming up soon. Remember, that's what crosses are: crossroads of decision.

Robin often looks at his Plain of Potential Relationships and bemoans the lack of crosses, but it's important to note that even Robin forgets that crosses come and go. Sure, there may not be any love relationships showing in his immediate future—but that doesn't mean there will never be any again. Remember not to jump to conclusions when you read your own palm—or anyone else's, for that matter.

Adding Together the Heart and Head Lines

When you add together the heart and head lines, you'll discover your level of emotional and intellectual expectations. We'd argue that the latter, intellectual expectations, may be more important to long-term love than the former, your emotional ones.

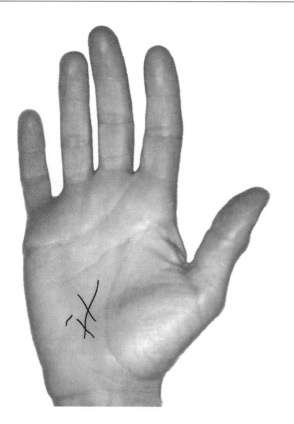

Crossing lines of relationships under Apollo.

Years ago, when Lisa's mother was newly widowed for the first time, she and Lisa made up lists of what was most important in a potential partner. Both put "sense of humor" in the #1 spot, and both put "smart" at #2. Chances are, Lisa and her mother aren't alone in what they think is important—most of us want a partner who will laugh with us, talk with us, and explore with us. Just read the personal ads and see.

A little later in this chapter, we'll be talking about what to look for in the heart and head lines in more detail.

Venus Is the Goddess of Love

How hot is your heart *chakra*? Is it full? Is it red, white, or pink? A strong mount of Venus (see Chapter 17) indicates that you've got a lot of love to give—so it's best to find a lover whose mount of the Moon is willing to receive it.

Don't underestimate this aspect: There are many, many people who for various reasons just aren't very good at receiving love. They may feel unworthy, or they may just not be emotionally inclined. Some people are afraid that if they show emotion they're revealing a weakness, and this manifests as rebuffing the love that's offered to them.

If you've got a strong mount of Venus, you understand what the goddess of love is all about—and your best relationships are going to be with those who also understand.

Helping Hands

Of course, there's always the possibility that one partner will have a heart line that rises into Jupiter, in which case that person could be perfectly happy to be the "power behind the throne"—if his or her Jupiter isn't otherwise strong.

Has Your Heart Got a Curve?

Of course, the heart line has a great deal to do with love. Does it have a curve? Is it deep and well marked? And, perhaps even more important, where does it end?

As you may recall from Chapter 11, when we talked about the heart line, a straight heart line indicates someone who's pragmatic when it comes to matters of the heart. That's fine—as long as both partners have the same configuration. Problems may arise when one heart line is straight and the other curves gently with expectation.

Similarly, the depth of the heart line can indicate the emotional depth of the person. Whether you cry at movies, weddings, and everything in between, or wonder why your lover cries at movies, weddings, and everything in between, is revealed by the depth of the heart line. In this case, though, true love makes accommodations: Lisa's husband Bob, for example, always knows when to pass Lisa a tissue—and Lisa knows that if she wants flowers or jewelry, she can always buy them herself.

Lastly, where the heart line ends is an indication of how you love. Do you have a serious Saturn end to your heart line, or a more idealistic Jupiter one? Will your lover need to live up to your practical expectations or some impossible ideal? Or, perhaps more important to you, will you need to live up to something you can't possibly achieve?

Balance is what's important here. While the heart line endings don't have to be identical, they do need to have similar styles and some degree of balance. It's always best to compare your heart line endings, and avoid unhappy endings—before they begin!

Is Venus Wearing a Girdle?

If you've both got Girdles of Venus (see Chapter 15), you can always go out dancing together. You'll have similar appreciation for the arts and will understand each other's needs in that regard.

When both partners have Via Lascivias (see Chapter 15), the equation's a little different. Who's minding the relationship while the lust is pursued? And is this relationship about love or lust? Of course, if only one person has a Via Lascivia, the problem could be worse, with two very different models of sexual expectation. But you've probably heard this story before: "She expected sex every day!" versus "He wanted sex only once a day!"

Little Lines of People

In Chapter 17, we talked about relationship and children lines, but we'd like to go into a little more depth here, and see if you can actually tell who those lines are. Robin believes you can, and, in the case of lines of children, you can find them before they're even thought of.

In addition to more permanent relationship and children lines, crosses of potential relationships will come and go below the mount of Apollo. Just as there's love all over your hand, there are people as well.

Relationships in the hand.

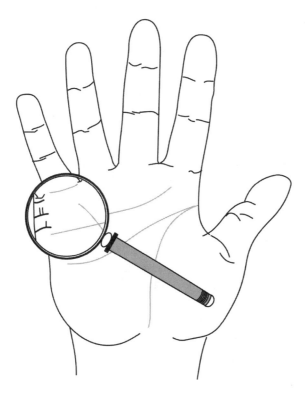

Relationships and Marriage

Do you have any lines that begin on the percussion of the hand on your mount of Mercury? And, if so, how many of these lines are there? These are the lines of long-term, committed relationships, sometimes called the lines of marriage, although these days, the two don't always go together like a horse and carriage, as they once did.

Now, let's say you've been married three times. Will three of these lines appear on your Mercury mount? Maybe yes, maybe no. How many of those marriages were truly long-term and committed? Was one of them with your high school sweetheart? Did one end in acrimony and bitter alimony debates?

Only lines of true, committed, long-term relationships will appear as relationship lines on the mount of Mercury, and so it's quite possible that despite your three marriages, only one line will appear (or, worse for your current marriage, none!).

Hand-le with Care

Robin once met a woman whose only relationship line was that of her long-term affair with a man she'd never married—and none of her four marriages appeared in her hand. Commitment comes in many guises.

A Line Does Not Your Child Make

Rising lines of children rise perpendicular to relationship lines—but sometimes they don't touch the relationships lines, and for good reason. Far too many of us have children from relationships that turned out to not be long-term or committed—so, while the children will of course continue to appear on our hand, the relationship will not.

Another reason that lines of children may not come out of a relationship line is that the children may not be your own. The committed schoolteacher with no children of his own may show his favorite students as child lines on his hand. So might the godmother or doting uncle. Lines of children, in other words, like relationship lines, reveal long-term, deeply committed relationships with children—whether or not they're your own.

What if you're planning to have a child, though? Can you find this child in your hand? The answer is yes, and this child will appear as one of these lines. Robin believes that a girl line will lean toward Apollo while a boy line will lean away from Apollo—and the child may well appear before he or she's even been conceived. As with all changing lines, you should assess the hand more than once to assess this matter of high importance.

Comparing Your Hands with Your Lover's

Just as Lisa and her mother made those lists years ago, before you compare your hand with your lover's, we'd like you to make a list of your own. In fact, it would be even better if you both made lists and then compared them. No fair peeking!

What I Look for When I'm Looking for Love

1. _____
2. _____
3. _____
4. _____
5. _____
6. _____
7. _____
8. _____
9. _____
10. _____

Finished? Okay! List in hand, let's find the lover who's right for you.

Assessing the Compatibility of Hands

Your hand and your lover's don't have to be identical for you to be compatible. Remember the old adage, "Opposites attract"? This holds true, to some extent, when it comes to hands as well. After all, "givers" will do best with "receivers," and "takers" will do best with "givers."

Again, the most important thing to look at when you assess the compatibility of hands is the thumbs. After thumbs, take a good look at the head and heart lines, the lunar and Venus mounts, and then, the phalanges of the fingers.

Assessing the Compatibility of Heads and Hearts

When you look at the heart line, you should also look at the head line. Why? Because a good relationship is ultimately as much (if not more) about mental compatibility as it is about emotional compatibility: Witness Lisa and her mother's list (and, quite possibly, your own).

Remember that the length of the head line isn't a measure of intelligence, but a measure of detail orientation. If your head line is long, indicating you pay a lot of attention to details, you might do best with someone who has a shorter line, who can look at the big picture because then you can complement each other. Someone's got to keep track of all those receipts for tax time, after all.

In the same way, there are some heart line aspects that just won't go "hand in hand," either. Someone with a pragmatic dip under Saturn won't likely do well with the lively sense of humor of a Mercury rise. A heart line that's straight likely won't do well with a definitive curve, and the chained heart line might not be best for the more definitive one.

325

Rising lines from head and heart can both be keys to whether you're a match made in heaven. Remember that a rising line from the heart line to Saturn may indicate materialism, while a rising line to Jupiter can mean idealism. Can idealism and materialism mix? You be the judge.

The best way to find out if the heart and head lines blend is to go back through Chapters 11 and 12 point by point. With this book in hand, assessing your compatibility—and possible points of contention—can be as easy as 1-2-3.

We Gotta Hand It to You

You don't have to be perfectly matched to be compatible. Jack and Janet had dramatically different tastes and interests—and all their hands had in common were equally "eccentric" Mercury fingers and narrow third phalanges in all of their fingers. This translated to a common taste for simple furnishings, uncarpeted floors, a thermostat set to 65°—and a strict macrobiotic diet. In addition, they always took their daily walks together with their rambunctious but beloved dogs. Sure, Jack collected antique guns while Janet was always adding to her unique library. What was important was that they'd found areas to share what was important to them.

How Do Your Phalanges Size Up?

Okay, students, it's review time. Which phalange is which? Just in case you've forgotten, here's a drawing to refresh your memory.

Now, following what we said earlier—that mental compatibility is the most important aspect of long-term relationships—which phalange do you think is most important? That's right, the second phalange—how you think.

Let's say you've got relatively long second phalanges, and that new gal you're dating has short second phalanges. Look out! Chances are, she's not going to share your interest in talking about the merits of impeachment versus censure (long second phalange of Saturn) or reforming the ministry (long second phalange of Jupiter). In addition, you should probably find different people to go to the movies with—you'll never like the same ones!

Similarly, the shape of the first phalange can make or break a relationship. Sensitive conic fingertips aren't always going to do well with more realistic square ones, unless something else draws the people who have them together. Still, some balancing isn't necessarily a bad thing, and one person's spatulate Saturn may be just what another's pointed Apollo needs.

Lastly, the third phalanges' narrowness or width can help determine whether you share material concerns. Again, a careful saver can do much to complement someone whose money seems to run through his fingers, so don't use this rule to rule someone out—just to assess the compatibility.

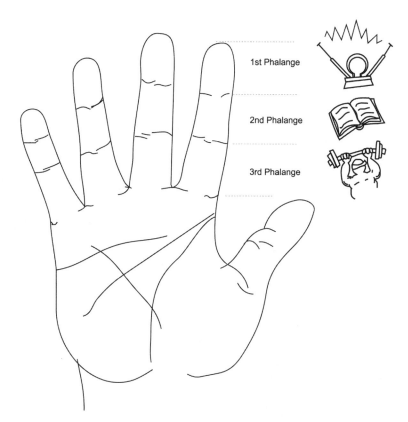

1st Phalange

2nd Phalange

3rd Phalange

Which phalange is which: your sensitivity, your thinking, and your materialism.

Pair Bonding: Sociology in the Hand

According to sociologists, *pair bonding* is defined as any cooperative relationship entered into by two or more people. With such a broad definition, it's clear that what we're talking about here is pair bonding, but what's sociology got to do with the compatibility of hands?

When it comes to committed, long-term relationships, pair bonds are about a lot more than mere cooperation. Here are some of the questions to consider when assessing whether your pair bond is a lasting one:

➤ Is your partner's well-being as important to you as your own?

➤ Do you put your partner's interests ahead of your own?

➤ Do you put your marriage's importance ahead of your children?

➤ Is your marriage more important than what your parents think?

➤ Is your marriage more important than your job?

Handy Words to Know

Pair bonding is a sociological term for any sort of cooperative relationship entered into by two or more people.

These are not easy questions. What's important is that both partners of the pair bond *answer them the same way*—and this can be revealed by comparing your hands. While we believe your marriage should be more important than all of the rest, and that your partner's well-being should be as important as your own, there are many strong and committed relationships with different equations.

What good relationships are ultimately about are compatibility, mutual respect, understanding, and, oh yes, love. After the first heady throes of romance comes the rest of your life—which is why most fairy tales end with "and they lived happily ever after." Why bore us with the details? We're living it every day.

Good relationships aren't boring, though. They're built by two people who understand the true meaning of what a pair bond entails. Like everything else, good relationships are in your hands.

Can Your Hand Tell You When You'll Get Married?

While your hand can't tell you when you'll get married, it *can* tell you when you'll fall into a committed relationship. This will appear as a cross below Apollo, which we discussed earlier in this chapter. When the relationship is a "go," the cross will be clear and well-defined.

Helping Hands

When it comes to crosses on rising lines of Saturn and marriage, Robin's more inclined to look on the passive hand than the active hand. Why? Because the legal contract isn't what's going to keep people together—it's commitment, and lasting commitment is far more likely to be an internal matter.

If, conversely, that same cross is part of a branching line to Saturn, marriage *is* likely because you believe in marriage and what it represents. If your Mercury finger is also straight and your Saturn finger is strong, a legal contract is practically assured.

Ask Your Palm About Love

Are you ready to ask your palm about love? Better yet, are you ready to ask both of your palms about love? Begin with your—and your significant other's—thumbs and work your way through the Venus and lunar mounts, the head and heart lines, and everything else we've discussed in this chapter. There really *is* love in the palm of your hand.

The Least You Need to Know

➤ There's love all over your hand.

➤ Your thumbs reveal how your wills will match up.

➤ You can look beneath Apollo to assess your expectations.

➤ Adding together the heart line and the head line can reveal your needs.

➤ Match up your Venus mounts and match up your love.

➤ You can find potential lovers and children in your hand.

➤ Pair bonding requires mutual respect, understanding, and love.

Chapter 22

There's Money All Over Your Hands

In This Chapter

➤ What's your "money style"?

➤ From elementary hands to mixed ones: hand shape and money

➤ Does money run through your fingers?

➤ Some lines about money

➤ "Mount"-ing a savings plan

➤ What your palm can tell you about money

After love, money is the next most often asked-about issue Robin comes across. Interestingly, like love, there's money all over your hands because not only can money come from a variety of sources, but your ability to use it or lose it depends on a number of factors.

Do you faithfully put the $2,000 max into your Roth IRA every December 31st? Or do you max out all your MasterCards and Visas and try to pay the minimums on them every month? What do you do when tough times strike? And when can you expect Aunt Ida's inheritance? The answers to all these questions—and more—are here, so let's find the money in *your* hands.

Your Money—and Other Peoples' Money

No one wants to hear that small change leads to larger change, and yet that's the way most people accumulate (or don't accumulate) their money. But when people ask Robin about the money in their hands, they want to hear about Aunt Ida, the lottery, and the No. 4 horse in the 6th at Pimlico.

No, your hand can't tell you which horses to pick for the Trifecta (if only horses had palms), but it *can* show lottery winnings, as we'll discuss shortly. It can also show how your fortune may be interconnected with others', whether it's marrying money or being promoted within a company.

In addition, your hand can reveal your "money style." Think about it: If you get an unexpected windfall, do you run out and spend it on a state-of-the-art CD player, or take it straight to the bank and invest it in a long-term CD (that's long-*term*, not long-*play*)?

Learning your money style can help you achieve your money goals. If you're someone who can't seem to hang onto money, for example, you may choose to turn over your paycheck to your more frugal spouse. If, on the other hand, you tend to patch the same pair of jeans over and over rather than buy a new pair, you may need a more frivolous spouse to encourage you that it's okay to buy new jeans occasionally.

The Shape of the Hand

The first place to look for your money style is in the shape of your hands. It's here, after all, that you'll find the best ways for you to earn money.

Remember back in Chapter 3, when we first talked about hand shapes? If so, you may also remember that we said shape wasn't the most important thing about the hand—and it's true. Still, hand shape is a fairly reliable indicator of what careers you'll be interested in, and, for that reason, it's a great place to find your earning potential.

The first thing to notice is how your hand shape matches up to what you do now, by referring to the following table. If it doesn't, do you like your job? Would you rather be doing something else? If that's the case, look at the career choices for your hand shape. If one of them appeals to you, perhaps it's time to call your local continuing ed program and see if some training can help you find a new direction.

If you need some keywords about what each of these hand shapes looks like, go back to Chapter 3 and find them.

Hand Shape	Some Career Possibilities
Elementary	Truck driver, minter, gardener, plumber, lapidarist, kennel master
Practical	Architect, teacher, LPN, middle manager, businessperson

Hand Shape	Some Career Possibilities
Spatulate	Project manager, engineer, ace mechanic, musician, computer whiz, carpenter, sculptor
Conic	Artist, landscape designer, interior decorator, writer, lawyer, problem solver
Philosophical	Philosopher, film critic, book reviewer, inventor, reformer, scientist, therapist
Psychic	Priest, prophet, poet, philosopher
Mixed	Any and all, but none forever

Putting Your Fingers on Money

The next place to look for your money style is your fingers. Which finger is strongest? Which phalange of each finger is longest? And is your thumb generous or cautious when it comes to cash?

Your fingers can quite literally answer the question of whether or not money will "run through your fingers," so let's look at them one at a time to see where your strengths and weaknesses can be found:

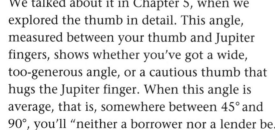

> **We Gotta Hand It to You**
>
> When you look at your fingers, pay special attention to the material third phalanges. This is, after all, a capitalistic society, and, like it or not, possessions are a measure of worth. The reason you collect particular things is an aspect of the length of your fingers' third phalanges as well, and, whether because they're useful, lovely, or because you're sentimentally attached to them, the things you collect can reveal a lot about your money style.

> ➤ *Thumb.* Remember the "angle of generosity"? We talked about it in Chapter 5, when we explored the thumb in detail. This angle, measured between your thumb and Jupiter fingers, shows whether you've got a wide, too-generous angle, or a cautious thumb that hugs the Jupiter finger. When this angle is average, that is, somewhere between 45° and 90°, you'll "neither a borrower nor a lender be." In other words, while you will be giving, you'll be practical about it as well.

> ➤ *Mercury.* How long is your Mercury finger? When it's longer than average, you can't help but make money—plus you can probably always get it for us wholesale. In addition, if your Mercury's low-set, you may have had some economic hardship as a child. A Mercury finger that leans toward Apollo can indicate an alert businessperson who'll have a certain flair, and the length of Mercury's third phalange can reveal how you express yourself materially.

> ➤ *Apollo.* The Apollo finger's not necessarily long on cash, but there is a knack for understanding what art is worth when the first phalange of Apollo is short. That's

because this can indicate someone who, while not artistically inclined, is very good at assessing another's artistic worth.

➤ *Saturn.* Not surprisingly, your Saturn finger has a lot to do with your self-discipline when it comes to money. If it's straight and upright, you'll never fudge on your taxes—or earn money in other than acceptable ways. A Saturn finger that leans toward Jupiter can indicate a self-made person, possibly even a ruthless one when it comes to her goals; while if it leans toward Apollo, she'll be more creative in how she approaches them. In addition, the Saturn fingertip can show your work ethic, especially if it's square, which indicates integrity's more important to you than monetary reward.

➤ *Jupiter.* The finger of leadership can not only lead you to money, it can manage others' as well. If the Jupiter finger is long, in fact, you may find someone willing to take risks with money—both his own and someone else's. Further, the successful entrepreneur will have not only a long Jupiter finger, but one that's well-shaped and well-proportioned as well.

Cross Your Palm with Silver

We don't mean this old gypsy phrase literally, but it is possible to find marks of money all over your hand. Whether it's…

➤ the triangle that reveals your potential earnings,

➤ the stars of unexpected winnings,

➤ the fraying of lines that can indicate hard times,

➤ or the often underestimated importance of stamina to be found in your life line,

…you can use cross your own palm with silver—if you know where to look.

Hand-le with Care

Let's face it—most of us want more than we have, no matter how much or how little we have already. It's easy to say it's human nature—but it's also worth a look at the plain of Mars—to see where this need for "keeping up with the Joneses" originates.

The Triangle of Earnings

A good place to look for money in your hand is the *triangle of earnings*. Found where your head line meets your rising line to Saturn, it's formed by the addition of a rising line to Mercury.

If this triangle is closed, it shows a capacity to hang on to money that comes in, while if it's not entirely closed, your money can figuratively escape through the gap. If there's no third side to the triangle at all, well, you probably already know what happens if you happen to come across any money!

Handy Words to Know

The **triangle of earnings** can be found where the head line meets the rising line to Saturn. If a Mercury line rises to form a triangle here, you can use it to assess your earning potential.

Another aspect of this triangle to consider is its size. If it's particularly large, you may have the potential for large earnings as well. Still, this doesn't necessarily mean you'll be a millionaire (billionaire is probably a more appropriate reference these days!)—you'll still have to work for what you earn. But the potential for wealth is there.

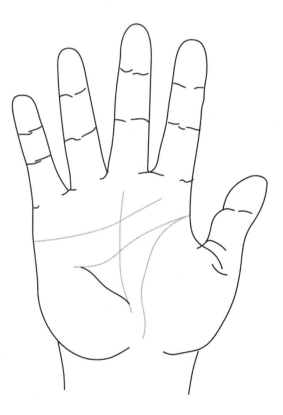

The triangle of earnings.

Helping Hands

Robin has actually seen lottery winnings in the hands of people. Four times, to be exact. None of these, however, was a life-changing amount of money. The most was $20,000; the least $400. Still, a windfall's a windfall, right?

Winning the Lottery

"Will I win the lottery?" Perhaps more important, do potential lottery winnings appear in the hand? The answer is yes—but Robin's never seen them change someone's life dramatically (but then, he's never seen a big winner's hand…).

You don't want to hear us qualify all this, though. You want to know what to look for. So, without further ado, here's the "formula" for windfall money in the palm:

➤ A star on the mount of Apollo

plus

➤ A star on the Saturn line

plus

➤ A triad on the mount of Apollo

In addition, these three marks should be "coherent in time," that is, all present at the same time.

We can't stress enough that lottery winnings have a great deal to do with the spirit with which one pursues them. Have fun. But don't spend your paycheck on Quick Picks for the big jackpot. And don't blame your palmist for not winning more money!

Hand-le with Care

This doesn't necessarily have anything to do with palmistry, but it is a true story, and a cautionary one having to do with the lottery at that. Lisa was once in line behind a man at a convenience store who bought 50 picks—all with the same numbers. Did he think he was improving his odds? We shudder to think.

Tough Times

When it comes to predicting tough times, Saturn's the guy to talk to. Whether it's the rising line to Saturn or the Saturn mount, these areas of the hand are going to exhibit the warning signs.

If there's a thinning, fraying, or break on the rising line to Saturn, it can indicate financial tough times in the offing. BUT these warning signs may be saying something like, "It may be best not to buy that new car now," or, "What's wrong with the house and mortgage you've got now?" In other words, these warnings may appear to tell you not to make unnecessary or unwise expenditures now—whether you want them or not.

What this means is that you can circumvent the problem by putting off the purchase. What actually happens, though, is that, when Robin suggests that a client not buy that diamond ring, he'll get a call a few months later, berating him for predicting the person would have trouble making the payments! Of course, the phrase "Shoot the messenger" may well have referred to a palm reader!

Any branching off the Saturn line is generally a choice that may affect the money flow. These choices can include anything from deciding to quit your job to paying off your credit card balance. No matter what the decision, the branching is saying "think twice." Pay attention to your Saturn—it knows whereof it speaks.

Assessing Your Potential

Beyond the triangle of earnings, the very basis of your story can be found in the lines of your hand. Not only can your heart line indicate your materialism, your head line can show the way you focus your energy, and your life line can show how your life force can be marshaled to shore up your earning potential.

Just like electric lines, the lines in your hand may be solidly grounded or less well connected. Knowing the potential your various lines show can help you learn still more about your money style.

Is Your Heart in It?

A heart line whose main branch heads toward Saturn will be very materialistic when it comes to love and romance. This includes strong self-discipline where money's concerned, as well as the desire to earn and hang onto money in order to feel comfortable romantically.

As we noted in Chapter 11, Robin likes to remind clients that instead of asking whether their potential beloved will have money, they should ask if the person can live within his or her means. For that matter, if you've got trouble living within yours, perhaps someone whose main heart line branch is toward Saturn may be just the person you need to help you save what you earn.

Is Your Head in It?

Once again, the Saturnian aspect comes into play when we talk about the head line. In fact, the short head line, which actually ends under Saturn, indicates a strong material focus. If this is your head line, you'd do well as a businessperson, entrepreneur, or a farmer who's committed to the bottom line.

337

Helping Hands

Does your landlord own a lot of properties? Take a look at her head line or heart line: Chances are, one of them ends under Saturn (although both ending there would be too limited). The person with this configuration understands the value of everything concrete, especially land and property. A peak on one of these lines would also represent this.

If your head line ends under Saturn, you're someone whose main mental focus is money, and you also know that the best way to amass and retain money is through your choice of career. You'll be no-nonsense in your approach to money, and you'll be a shrewd investor who knows how to use money to make more money.

Another head line configuration that can translate into strong earning potential is one that ends in the mount of Uranus. This mount, remember, is where you'll find people who understand the latest in inventive communication, and when the head line ends here, there's the potential for making a lot of money with this talent as well—especially if the person has a practical side to go with it.

Being Healthy Never Hurts

The depth of your life line comes into play when it comes to your earning potential, not because it reveals a material sense, but because it's a measure of your overall health and well-being, and being healthy never hurts.

In fact, the amount of *chi*, or vital breath, you have has a great deal to do with how others will act and react with you, which in turn can translate to financial success. A deep and well-formed life line can compensate for all sorts of other limitations in the hand, and it's an indication of an inner strength others will envy and seek to emulate.

Another place to check your *chi* is at the tip of your thumb. When the flesh at the tip of your thumb isn't bouncing back as it should, you may need to take some time off from work—and this, in turn, could affect your earning potential, at least in the short term. If, on the other hand, your thumb *chi* is resilient, it's an indication of your own resilience as well.

The Role of the Planets

The planets, of course, have given their names to not only the fingers, but the mounts and rising lines as well, and their roles in your money style cover everything from your temperament (Mars) to your responsible nature (Saturn), and your leadership (Jupiter) to your capacity for commerce (Mercury).

First, to test your knowledge of the planets, see if you can determine which mount covers which characteristics in the following list. No fair peeking!

1. Do you understand value?
2. Are you driven?

3. Are you pragmatic?

4. Are you optimistic?

5. Are you clever?

6. Do you stand out in a crowd?

Answers:

1. Venus

2. Mars

3. Saturn

4. Jupiter

5. Mercury

6. Apollo (the Sun)

Which of these characteristics are required for material success? At least some of them, and, perhaps, all of them. Read on.

Value Your Venus

What are your values? What are your material desires? Do you know that a degree in economics will change your life? Or that a Lexus in the driveway will make a statement to the world about you?

Your mount of Venus is about your material desires and goals, which can help you focus your monetary desires on something tangible, and pull all the other planets into line to do so. Venus understands the value of acquisition—not just for acquisition's sake, but because your possessions make a statement about you.

Marshal Your Mars

Question: What's a stumbling block?

Answer: A great place to leap off from.

The three mounts of Mars can be thought of as glasses half full or half empty (depending, probably, on your Jupiter mount). How you use this Martian energy can mean the difference between wallowing in self-pity or marshaling your Mars to achieve something bigger than you ever imagined in the first place.

First of all, there's the self-discipline of active Mars. Even if you've got a bad temper, learning to control it can be a great asset for furthering your material desires.

Then there's the "holding your own" found on passive Mars. Do you tend to let others walk all over you rather than confront them with the force of your own convictions? If you've got a strong passive Mars, you're not going to knuckle under to the rest of the gang.

Lastly, there's the plain of Mars, that lively area of activity where you meet the world. How well do you deal with everything the world shovels out? When you see a pile of manure, do you just know there must be a pony? Or do you just see a mess you'll have to clean up?

Mars is tough, aggressive, and cocksure—and if you're going to succeed, marshaling your Mars can give you just the head start you need.

Helping Hands

If your Saturn line breaks before it reaches the head line, a job change may be in the offing, especially if it occurs where the rising line to Saturn parallels the life line.

Support Your Saturn

As you've probably gathered from other discussions in this chapter, no planet plays a more important role in your "money style" than Saturn. Among the three areas of Saturn, the finger (which we've already discussed), the mount, and the rising line, it's the rising line that may make you or break you.

The rising line to Saturn is a measure of your standard of living, your potential for material wealth, and your relationship with authority—including your own. If this line rises all the way to the mount of Saturn, in fact, you may be too responsible—and unable to let go of connections that are no longer doing you any good.

In general, a reasonable rising line to Saturn indicates reasonable success from hard work and diligence. This isn't the marking of overnight success, but you won't starve with it, either. You may, though, have to do it "their way" because this line will work within the system.

In addition to the Saturn line, the Saturn mount is a good place to find how well you do within organizations and systems. Are you responsible? Do you follow the rules or buck the system? Remember, when it comes to earning potential, sometimes some system-bucking is a good thing—and less Saturn mount is usually best.

Joy from Your Jupiter

Your mount of Jupiter can make the difference between enjoying your life and merely living it, because it's here you'll find your optimism, will to succeed, integrity, and skills. Are you self-confident? Have you got a little bit of *chutzpah*? Are you ambitious? Do you inhabit your life or merely live in it?

It takes strength of character to succeed, and the mount of Jupiter is the location for everything from your ideals to your enthusiasm. Look at it another way: Do you take responsibility for your mistakes? If you look at mistakes as lessons rather than locked doors, your Jupiter can lead you wherever you want to go.

A strong mount of Jupiter indicates a leader, and someone who uses her head. There's also physical strength, optimism, ambition, and the charisma that goes with self-confidence. A strong Jupiter can translate to much success—as well as much joy from that success.

Making Your Mercury Work for You

If the mount of Mercury is full and inflated, you can be sure there's a profit to be made. The person with a strong Mercury mount can get it for you wholesale, will choose to take the class in summer school because it will be easier then, and can diffuse tension with just the right joke.

Helping Hands

A strong Jupiter mount gives you an extra something to fall back on. In fact, Jupiters don't fail! Sometimes, their success is delayed, but it will arrive. No ifs, ands, or buts. Show us the money!

Marks on Mercury can further indicate quite specific career choices, whether it's the health orientation of the medical stigmata or the born teacher found with the Mark of the Teacher. Other markings on Mercury can show what's needed for commerce at the moment, such as the temporary business partnership indicated by a cross, or the need to slow down indicated by a square.

The Sun Is a Question

Sometimes, you can be *too* attractive for the job. Unless you're a supermodel, you won't get by on looks alone, and the wise Apollo will always have something else going for him besides the beauty of his youth.

The question with Apollo is whether the talent is balanced by a will to succeed. Talent alone isn't enough for material success, but when it's balanced with some Saturn, a strong thumb, or a good Mercury line, the answer can be creative success.

It's Better to Be Consistent Than Lucky

Consistency can be found on Saturn, while your luck resides on Apollo; and while a little luck never hurts, it's better to be consistent than lucky. In fact, setting goals and meeting them is an aspect of Saturnian consistency rather than Apollonian luck—and "luck" never lasts.

We Gotta Hand It to You

Strong Apollonians will often be the ones to set up the situation, design the office, select the logo, and even possibly hire—and inspire—the first people on the job. They'll be the ones charming the clients at the opening gala—but they won't be there for the mundane, day-to-day operation. It's challenge they crave and drama, rather than routine. They may even create a bit of drama just to keep things from becoming routine, and without an audience, they're just not at their best.

The truly lucky won't necessarily fail, but they really never know where or when they'll succeed, either. They may, in turn, be unlikely to set new goals for themselves—because things seem to go their way without trying. If you've ever gotten something without working for it in some way, you may well know how unearned such luck can seem. It truly is better to be consistent than lucky. Remember Aesop's fable about the turtle and the hare: Slow and steady wins the race.

Ask Your Palm About Money

Do you have a money question you'd like to ask your palm? Maybe you want to know if you'll get that raise, or whether your current career path is the right one for you. Phrase your question in a way that your palm can answer, such as:

➤ What are some career possibilities that I'd enjoy?

➤ Where do my talents lie?

When you're ready with your question, go back through this chapter to find the answer. As always, it's in your hands.

The Least You Need to Know

➤ You can find your "money style" in various areas of the hand.

➤ The shape of your hand can show you the best ways to earn money.

➤ Your fingers can show whether you'll hold onto money or whether it will "run through your fingers."

➤ The lines on your hand can show your earnings potential.

➤ Your mounts can help you hang onto what you earn.

➤ It's better to be consistent than lucky.

Chapter 23

The Pursuit of Happiness

> ### In This Chapter
>
> ➤ What is happiness?
>
> ➤ Finding your comfort zone
>
> ➤ What's your heart's desire?
>
> ➤ Finding the happiness in your hand

According to philosopher Emmanuel Kant, the formula for happiness is, "Something to do, someone to love, and something to look forward to." Put in this perspective, it doesn't seem that the pursuit of happiness should be so elusive, and yet, to many of us, a pursuit is all there ever is.

Why is this? What is happiness? Is there a magic formula for finding it? Perhaps more to the point, can you find your potential for happiness in the palm of your hand?

What Is Happiness?: A Zen Koan

What is happiness? We might as well ask, "What is an adjective?" In writing classes, students are taught to "Show, not tell," and that means banishing nondescriptive adjectives from town. What does "the beautiful seashore" show, after all? Not nearly as much as "white sand, tall graceful palms, gentle waves, and the turquoise water." (We won't go into that "tall, dark stranger" here...)

Handy Words to Know

Zen koans pose answers to seemingly unanswerable questions, such as "What is the sound of one hand clapping?" Meditating about the meaning of (rather than the answer to) such imponderables can help you understand yourself better as well.

The question "What is happiness" might be better understood as a *Zen koan*, a way of pondering something seemingly imponderable. Happiness means different things to different people, and understanding this is the most important thing you can learn about happiness. That said, in this chapter we're going to explore how *you* can find your own particular heart's desire.

Taking a Good, Hard Look at Yourself: A Quiz

There once was a man who kept asking his wife what was the secret to happiness. "It's inside you," she told him, again and again. And each time, the man became angry. "Why won't you tell me?," he'd cry. "Why are you keeping it a secret?"

As that woman knew (and that man sadly did not), it's not a secret at all: The secret to your happiness is inside you. The hard part is finding out just what that secret is, and methods for doing so include everything from psychoanalysis to biorhythms to astrological birth charts to reading your palm. Before we show you how to use your palm to find your heart's desire, though, let's see what you know about yourself already.

1. Which of the following statements is most true of you?
    a. I just want my family to be happy.
    b. If I had a better car, everything would be all right.
    c. I'd stop complaining if my boss would leave me alone.
    d. Someday my prince/princess will come.
    e. My home is my castle.

2. What would make you happy *right this minute*?
    a. a hot fudge sundae
    b. a million dollars
    c. no mortgage
    d. a love to call my own
    e. a day off

3. What would you do to achieve happiness?
    a. go back to school
    b. look for a different job

c. move to another town

d. go shopping

e. break up with my boyfriend/girlfriend

4. What could others do to make you happy?

    a. remember my birthday

    b. pay off my debts

    c. get off my case and let me do my job

    d. Listen, just listen

    e. buy me a Porsche and send me (and the Porsche) to Hawaii

5. What would make you think you'd arrived at "happily ever after?"

    a. a storybook wedding

    b. having the money for the rent on time, a car that runs, food in the fridge, and a month's supply of cat food

    c. a loving spouse, a job I love, money in the bank

    d. looking forward to going to work every day

    e. good health and good cheer

You may have figured out that these questions are meant to show what areas of your life seem to be most important to you when it comes to the idea of what happiness is. After you use the scoring that follows to find out, the rest of the chapter will show you how to use your palm to find out how well you really know yourself—and how to begin to achieve your own particular brand of happiness.

<u>Scoring</u>

Each answer is assigned a letter. After finding the letter for each of your answers, determine which letter you have more of than any other. This letter will be your "happiness keynote."

1.		2.		3.		4.		5.	
a.	F	a.	G	a.	P	a.	G	a.	D
b.	P	b.	D	b.	W	b.	P	b.	P
c.	W	c.	P	c.	D	c.	W	c.	F
d.	D	d.	F	d.	G	d.	F	d.	W
e.	G	e.	W	e.	F	e.	D	e.	G

Which letter did you choose the most? That's your "happiness keynote." Note: If there's a tie, be sure to read the descriptions for both (or all) letters in the following list.

➤ *Family/Love.* Nothing's more important to you than the love of a good family, and this includes not just a spouse, but children as well. Maybe you're still looking for Mr. or Ms. Right, or maybe you believe that part of this equation is having a job you love and money in the bank, but to you, happiness is synonymous with domestic bliss. You'll want to see if your mount of Venus and Saturn finger agree with your self-assessment, and read the upcoming section "The People in Your Life" to see if others truly are the way to your version of happiness.

➤ *Practical.* Sure, love's important—to other people. What matters to you is doing your job, paying the bills, food in the cupboard, and everyone leaving you alone. Chances are, you've got a strong and serious Saturn nature, as well as a rising line to Saturn to help you get things done. Does "All work and no play make Jack a dull boy"? Read the upcoming section "Security Is an Illusion; Adaptability Is Survival" to find out if happiness can also bring some joy.

➤ *Work.* It sounds as if your job isn't what you'd like it to be—and yet your life revolves around your job. Is this because you're so unhappy with your job that it seems if things went better there, everything else would be all right, too? When it comes to finding the career that's right for you, you'll want to assess everything from your fingertip shape to which finger's dominant, as well as that finger's strongest phalange. You can find the job you want—but first you have to know just what it is. Look in the upcoming sections "Job Security" and "There Are People Who Love Their Jobs" to find out what it might be.

➤ *Dreamer.* There's nothing wrong with dreams—as long as they're tempered with some reality. Do you really think you'd live happily ever after on a tropical island? Do you really expect your prince to come riding up on a white horse and carry you away? Maybe it's time to move from the "Romance" section of the bookstore to the "Self-Help" one. There are some terrific books for helping you find your heart's desire, and we'll be discussing some of them in a moment, in the section "Somewhere Over the Rainbow: Obtaining Your Heart's Desire." Meanwhile, take a look at your lunar mount and see if it needs some reality thrown in. Maybe you should look at your Mercury mount, too—and see if you're trying to pull our leg—or your own.

➤ *Gratification.* Gratification, as in "immediate gratification," we should say. You live for the moment, seek to fix things as they break, and never look very far into the future. When we talk next about "Comfort, Contentment, and the Zone of No Challenge," you'll want to pay close attention. Maybe it's time to marshal your Mars and get moving.

Comfort, Contentment, and the Zone of No Challenge

According to early-20th-century American novelist Theodore Dreiser, a desired object once obtained is no longer desired—or desirable.

What do you do when you get where you wanted to go? Do you kick back and relax, bask in comfort and contentment—and never go anywhere again? What's wrong with basking, anyway?

Nothing's wrong with a little well-deserved respite after achieving a goal, but when you don't move on to the next goal after a while, you may settle into the "Zone of No Challenge."

If you're living here, your palm may show a lack of any color, a flaccid thumb, or an uninfluenced (that is, without other lines or markings) head and heart line. While your Saturn line may be somewhat strong, you may be lacking an Apollo or Jupiter line to temper it.

Happiness is not a rut. Nor is it not thinking about the future and living from moment to moment. There's nothing like a goal—something that you desire—to get you motivated.

What motivates you? The answer may lie in your active Mars. What makes you angry? What would you change if you could? If something is important enough to anger you, chances are it's important enough to consider changing it in some way. Sure, you can't change your in-laws—but you can move to another state. Sure, your congressperson did or didn't vote for impeachment—but you can work to vote him or her out of office next election.

Somewhere Over the Rainbow: Obtaining Your Heart's Desire

We are here to tell you that you *can* obtain your heart's desire—once you know just what your heart's desire is. You may think you just want a spouse, or the right job, or even the month's rent, but each of those may mask your true heart's desire. In fact, "somewhere over the rainbow" may be, as Dorothy discovered, "right out in (your) own back yard."

In addition to books that help you figure out what it is you want, it's possible to find your true path in your hand. You can answer the following questions by looking to that area of the hand.

We Gotta Hand It to You

There are some wonderful books out there to help you find your true path, such as Barbara Sher's *Wishcraft* (Ballantine, 1986) and Louise Hay's *You Can Heal Your Life* (Hays House, 1987). These books take you step by step through exercises that help you to visualize what your ideal day might be—and then discuss how to confront what you imagine to be standing between you and that ideal day.

What's most important to me? What mount, finger, and line are strongest?

What do I want in a spouse? Is Apollo, Saturn, or Jupiter strongest? Do I need to be entertained (mount between Apollo and Mercury)? Do I have a Via Lascivia?

What career would I do well in? This depends on what's emphasized:

➤ Check both your Jupiter and your thumb. Are you ambitious enough to pursue something, or would you rather be given something?

➤ Is Saturn strong? If so, you probably require the security of a bureaucracy or large organization.

➤ Does your head line rise to Mercury? Sales or business may be your forte.

➤ Is your head line flat along Mercury? This can indicate the accountant, librarian, or researcher.

➤ Do you have medical stigmata? A career in medicine may be lined up here.

➤ Is there a Jupiterian animal influence? Consider a career that will involve animals in some way.

➤ Is there a lunar emphasis? You'll want to put your imagination to work.

➤ Is there a rising line to Apollo? Creativity will be a given in whatever career you find to love.

What goals would excite me? First, check which mounts are strongest. You should also see if you have an idealistic heart line, along with spiritual energy inside the heart line.

What activities make me happy? Again, check the mounts. Apollo = performance and arts. Mars = competition. Saturn = hard work. You get the idea here, right?

Whether it's profession, people, or passion, what matters most to you is written in your palm. Once you find your heart's desire, you can begin to design a path to take you there—a path that can make you as happy as the goal itself.

Home and Hearth

What is a home? For some, it's an ever larger house in an ever better subdivision, not too far from the country club. For others, it's wherever the shoe drops or the road runs out for the night. How do you determine what "home" means to you? Look to your Venus, your Saturn, your Apollo, and your heart line, as well as your life line and your head line.

Hand-le with Care

Americans seem to think that "owning a home" means something much greater than it actually does. Perhaps if this is your goal, you should check your palm to see if it's your dream or someone else's. Sometimes people get larger homes than they need—or really want. You could save yourself a lot of disappointment down the line.

Building a Comfortable Nest

If your hand says that buying a home is what you want, and if your bank account says it's time, look under your Mercury to see if the time is right. This is where a cross, triangle, or square will appear if some negotiations are in the offing.

If you're thinking of building, these same markings will appear in your Neptune or lunar mount. These are the areas where you'll find your actual "nesting" instinct, and building your home really is feathering your own nest exactly as you want it.

If you're designing a more unusual home—remodeling a church, building underground, or creating a modified geodesic dome—your Uranus may well come into play as well.

A Place to Retreat

Nowhere is your desire for retreat and solitude more clearly shown than on your life line. Any branching inside the life line, in fact, shows a need to get away from it all.

When the branching in toward the Venus mount is clear and well-defined, you may well have taken this desire one step further, and purchased a cabin in the mountains, a place by the ocean—or a state-of-the-art RV.

Drop By Any Time

Of course, those life line branchings may go the other way, away from the Venus mount. This indicates a need for other people and for socialization. When your house is the place where everyone gets together, you'll find other influences as well.

First, there will be a strong Apollo—a love of entertaining and of people. You'll also exhibit a strong Jupiter, and enjoy having several things going at once. Lastly, your Mercury will show a knack for communication, for putting together the right mix of people as well as—sometimes, playing the matchmaker.

Job Security

Ten years ago, Lisa was a secretary. One day, she saw an ad in the paper for someone to teach computer basics at the local community college. To make a long story short, she got the job, realized she loved teaching, and went back to school so that she could teach writing, the first love she'd abandoned 20 years before because, according to everyone else, it "wasn't practical." Before she'd even gotten her MFA, she was teaching at a four-year college, as well as writing and publishing. She still types fast (you don't lose something like that), but now she's editing her own words instead of someone else's.

What's more important to you—job security or finding a job you love? Leaving the known is a scary, scary thing, especially if you haven't got a savings account (or relatives who do). But what if the company you've been with for 15 years transfers you halfway around the world when you just want to live with your wife in Des Moines? What can your palm tell you then?

The truth is that warning signs that it was time to part ways with this company have probably been appearing on your hand for some time. Maybe when you first decided to move back to Des Moines a cross appeared on your life line, or a branching line. Maybe a cross also appeared along your rising line to Saturn, or on your Saturn mount, indicating a problem with those in charge. (Maybe all your Tarot readings indicated this, too, but that's another *Complete Idiot's Guide*.)

Meanwhile, you and your wife were becoming more and more depressed. Your wife, a quick decision maker and a sometimes foolhardy risk taker, never would have gone overseas in the first place—but she would never have worked for the same company for 15 years, either. "You can do anything," she kept telling you. "And I make enough to support us." Both of these were true. And yet, something kept holding you back. What? The illusion of security.

Security Is an Illusion; Adaptability Is Survival

It doesn't matter where you work, what company you work for, what your job title is, or how much money you've made for the company you work for: Job security is an illusion. It doesn't matter if you love you job; keeping it, unless you own the store (and sometimes even if you do!), is not up to you.

When the man in our story finally told his boss he wanted to go home, the check for his Christmas bonus was cancelled, the boss refused to discuss the possibility of the man being transferred to another division in Des Moines, and 15 years of great work went right out the window. Ah, gratitude. Ah, the illusion of security.

BUT. Here's what happened next: The man went home. Within a week, he'd found a job using all his project-management and troubleshooting skills. Yes, he took a pay cut. But he also went home for dinner every night, formed a band now that he was living in one place (he hadn't been able to keep up with his piano while traveling with his job), and he got to sleep with his wife.

Adaptability is survival. Sometimes, you have to take a risk to get to what you want.

There Are People Who Love Their Jobs

Lisa loves her job. Robin loves his job. So there are two of us right off the bat. We both make a living doing what we love, although we have different criteria for what "making a living" means. Lisa can pay her mortgage and her bills with what she makes, plus keep a healthy savings account; Robin can pay his rent on time, buy another decent used car whenever his current one finally dies, and keep his many pets in food and water.

This is not to say that there aren't days when Lisa wishes her computer would blow up and her deadlines would disappear. Nor is it to say that Robin has days when he doesn't care if he ever sees another palm. We're human just like you—and no one loves his or her job *all* the time.

But you can find a job you love most of the time. It's in your hands.

Finding Your Job Potential in Your Hand

Just because your mounts or lines show a specific career potential doesn't mean you'll have the guts, luck—or time—to move ahead with it. There is, however, more than one career in every hand. Finding the job potential in your hand means looking at your hand often, and noting where changes, especially markings, occur.

Crosses, triangles, and stars are good indications of something coming, and where these markings appear can reveal career potentials as well. Which mount is marked can indicate which career might work for you.

Area of Influence	Job Potential
Saturn	Anything in a bureaucracy or large organization
Mercury	Sales, business accountant, researcher, teacher, medicine, writer
Jupiter	Veterinarian, CEO, self-employed
Moon	Therapist, counselor, or anything where you use your imagination
Apollo	The arts

The People in Your Life

What do the people in your life have to do with happiness? You already know the answer to this question. From the true love you haven't yet found to the coworker or neighbor whose life mission seems to be to drive you crazy, your interactions with others can make or break not only your day, but how you view everything else.

Whether you seem to repeatedly make the same bad choice of lover or friend, or your parents or children can't seem to make a decision without you, the people in your life appear in your hand in a variety of ways. Once you understand the ways that others can make you happy, you can work *with* the people in your life, instead of against them.

Ruts and Circles: Finding and Breaking Patterns

You may recall from Chapter 11 that a fixation on a certain type of person can be found in various rising and falling lines from the heart line. Do you tend to try to fix those who are "broken" in some way? Chances are there's a rising line to Apollo. Maybe the tendency is for healing others: This would be found in a rising line to Mercury. Or, if there's a love of anyone in uniform, the rising line will be to Saturn.

While falling lines from the heart line can indicate whether you'll prefer your closest companionships with your own gender or those of the opposite sex, dips can indicate you'll be more practical in particular areas. Similarly, squares and ovals can involve protection from your own worst interests, and so you could actually think of these markings as signals for finding and breaking patterns.

But you don't need a mark to reveal where your inclinations lie: The very existence of the rising line off the heart line is enough to indicate a pattern. Now, if you like dating washer repair people (because your rising line to Saturn says you love uniforms), you probably don't need to break the pattern. If, however, you're breaking your washer just to meet them, that's another story.

Helping Hands

If your sibling's also your business partner, you may find him or her under Mercury. If your spouse is your business partner, a square may appear on Jupiter as well.

Friends, Lovers, Brothers, Others

Everyone's on your hand: your mother, father, lover, brother, boss, neighbor, milkman (do people still have milkmen?), doorman. Once you know which relationship is which, you can also note if any markings are signaling that there's something you should be paying attention to there.

Here's a simple guide to who's who on your hand.

Who	Where You'll Find Them
Mother	Red or pink line on lunar mount
Father	Branching on mount of Saturn
Sister	Pluto toward lunar mount
Brother	Pluto toward Venus mount
Husband	Rising line from lunar mount to Saturn or lower Apollo; also, relationship line on Mercury
Wife	Cross on Apollo, relationship line on Mercury
Female child	Rising line from relationship line away from Apollo
Male child	Rising line from relationship line toward Apollo
Lover	Color of heart line, intensity of Jupiter, cross on Apollo low in hand
Grandmother	Deep in lunar mount
Grandfather	On Saturn line at bottom of hand, or branching on mount of Saturn similar to father
Cousin	Above lunar mount, depending on relationship
Neighbor	Color tone on life line, or coming to Saturn line from life line
Boss	On Saturn line
Coworker	On Saturn line or, if more personal, on life line side toward Saturn

Lord, I Was Born a Ramblin' Man...

And then there are those for whom the grass always looks greener on the other side. Is wanderlust in your blood? Or do you just need a vacation every six months or so to give you the adrenaline boost you need? Do you travel as a career or does the idea of leaving the house make you weak in the knees?

How you feel about being a ramblin' man (or woman) may be a key to your happiness. This is one of the areas that's easy to study in the palm, and yet it's one that's often ignored by counselors and therapists. Let's find out if your happiness depends on an island, boat, or journey, or if you've got wanderlust as a disease.

Islands, Boats, and Journeys

The curve of your life line will show whether wanderlust is in your blood. If your life line hugs your thumb, you're someone who prefers to stay closer to home, while a widely arcing life line is a sure sign of the ramblin' man.

Helping Hands

There are people with wanderlust in the blood who never leave home. A good example of this can be found in Anne Tyler's *The Accidental Tourist* (Berkeley, 1998), whose protagonist writes travel books for the armchair traveler—including himself.

Then there are "travel lines." These appear as fine lines perpendicular to the life line. They don't necessarily cross it, and, perhaps more importantly, they show possibilities rather than actual journeys. If you've got lots of travel lines, though, you do have wanderlust in the blood.

It's important to note that if you travel for a living, you may well have no travel lines in your hand. Remember, "business as usual" won't appear as a marking—it's the unusual that will show up.

Wanderlust as Disease

Let's take the word apart: Dis-ease. That's right. "Dis-ease" means "lack of ease." And what has this chapter been about? The pursuit of happiness.

There are those who believe that if things aren't working out here, it's time to pack up and move there. Or go there. Or run away to there. Running away will never appear as a triangle on your hand—because running away is not the way to approach and solve your problems.

Instead of running away, the next time something seems insurmountable, use your hand to find your strengths. Whether it's a strong thumb or a great imagination, the tools for turning your "dis-ease" into "ease" are in your hands for you to use.

Ask Your Palm About Happiness

So you want to know what will make you happy. Go ahead. Ask your palm. What career would you love? What kind of home? What friends? Travel or homebody? Your happiness can be found in the palm of your hand!

The Least You Need to Know

➤ Happiness is different for everyone.

➤ It's important to have goals and desires.

➤ The emphases in your hand can show you where your happiness lies.

➤ Whether you need travel or prefer to stay closer to home is written in your life line.

Part 6
The Bigger Picture

The future of a generation is in everyone's hands—and we can all make a difference in our own way, once we know our strengths and weaknesses. We'll look at a hand from Leonardo da Vinci's generation—and then you can compare that hand to your own. Reading palms is about more than just you—it's about your place in your world and your interaction with those around you.

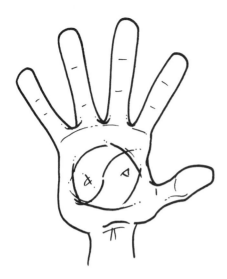

Chapter 24

Learning to See the Gestalt: The Whole Picture

In This Chapter

➤ Looking at the whole hand to see the bigger picture

➤ Finding what's dominant in your own hands

➤ Using your intuition to read your palm

➤ Learning to read your own warning signs

We've given you the tools, now it's up to you to use them. In this chapter, we're going to show you what to do the first time you encounter someone's hand, including looking at the whole hand, finding what's dominant, and encouraging people to seek and live up to their potentials.

Most palmistry books stop here and say, "The rest is up to you." But we know there's a lot more to reading palms than just book learning, so, in this chapter, we'll let you in on some of Robin's inside secrets.

How to Look at the Whole Hand

In Part 1 of this book, we introduced you to the concept of the self as macrocosm and the hand as microcosm. We've come full circle now: We've explored every aspect of the microcosm of the hand, from the fingers to the various marks, so it's time to return to the macrocosm of the self.

The first time you look at someone's hand, look at the whole hand. This isn't as easy as it sounds: You'll be tempted to notice the fingers, the lines, which mounts are strongest. It may help if you think about those "Magic Eye" drawings that look like nothing at first, but which, as you stare at them, suddenly assume some form (of course, some of us have never been able to find the tiger in the forest in those things).

When you first look at a hand, take this same kind of mental stepping back and just look. Here's where your intuition's going to come into play, as well as your powers of seeing. Don't look for the obvious or the dramatic: Just look at the big picture.

Some of the things you might notice as you do this include:

➤ How many or how few lines the hand has

➤ How strong or how weak the mounts are

➤ How long or short one or more fingers are

➤ Whether the thumb hugs the fingers or leans far from them

➤ Whether the hand is relaxed or tense

➤ The color of the hand

Then listen to your inner voice, your intuition, and go with what it tells you.

Hand-le with Care

Your first impression of a hand is the most important one. Just as you get used to looking at the street where you live and so don't notice it holistically anymore, the more you look at a hand, the less likely you are to see its gestalt, the whole picture, as well. That's why you should take your time at this point.

Being Systematic

First, let's be realistic. Your first attempt to cook an egg over easy probably had a broken yolk, right? Just as you have to crawl before you can walk (or run), you have to start out slowly when you're learning to read palms.

Second, be aware that your friends' and relatives' palms, while your obvious first choices for first readings, will also be subject to your preconceived truths, family myths, and personal prejudices (both pro and con), just as your own palm is. Still, these people are good ones to start with. Just be sure to let them know you're a beginner!

Okay. Ready? Take a deep breath. Take a good look—at both hands. What do you see first?

Handy by Design

A long and gracefully curved head line? A branching from the life line? Take another deep breath. Look again. *Every hand has several strong and positive points. Every hand.*

Here are some things that Robin commonly checks and notices first:

➤ Check for thumb stiffness.

➤ Look at the angle of generosity.

➤ See the heart line and look at the idealism (or lack of it).

➤ Check the fingertips.

➤ Look at the mounts, especially Venus and the Moon.

Now comes the big step. Ask your intuition. Hopefully, before this big moment, you and your intuition have had a long talk or two. You've tried to acknowledge your own limitations and shortcomings, too, because your intuition will be limited by your prejudices. Still, it's the best compass you have to read the map of the hand.

After you've discussed what you've noticed first, look yet again. Think of it as peeling away one layer of the onion and looking deeper. Maybe you noted a line in the lunar mount as a rising influence of the mother's attention. Your second look makes you read it as a potential for kidney infection. Both of these interpretations are there—the hand is as complex as the person it belongs to.

Helping Hands

Just as the experienced horse person sees more in a horse in 30 seconds than the rest of us may ever see, so the experienced palm reader sees more in every palm. Robin's looked at thousands of palms, so he quickly sees things that will take you at least 100 tries to see.

Helping Hands

Your intuition is your compass to the map of the hand. Honing it—and making it available on demand—is one of the great unsung skills of the best palm readers. Learn more about intuition by reading *The Complete Idiot's Guide to Being Psychic* (Alpha Books, 1999).

One of the most important lessons of palm reading (or, for that matter, of life) is that it's okay to say, "I don't know." It will take at least a hundred hands before you feel at all self-assured about reading palms, and at least that many, too, before you know which questions to ask. Encouraging dialogue, in fact, is one of the keys to a good reading.

Hand-le with Care

What if you said, "Your active Mars shows both courage and temper," and then see in the life line and Saturn a desire to retreat. Don't let seeming contradictions like this confuse you: Chances are, they're aspects of internal conflict and that's how they should be read.

We Gotta Hand It to You

Here's an example: Jack wants to know if he'll be working for the bank or for the university loan office. Robin would first look to see if Jack has a Mercury peak toward service or education. If he doesn't, Robin would tell him the bank seemed more likely. Still, Robin might use a pendulum (which we discussed in Chapter 3), or a tarot deck to help clarify this "close one." After all, both are fiscal organizations that are large and faceless, and both are cogs in the wheel—and so will have similar manifestations in the hand.

Encouraging Dialogue

If someone's asked to have her palm read in the first place, chances are she'll be eager to tell you who's who and what's what on her hand. "Oh, that must be the woman at the next desk," she'll explain when you note a conflict at the office. Or she'll tell you that yes, she did fall off a ladder last year and break her foot.

You should encourage people to ask other questions as well, and when they do, you should look in all areas pertinent to the question before you answer. In fact, a second look may well be necessary to find the whole answer, or the answer may not yet be in the hand. If this is the case, don't try to find one that doesn't exist.

You should ask questions, too, such as whether the person has moved in the last year or if there's a major job change planned. These questions will help you determine what a branching off a rising line might mean.

It's important to remember that everything in the hand is a product of a choice, some of which may be karmic choices. Yes, people will do the unexpected, but even the unexpected is a choice. In this context, it's truly amazing that you'll get things right when you're reading a palm—but you will. And you'll be right more and more often, the more palms you read.

What's Dominant?

Using the guidelines we've just provided, it's time to test your palm reading skills. Here are three sample hands for you to study. Take a look at each one and then list what's dominant in each hand. No fair looking ahead!

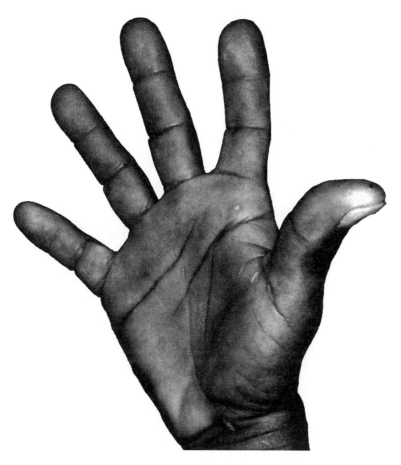

Sample hand #1.

Dominant characteristics:

1. _____
2. _____
3. _____
4. _____
5. _____

Sample hand #2.

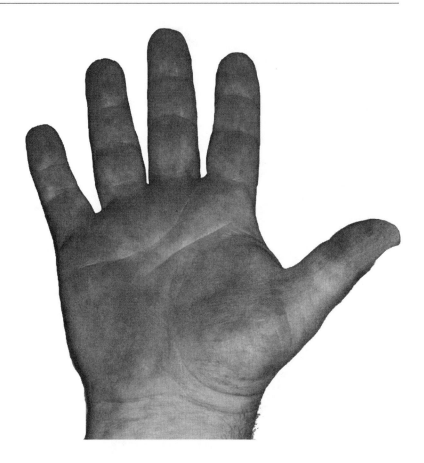

Dominant characteristics:

1. _____
2. _____
3. _____
4. _____
5. _____

Sample hand #3.

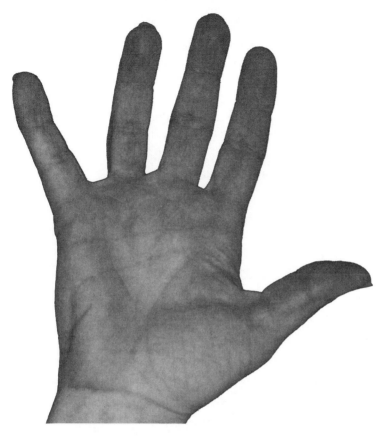

Dominant characteristics:

1. _____
2. _____
3. _____
4. _____
5. _____

Determining Dominance

Now, we're going to look at each of these sample hands and tell you what we believe is dominant. We'll list more than five items for each sample because in each case, there's room for more than one interpretation.

See if your discoveries match ours. Where they don't, go back and decide what it is that made you decide a certain characteristic is dominant. If you still believe you're right, you probably have a point. If you believe we're wrong, though, you may just be stubborn.

In sample hand #1, the following aspects are dominant:

➤ Strong, simple, deep lines
➤ Lack of modifying lines
➤ Strong and stubborn thumb
➤ Head line not long
➤ Low upper Venus
➤ Elemental hand shape
➤ Short life line
➤ Saturn-oriented heart line
➤ Short, impulsive fingers
➤ Pluto activity regarding brother

In sample hand #2, the following aspects are dominant:

➤ Strong lunar and Venus mount activity
➤ Heavily accentuated lunar mount for intuition
➤ Well-scribed lines
➤ Eccentric Mercury
➤ Low-set thumb
➤ Mottled appearance (emotionalism)
➤ Branching Saturn/Jupiter heart line
➤ Short life line

In sample hand #3, the following aspects are dominant:

➤ Amazingly rich (that is, full and well-marked) mounts
➤ Markings on Apollo, including the Mark of the Historian
➤ Strong Mercury line
➤ Strong Mercury mount activity
➤ Head line very, very long

➤ Strong Saturn line

➤ Eccentric Mercury

➤ Active Mars unusually strong for a woman

It's Better to Be Lucky Than Good

As you look at someone's hand, you're going to notice some bad along with the good. How do you deliver that news? While it's important to warn people of possible problems or roadblocks, there are ways of phrasing such things without scaring the living bejesus out of them. After all, what you're seeing is a possibility, not an absolute.

Here are some things you might see in the hand, and good ways of phrasing their appearance to their holders:

➤ *A star on Apollo.* "You have the potential for great success in your creative endeavors, but take your time and don't forget your old friends along the way."

➤ *A grid on Jupiter.* "Now might be a good time to pay a visit to your dentist for a routine checkup."

We Gotta Hand It to You

You can temper almost any bad news—and maybe even turn it into good news. You might see some kind of car trouble on the mount of Mercury, and suggest the person not buy the first car he sees or that he should be careful when he's driving back to school. Or, if you see a grid below Apollo, you may suggest that the couple plan a long engagement. Both of these suggestions can save the person from future difficulties.

➤ *A chained heart line.* "Your love life is not without its ups and downs. But look at how strong the *chi* of your life line is—you have the strength to face anything."

➤ *A cross on the Saturn line.* "There's the possibility of some difficulties with a person of authority, but this can work in your favor if you think things through."

The Hand as Life Path and True Destination

In Parts 1 and 5 of this book, we talked about how archetype and myth can help you understand yourself and the society you live in, and gave you some examples of contemporary myths. In this section, we'd like to bring that concept full circle, and have you use archetype and myth to explore your own life path and true destination.

For this exercise, you'll first need to come up with a situation in your own life you'd like to explore. Is there a situation in your workplace you'd like to analyze using your palm? Or are you facing a personal decision in the near future? The best situations for this exercise are those involving a group of people).

So, what's your situation? Start by giving it a title:

Risk Takers and Security Seekers

Who are the archetypal characters in your situation? Let's say it's a job question. You'll be the hero or heroine, while your immediate superior may be either the villain or the mentor, depending on the situation.

The Hero or Heroine: _____

The Villain: _____

The Trickster: _____

The Friend or Helper: _____

The Mentor: _____

The Innocent: _____

Now we're going to find each of these characters in your palm. For example, if the hero or heroine is yourself (which is probably the case), you'll find this particular moment in time on your life line.

The villain of the piece is going to appear as a grid, black dot, horizontal line, or other energy working at cross-purposes to you in the area where the blockage is taking place. Is there a problem at work? Look along the rising line to Saturn? Is there a problem at home? Try the lunar or Venus mounts.

The other characters will often appear as crosses in your hand, people who will either help you toward your goal or seem to stand in your way. Now that you understand what appears where on your hand's map, though, you'll probably have no problem finding where these folks stand.

Dependence and Independence

The second part of this exercise involves your journey toward your goal. You may recall the hero's journey that we discussed in Chapter 2—no matter what your decision, your journey will cover a similar archetypal path.

Here are the steps of the hero's journey. Use these spaces to fill in the metaphorical steps of your own situation. If you haven't yet arrived at a particular step, go ahead and fill in some possibilities: The more, in fact, the better. It's likely that you'll encounter more than a "roadblock" on any journey.

The call: _____

The initial refusal: _____

The help of a wise advisor: _____

The entrance to the "other world": _____

Meeting the enemy: _____

Destroying the enemy: _____

Returning to one's home, victorious: _____

In order to illustrate how this might work, let's use the example of a couple who's decided to build a new home. We've filled in the blanks for them, so that you can see how this particular situation fits into the hero's journey.

➤ The call: *We call the architect and meet to discuss house plans.*

➤ The initial refusal: *We don't like his first plans. Should we get another architect? Should we not build at all? Should we meet with him and discuss our differences?*

➤ The help of a wise advisor: *Sam at the bank says Tom's a great architect, and encourages us to let Tom know what our misgivings about the initial plans are. We do, and mention to Tom that Sam suggested it. Tom's pleased. So are we, with the revised plans.*

➤ The entrance to the "other world": *Plans approved. Loan approved. Contractor selected. Ground broken. Oh no! We're committed!*

➤ Meeting the enemy: *Great-grandma's breakfront isn't going to fit in the media room. Do we tear that wall out? These windows don't look at all like how we pictured them. Can we install others instead? The contractor wants us to decide where we want the outlets NOW.*

➤ Destroying the enemy: *Okay, we'll put the breakfront in the guest room. We can't afford other windows—we'll get used to these. We walk through and decide where we'll need outlets.*

➤ Returning to one's home, victorious: *It's finished! We've moved in. We still haven't found the best place for great-grandma's breakfront, but the views are spectacular, and the house is more than we ever imagined it would be.*

You can see that you can use this template to turn any situation into a hero's journey. And you can use your palm along the way as well. Each of these steps will appear as a cross on your palm (as well as your spouse's, if you're in this together). And, if you, too, are building a home, it's going to appear on your mount of Neptune.

> **Helping Hands**
>
> No situation is without its ups and downs, pitfalls and triumphs, joy and sadness. Using the hero's journey to plot your course can help you deal with the downs, pitfalls, and sadness without the trip turning into a disaster.

Encouraging Potential

It's simple to stick with the status quo, to do the same thing, eat the same thing, even say the same thing every day, but it's not terribly interesting or life-affirming. When it comes to stepping out and trying new things, though, most of us are just a little scared.

As Franklin Delano Roosevelt said, "There's nothing to fear but fear itself," and this especially applies to the potential in your own hand, and in others' hands. It's one thing to say, "I could be a painter if only..." and quite another to say, "I'm going to be a painter."

But how do you encourage potential without letting the fear take over? The answer, not surprisingly, is right there in the palm. In the case of the potential painter, you might point out the strong rising line to Apollo, coupled with the distinctively pointed Apollo fingertip. Or, if someone is thinking of leaving her clerical job to become a doctor, you might point out how strong her medical stigmata already is.

As a palm reader, you must point out the potential pitfalls as well as the eventual glory. If you see a possible delay crossing someone's Jupiter mount, let him know. But let him know, too, that the delay is only a setback, and that he can be all that his potential suggests. Show him where his future is in his hands.

The Gestalt of Your Hands

The gestalt of your hands is the equivalent of your big picture. It involves adding together everything you've learned about your hands to draw the bigger picture of who you are. It's here you add your long first phalange of Mercury to your rising line to Apollo and discover that you really do have a talent for the written word. It's here you connect your deeply channeled life line to your strong passive Mars and understand where your inner strength comes from.

Gestalt is a school of psychology that originated in Germany with psychologists Fritz Perls, Kurt Lewin, and Wolfgang Köhler. Gestalt therapy takes a look at what we do and think and considers all of our thoughts, actions, and habits in the context of our "whole" self. In fact, *gestalt* is a German word meaning "shape" or "form." Dreams are often the subject of gestalt analysis, as they are believed to represent a hidden or disowned part of our conscious personalities that needs to be understood and integrated into our waking experiences.

Studying your dreams and studying your palms are both methods for exploring the gestalt of your self; each is a powerful metaphor for revealing your whole nature.

Finding the gestalt of your hands is a curious combination of arithmetic and holistic understanding. It's adding seemingly unconnected aspects together to arrive at some larger whole. As human beings, we're complex and ever evolving. With the maps of our hands to guide us, we can also understand how we work.

The Least You Need to Know

➤ When reading a palm, look at the whole hand first.

➤ Have a system of reading palms and use your intuition.

➤ Reading the warning signs doesn't have to be dangerous.

➤ You can use archetype and myth to understand your own situations.

➤ Encouraging potential is your responsibility.

➤ The map of your hand is a portrait of your gestalt.

Turning Self-Sabotage into Self-Fulfillment

Who's the villain in your story? Is it possible that you're the one standing in your own way? Can you find the stumbling blocks in your hand and turn them into places to leap from instead?

We may blame others, but most of the time, what happens to us is in our own hands. If it seems as if you get to a certain "door" over and over and never move beyond it, the person with the key to that door may well be yourself. In this chapter, you'll learn how to uncover the self-sabotage in your hand—and turn it into self-fulfillment instead.

Who's Hurting Whom?

Let's go back to Mars—active Mars, passive Mars, and the plain of Mars—and see if you're your own worst enemy. First, let's review these three mounts:

➤ Active Mars: your temperament and your temper

➤ Passive Mars: your self-assuredness

➤ Plain of Mars: how you deal with slights (and not-so-slights)

Helping Hands

A very good way to build up your self-esteem is to take a look at the hand of the person you believe is making you feel inferior. Chances are, the feeling of inferiority is coming from your passive Mars—not from a superiority anywhere in the other person's hand. We truly are our own worst enemies.

You may think that taking a swing at whomever angers you hurts them more than it does you, but the truth is that in the long run you'll be left with no one to swing at—or worse, in jail where people are swinging with far more than their fists. If you know you have an inflated active Mars, you can look for warning signs and channel your anger in more constructive directions.

If, on the other hand, your active Mars is deflated, you may have passive-aggressive tendencies. This can mean you'll let people walk all over you for far too long and then suddenly reach the end of your rope and blow up. These blowups don't have to catch you by surprise, though—a red line, star, or blue dot can alert you to the build-up before it reaches the point of no return.

Passive Mars, the area of your self-assuredness, is so often not accented these days that we wonder if we've become a society of people with low self-esteem. If the self-help section of the bookstore's any indication, this may in fact be the case.

What makes a person self-assured? How can you inflate your passive Mars and make yourself more resistant to the unreasonable demands of others? We'd suggest taking a look at your hand, and then listing its strengths. Every hand has strengths, and finding yours will remind you of the areas where you shine.

The next time you're feeling like someone's doormat, instead of taking it lying down, remember where you're strong. Do you have a good sense of humor? Diffuse the situation with a joke. Are you a responsible Saturn sort? Remind her what the rules are.

One last Martian territory to explore is the proving ground of your plain of Mars. Envy and revenge are ultimately expensive propositions—especially to yourself. Remember, "living well is the best revenge." Keep a vengeance notebook, make lists of who's pissing you off—but confine it to your plain of Mars, rather than let it spill into your active life.

Standing in Your Own Way

Can your belief system limit you? Yes, almost always. That's because any belief system you have carries with it a set of givens that you believe can't be changed or challenged. Whether you believe that breaking a mirror brings you seven years' bad luck or that God created the world in seven days and forget about the theory of evolution, any challenge to your belief system is a challenge to your self-image. And that in turn leads to a fear of change.

Now, hand in hand with this is the picture you have of yourself. Do you see yourself as someone so devoted to your company that the thought of making a change, even one that might bring you a higher salary, makes you weak in the knees? Do you see yourself as the life of the party—and force yourself to act that way, even when you don't feel like it?

If your head line's straight, your life line hugs your thumb, and your thumb is rigid and high-set, any change will be difficult for you. But for the vast majority of us who don't share all three of those characteristics, the possibility of change should be looked at as an opportunity rather than something scary.

Next time you're faced with something you think you can't do, examine why you feel that way. Does your stubborn thumb stand in your way? Or is it your straight dogmatic head line? You can learn to use what you have to your advantage, instead of allowing it to stand in your way. Try it and see.

Karmic Signposts

Karmic signposts are all over your hands, whether as dermatoglyphics, triangles, or sister lines to the life line. When you've got good karma on your side, you have the strength to climb every mountain and ford every stream. And you don't even have to sit through *The Sound of Music* to do it.

First of all, there's the karmic courage of whorls. Anywhere these marking appears, you'll have the strength to face adversity—even though it may not be easy. If these whorls hook loops, they indicate lessons you'll have to learn—but you can learn them at your own pace. Bull's-eyes can show you've already done a lot of work—and the more bull's-eyes you have, the more karmatically blessed you are. Of course, bull's-eyes can mean you'll be given more karmic work to do, too, but you *will* come through it, and much stronger every time.

Next, there's the assistance that can come from shapes like squares and triangles we discussed in Chapter 16. Squares will enclose otherwise difficult energy, and help you get through the tough times. Triangles are karmic tools for advancement, whether it's a raise or a shovel you need.

Lastly, there's the sister line to the life line. This parallel line is considered a karmic support system, a spiritual "something to lean on," no matter how tough the going gets.

Hand-le with Care

Note that none of these karmic signposts mean you'll avoid the bad times. They'll just help you get through them. Karmic signposts are the marks of the survivor. If you've got them, you know who you are.

Where to Look for Signs of Self-Sabotage

As an example of self-sabotage, we have the story that Robin likes to call the "black widow." Margaret's first husband died on their first anniversary—in combat in Vietnam. Her second husband disappeared after a month of marriage, possibly due to some bad debts to some "independent lending institutions." He appeared in Margaret's hand as a cross under Saturn in a dark spot. By the time she'd met her third potential husband, her guilt over the first two was a tangible thing: She truly believed men who loved her couldn't survive. True to her belief, this man died a week before their marriage—in a spontaneous car race on a country road.

Now, Margaret's head line descended well into the lunar mount, which meant she couldn't always differentiate between her imagination and her reality. In addition, her plain of Mars was both narrow and well marked, indicating a great deal of superstition.

What eventually saved Margaret was the self-reliance evidenced by her strong, high-set thumb. She'd never let go of her first husband (which was indicated by dots on her heart line), and she'd punished herself by selecting two other husbands she knew had very dangerous lifestyles. Once Margaret became aware of the self-destructive pattern she'd set for herself, she was able to break away and marry a man who didn't drive fast cars, wasn't drawn to combat in the military, and had no shady connections.

Once you acknowledge your self-destructive patterns, in other words, you have the power to change them. But where do you look for self-sabotage?

Signs Along the Head Line

Obstinacy begins in the head, and whether it's the foolhardiness of a head line that starts inside the mount of Jupiter or the rigidity of a straight head line, signs along the head line are guideposts to those who are standing in their own way.

The length of the head line alone can point to self-sabotage: When it approaches the percussion of the hand, you may be so consumed by details that you can't see the bigger picture at all. People like this who "can't see the forest for the trees" might do well setting alarms for themselves to keep from getting lost among the details.

A straight head line can indicate extreme focus, but along with that focus can come rigidity and a refusal to compromise. People with straight head lines are unyielding in the extreme, and will have a personal certainty that they're correct—and everyone else is wrong.

Head lines that descend toward the lunar mount pose the opposite extreme: the vivid imagination. This particular method of self-sabotage involves always assuming the worst, and, at its worst, belongs to someone whose obsessions alienate even those who care about him. A head line that descends into the lunar mount just "knows" things will never get better.

Hand-le with Care

Other signs of potential obsession include dips, dots, and dark spots on the head line. If you lie awake at night, going over and over what you "should have said"—or possible scenarios for confrontations that haven't occurred yet—you should pay close attention to these warning signs. As you know, the reality is rarely as bad as what you've obsessed about.

It's a Mad, Mad Mount of the Moon

As we've already mentioned, if the head line descends into the mount of the Moon, there's a vivid imagination at work. But even with a head line presence, the lunar mount is the area of your emotional life, and so is bound to have its ups and downs.

Nearly everyone is sad sometimes, but it's on the lunar mount that you'll find the capacity for chronic depression, or "the habit of sadness." A dark shading or a series of horizontal lines can be signs of chronic depression—or mineral deficiency (which can be corrected with lifelong mineral supplements). If the head line is also wavy, the distinct pattern of ups and downs can indicate manic depression or bipolar disorder.

Helping Hands

Just as they are in other areas of the palm, marks on the lunar mount can be warning signs of problems to come. A grille may warn of gastritis, weak stomach, too many fluids, kidney, bladder, or prostate problems, or pending exhaustion, while a blue or black dot may point to a lack of energy or weakness. Pay attention to marks on your lunar mount, and cut off the bad energy before it gets out of hand.

Two places to look for trouble signs in the lunar mount are in the second and third realms. If the second realm is highest, you may be obsessing about an emotional issue, while if the third is emphasized, your obsessions may be spilling over into your health.

Criminal Behavior

There are those who believe that the potential for criminal behavior exists in all of us, but this idea also depends on what your definition of "criminal behavior" is. Do you count every little white lie, or do you believe fibbing is criminal only when it's perjury?

Whether or not we're all potentially larcenous, you can find potentials for criminal behavior in the hand. When criminal behavior is a given, though, is harder to pin down; perhaps it's when all of these aspects appear in the hand. But, even then, some saving grace can keep the person from crossing over to the wrong side of the law.

Sign	Possible Manifestation
Long, Saturn-leaning Mercury finger	Dishonesty
Short Mercury finger, bent to percussion	Need to screw things up, potential for sabotage
"Murderer's thumb"	Loss of personal control
Saturn-oriented heart line	Law obsession, litigious
Inflated or well-marked lunar mount	Delusion, moody inconsistency, not good to word
Deflated or unmarked lunar mount	Lack of emotion or passion of satisfaction
Plain of Mars emphasis	Tendency to plot revenge, too much attention to past
Waisted thumb	Too much thought with cold calculation, no acceptance of common human bond

Now, notice that no one can possibly have all of these configurations. Your lunar mount can't be both emphasized and deficient, nor can your Mercury be both long and short. The important thing to remember about potential criminal behavior is that the power to change it is also in your hands—so look for those saving graces as well.

Sex Is Not So Simple

Whoever said sex was simple? We've already mentioned that old joke, "She expected sex every day!" versus "He wanted sex only once a day!" There are a number of things to consider when it comes to sex: compatibility, obsession, and deviance.

Compatibility's the easy one: Check both heart lines for coherence, and see if either of you has a Via Lascivia. You can also look to the mounts of Venus and the Moon for further corroboration, if you aren't sure about the heart line compatibility.

The potential for sexual obsession occurs when the Via Lascivia is a dominant line in the hand—even stronger than the heart line. If this configuration exists, it may be best met by someone with a similar Via Lascivia.

And then there's sexual deviance. Of course, we hasten to add, one person's deviance is another person's pleasure. If no one's getting hurt in the process and there are two consenting adults, perhaps the key is finding that other consenting adult. Can you find this in the hand? This may show up as a Venus-Mars line inside the life line, which is probably a bit broken.

If your pleasure involves whips and chains, look for an obsessively long head line, some waisting on the thumb, an extremely understated passive Mars and some Apollo activity—for the acting out this requires! There may also be some black dots on the Venus mount.

Remember, though, what's "extreme" for some is the norm for others. Ultimately, whether the second set of sheets is satin or rubber is entirely up to the couple who's making the bed.

Is It Sex or Is It Love?

Sex is about lust, and will manifest as a red dot on the heart line. Love is about much more—companionship, devotion, caring, and yes, sex as well—so it will be located in more areas of the hand and in more ways.

Ideally, nearly all of the following signs should be present in the early stages of the relationship to equal love:

➤ Mounts of Venus equally broad or narrow

➤ Lunar mounts equally emphasized

➤ Equal or similar thumbs

➤ Both head lines with some similar configurations

➤ Both heart lines with some similar configurations

➤ Similar emphases in the fingers

➤ Similar emphases in the mounts of the fingers

➤ Similar tastes in which phalanges are long or full

Helping Hands

It's worth noting that if a couple is meant to be together, there's no power on heaven or earth that can keep them apart!

Looking for Love in All the Wrong Places

Remember, it's best to look for love in the head line and thumb, not the heart line. In addition, compatibility is best assessed in the thumb and fingers, where similar tastes and needs will be found. Remember, too, that love doesn't "make sense": It's emotional, not rational, and so can't be measured with a mental yardstick.

If you love Puccini and she'd never miss Garth Brooks when he swings into town, all is not lost. Maybe you both share a passion for pedigreed Bull Mastiffs (found on your mount of Jupiter) or never miss an episode of *Law and Order* (which may well show up on your mounts of Saturn *and* Apollo). Her down-to-earth practicality may temper your vivid imagination, or her handiness with tools may help with your tendency to break things.

Hand-le with Care

While some of your emotional needs and tastes can be met outside your primary relation-ship, your heart lines should still be companionable in some way for your relationship to be strong and long lasting.

Love is all over both of your hands—it's what's most important to each of you that's important to your relationship. You know where you can compromise and where you can't. Make sure you know where you both stand when it comes to children and child rearing, in fact, and you're three-quarters of the way there.

Handy Words to Know

Psychometry, a method of interpret-ing vibrations by feel, is a more dubious practice when it comes to reading the palm.

Psychometry and the Hand-Holding Palmist

It's time to talk about the "hand-holding" palmist, who uses *psychometry* while holding your hand. Psychometry's a way of reading vibrations by feeling rather than sight. It's Robin's belief that you should approach a palmist who "reads" your palm this way with a grain of salt and a gallon of trepidation.

Of course, touch is required to read a palm thoroughly, but constant hand holding isn't needed—or useful—for reading palms. A palm reader will check the texture and thickness of your skin, as well as your resilience. He may trace certain lines or point to certain markings. But, as we stated in Part 1 of this book, the most important tools for reading palms are sight and light—and the hand-holding palm reader makes use of neither. We won't discount psychometry's possibilities in other areas, but reading palms means "reading," not touching.

We'd like to add that Robin has used psychometry for other uses, such as determining the previous owners of antiques. In one case, he correctly "read" some beads he was handed as old and French, but they weren't French—the seller was! In another case, he read that a watch sent to him for a psychometric reading had belonged to a woman and a recluse, but it turned out that the medical connection he read was incorrect—the packing cotton had come from a hospital! Robin adds that the fresh energy of more recent owners is often much stronger than older energy, and so much easier to pick up.

Hand-le with Care

Your palm reader may well be psychic, but she can't close her eyes to read your palm. Any palm reader who professes to do so is a fraud. No ifs, ands, or buts. While she may be psychic, she's not a palmist.

Nobody Owns This Life But You

What's best for you? And who knows what's best for you? Your hand holds the answers to both of these questions—your potentials as well as your possible problems. Nothing in your hand is forever—it's up to you to take charge of your life and use those crosses of decision as helpers rather than hindrances.

Time after time, others will try to tell you what they think is best for you. Often, they'll truly think they do have your best interests at heart (especially if they're your parents). The truth is that nobody owns this life but you, and hard as it may often be, your future is in your hands.

Recognize the signs of self-sabotage and turn them to your advantage. Knowing where to find them ahead of time can help you become stronger, more self-assured, and yes, happier, in your life.

Signs of Self-Sabotage in Your Own Hand

Do you have the potential for self-sabotage in your hand? Chances are there are some problem areas you should be aware of. Whether it's an active Mars bad temper or a long head line tendency toward obsession, you can use this chapter to chart your own self-sabotage potential. As you go back through this chapter, make a note of your problem areas, and then chart new ways to stop stopping yourself.

The Least You Need to Know

➤ The only person ultimately hurt by your revenge is you.

➤ You don't have to stand in your own way.

➤ Sex and the potential for violence are in all of our hands.

➤ Beware of the hand-holding palm reader.

➤ Use your potentials to your advantage, not your detriment.

The Future of the World Is in All of Our Hands

Every generation has a story, and your hands will reflect the story of yours. Whether it's the idealism and cynicism of the baby boomers or the disillusionment and confusion of Gen-X'ers, a generation's future is in the hands of all of its constituents.

What this means is that we all have a hand in shaping our future. Whether you choose to join the Peace Corps or live a "life of quiet desperation," though, is entirely up to you. In this chapter, we'll look at how we each have a hand in the future.

We Move Toward a Story of Our Own Making

Whether it's buying Liberty Bonds or junk bonds, every generation moves toward a story of its own making. Individually, we define our lives by the fruits of our labors, but on a larger scale, our lives are defined by the fruits of *all* of our labors—no matter what their implications.

Do baby boomers want to be defined as a generation of people who would rather sue each other than try to work things out? This is but one contemporary issue—is it in our hands as well?

We can look at baby boomers' plain of Mars, active Mars, Saturn energy, and thumbs to help us understand how we got where we are, and where we can go from here. These days, most of us have heavily marked plains of Mars, expressing a memory for slights and insults and an energy for revenge, as well as a bad-tempered full active Mars. We're also sporting rigid, unyielding thumbs and a little too much judgmental Saturn, thinking that more laws might be the "answer."

Maybe what's called for is a little more compassion. Maybe it's time to let our thumbs' third phalanges take over for a while. How does your mount of Venus react to this idea? Perhaps more importantly, how does your active Mars take it? Why are so many so angry? Part of the answer is that our world is far different from the world of our parents and grandparents.

Helping Hands

One easily noticed generational difference can be found in the idea of what money's for. While baby boomers' third phalanges reveal their love of comfort and luxury, their parents' Saturn lines show a need for the security money can bring.

The Difference Between Our World and Theirs

For our (and by our, we mean Robin's and Lisa's and other baby boomers') grandparents, it was World War I. For our parents, it was World War II. For many of them, too, the Depression taught them to be satisfied with less. For us it was the Vietnam War, along with a decade of assassinations and upheaval none of us will ever forget, which resulted in unanswered questions, and an undercurrent of paranoid fear of government.

Are all generations defined by a war? Hopefully not. The jury's still out on what will be the defining history for the "Gen-X" generation. Perhaps it will be the Clinton impeachment trial, which, to our minds, would be far preferable to another world war.

What's the difference in each of these generations' hands, though? If war does define them, can we look to their Mars style and find all somewhat similar? Or can we look to their Jupiters to find their style of idealism, or to their mounts of Venus to explore the nature of their love?

The answer to all of these questions is "yes." A generation *is* defined by its hands—and its future is there as well.

The Future of a Generation Is in Its Hands

Documentation indicates that in 1914 England, palm readers were becoming more and more uncomfortable with what they were seeing in the hands of male youths: It appeared that half the young men of an entire generation were going to be lost. By 1918, this sad prediction had come true.

So what do palm readers see in the hands of the generations who are living today? Robin has looked at thousands of hands, and here are some of the patterns that he's noticed.

The WWII Generation

In the hands of those who lived through World War II, Robin's noticed a willingness to serve a cause or purpose, and the patience to pursue a goal. These people have realistic expectations for using the tools at hand, as well as a willingness to keep their secrets—and not confess them on national TV.

The hands of people from the WWII era have thicker skin, which is less inclined to bruise or be wounded. Their thumbs are lower set, too, because they were less specialized than we are today, and their low unmarked Apollo mounts show their lack of risk taking. If mothers from that era were our contemporaries, they'd have more Apollo— because they'd be in the band instead of the kitchen.

This generation also has very deep Saturn mounts and an understated Jupiter heart line configuration (in other words, it's not prominent). Uppermost in their hearts are material and security issues—and while theirs was a generation of *romantics*, they weren't *optimists*. Lunar head lines aren't common either because there wasn't much time to dream in those days.

The Baby Boomers

In the hands of the baby boomer generation, Robin's seen a certain idealism, tempered with both cynicism (crooked Mercury fingers) and resignation as they've grown older. This is shown in their Jupiter-tending heart lines, as well as the anti-authority eccentricity found in the Mercury (and other) fingers. In addition, the frayed lines on their Saturn mounts show both their bad backs and legal troubles.

Baby boomers' tendency to travel—and to move—shows up and down their life lines. Their shrewdness with money appears as extensive Mercury activity under and near the head line. And their very powerful Uranus mounts show their idealism, the role of the media in their lives, their interaction with electricity (they take it for granted), and the particular androgyny of their generation.

The Next Generation

The hands of Generation X show a high expectation for "how it's supposed to be." This is found in their high, rigid thumbs and short, straight head lines. In addition, their seemingly endless appetite for taking risks is based on the idea that they're impervious to injury.

You'll often find a star on Jupiter with a connecting line to the life line, which shows a tendency to drift mentally. Is this related to a childhood spent watching television? It's possible. Other manifestations of this TV generation can be found in their capacity for visual input—many of them, in fact, bear the visual talent marking of the Camera's Eye we discussed in Chapter 16. You'll also see Gen-X'ers with many branches on their head lines—that is, more than three—indicating a lack of mental discipline.

The libidos of this generation aren't terribly high, and their Venus mounts tend to be flat, and sometimes blue. You'll seldom see either a Girdle of Venus or a Via Lascivia. It seems the androgynous aspect of the parents' generation is moving to the next level.

A Lack of Catechism (We Are Responsible)

Television aside, it's highly unlikely that (a) we'll be rescued by Roma Downey of TV's *Touched by an Angel*; (b) we'll be invaded by aliens among us (or rescued by Scully or Mulder); or (c) we'll have the option of being "beamed up" (especially now that *Deep Space Nine* has been cancelled). Nor will anything in our life be tidily solved in the 23 or 48 minutes a typical television program spans.

There's nothing wrong with a little escapism now and then, so long as we bear in mind that we are responsible—that it's our choices that brought us to "here." In this late 20th/early 21st century, there's no handbook or catechism to teach us how to go about being responsible.

Each of us chooses his or her own way to make it through life, but there are some current fads that bear examination. Are they in our hands? Yes. And for that reason, it's worth examining their deeper meanings and implications.

Little Disasters

"Instant" television news is partly to blame for making little disasters everyone's disasters. Yes, disasters are tragic. Disasters are sad. Disasters are, well, disastrous. But years ago, one man's heartache didn't make the 6 o'clock news.

We've become a society fueled by disaster. The weather, which used to just happen every day, now becomes a major news story at least once a week—whether it's ice storms in Texas or drought in Iowa. Even a river flooding in China can headline the U.S. news. If you believe in global warming, then you'll agree with the position that humankind has achieved the power to alter the Earth's environment, perhaps profoundly affecting weather patterns (however unwittingly). It seems the weather just isn't as predictable as it used to be—and we're all feeling the consequences.

This tendency to focus on the negative appears in all of our hands as dips and dots on the heart line, and a flat lunar mount, Venus mount, or even Jupiter mount. "I don't care," these mounts are saying. "What I think isn't important."

This in turn is part of why we're so angry. Do we truly believe that what we do has no bearing on the bigger picture? And how might we change this perception, if it's so?

Once again, find your strengths. Can you write one hell of a letter to the editor? Can you write one hell of an *Idiot's Guide*? One thing we now do have the power to do is to send e-mails when we care about an issue. No matter what your method of voicing your opinion, though, it does matter. And we can make a difference. We *do* make a difference. Every day. If you're in doubt, just watch Frank Capra's *It's a Wonderful Life* just one more time.

Second Comings and Other Myths

If you sometimes think the world's going to hell in a handbasket, it's human nature to seek solace in the spiritual. Sometimes, though, it seems as if "rational" types are there to remind us that there is no God, that goddess cycles are New Age bunk, and palmistry is just one more misguided attempt to "explain" the unexplainable.

People's need to understand what's going on helps explain why certain "stories" seem to capture the mass imagination. It's comforting to believe in them—whether they're playing out a disaster scenario or a more hopeful one. These days, one such story is Y2K: Our computers crash; our utilities cease; our food supplies disappear; our airplanes fall out of the sky.

If you look at the hands of the doomsayers and stockpilers, you'll find similar configurations appeared in the hands of those who were building fallout shelters in the late 1950s and early 1960s. Remember them?

Hoarding itself appears as small branches from Saturn toward the life line, while the need to create excitement is found with a small curve in the head line along with a widely curving life line with a branching line as well. Those fallout-shelter people had rigidly strong Saturn lines, an aspect of their belief in their rightness—and we'd love to check the hands of some Y2K disaster folks for the same marking.

Hand-le with Care

Does anyone remember Edgar Cayce? He predicted all sorts of disasters. But those years have come and gone and few of his predictions—such as California (and Japan) falling into the ocean—came to pass. In other areas, such as health, we should add, his accuracy was uncanny.

We believe that we'd do far better to focus on the positive rather than the negative—the excitement and challenges of the new millennium. Let's look to the optimism and spiritual hope of our Jupiter mounts.

Still, it's interesting to wonder why a generation gets so caught up in its myths. We think the answer is a lack of catechism: Without a handbook, it's hard to know where to turn. But we do have our hands to guide us.

From Leonardo to You

Let's go back 500 years and take a look at some hands drawn by Leonardo da Vinci. This drawing, *Hands of Ginerva de' Benci c. 1474,* is a good illustration of what the hands of Leonardo's generation looked like. His famous painting, *The Mona Lisa,* shares the same characteristics.

These hands, drawn by Leonardo da Vinci, reflect both his genius and his generation. (Hands of Ginerva de' Benci c. 1474, *Leonardo da Vinci. Reprinted with permission of Royal Collection Enterprises Limited. Copyright© Her Majesty Queen Elizabeth II.)*

This drawing of hands reflects Leonardo's generation very well. Notice the strength in the long and conical thumb, as well as the strong active Mars, long third phalanges (for manipulating one's physical environment), and the equally long and pointed first phalanges for sensitivity.

What were some of the beliefs that were common during Leonardo's time? The hierarchy of society and the authority of city-states. The supremacy of the male—though a look at Ginerva de' Benci's or Mona Lisa's hands reveals that the genius of the generation was not limited to just one gender. Mona Lisa's mysterious smile may just reflect a bit of that self-awareness! The flatness of the world—around which the other planets revolved. No one had even thought of the speed of light, and if people were treated for illnesses, they sometimes were bled. Ugh!

History's full of episodes of fear, panic, eccentricity, and lack of grace—but it's also filled with episodes of hope, enlightenment, consensus, and epiphany. Perhaps it's time to find the hope in our hands. Perhaps it's time to compare our hands with Leonardo's generation—he was, after all, one of the greatest minds of the High Renaissance, or indeed, of any era. The artistry and scientific curiosity expressed through Leonardo's hands remain virtually unmatched throughout recorded human history. Until, maybe the 21st century? Stay tuned.

A Hand in the Future

Using Leonardo da Vinci's drawing as a guide, compare your own hand to the hands of the 15th-century High Renaissance. Sure, you can check for genius, but this exercise is as much about generational differences as it is about whether you can invent a better flying machine.

Next, compare your hand to someone else's of your generation. What you're looking for is your generation's tendencies in the hand, whether it's that Jupiterian idealism, Saturnian cynicism, Mercurial eccentricity and shrewdness, or something in between.

Here, for example, are the hands of two women, a grandmother born in 1909, and her granddaughter, born 50 years later in 1959. You can use these hands to begin your generational study, if you haven't got anyone else's handy.

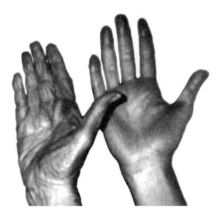

Now, if you wish, compare your hand to someone younger than yourself. This could be your child, your grandchild, or the kid you baby-sit for. How does that generation's heart line stack up? Is there hope for the future in his or her hand? Your child's hand is a mass of potential—and the future's yet to be seen.

A child's hand is all about possibilities. It's a picture of the child's true self, not the guidance (or battering) that life will manifest through the interaction of nature, nurture, and environment. In an infant's hand, Robin will see basics, but defined basics, either the leader or the follower, art and music, or mechanics and engineering.

Separating the Wheat From the Chaff

What's important? How do you separate the wheat from the chaff? When it comes to your hands, remember, we all have our strengths and our weaknesses.

What's strong? What do you have that you can use to your advantage? What's weak? And how do your strengths temper that weakness—or even turn it into an advantage?

Then, there's the hands of your generation. What are they trying to tell you—and all of us? Can we learn our lessons this time? Are we really cynical, and certain that what we do doesn't matter at all? Or do we believe, like Anne Frank, that "in spite of every-thing, people really are good at heart"?

We do believe that people really are good at heart—it's in all of our hands. So is the potential to believe that we can't trust our leaders, or that one person can't make a difference. But there are also, in each generation, group strengths and individual strengths that we can use to make the future a better place for all of us.

Being True to Yourself, Your Heart, and Your Passion

For your own happiness, you must follow the path you choose *with your heart*. Every path worth following will be challenging in some way, and challenge means that you won't always be secure.

If you're heart's in it, though, you'll be *passionate*, and so, true to yourself. When you have passion, you can overcome just about anything. Every life has its ups and downs—and those who are following their true paths know that the ups are well worth the downs.

You can choose to follow the path of least resistance—or you can choose to live a passionate life. Your choice is in your hands—both literally and figuratively.

The Least You Need to Know

➤ Every generation's hands reflect its unique genius and possibility.

➤ You can compare your hands with your parents' and children's.

➤ The future of a generation is in all of its hands.

➤ You can change the future.

Some Good Palmistry Books to Check Out

While we like to think we've written such a great palmistry book that you'll never need another, if we've whetted your appetite, you may well want to check out some others. Here are a few of Robin's "Holy Bibles" of palmistry:

Benham, William G. *The Benham Book of Palmistry*. North Hollywood: Newcastle Publishing, 1988.

Campbell, Ed. *The Encyclopedia of Palmistry*. New York: Berkley, 1966.

Cheiro. *Cheiro's Language of the Hand*. New York: Prentice Hall, 1987.

Costaville, Maria. *How to Read Palms*. New York: Crescent, 1988.

Gettings, Fred. *Palmistry Made Easy*. London: Bancroft & Co., 1966.

Palmistry Online

If you're reading this, you probably already know how to find things about specific subject matter online, so we're going to cut to the chase and give you information about some of the more interesting palmistry Web sites we've discovered.

http://home.earthlink.net/~y/gile/

See anything familiar in that address? You should—it's Robin's Web page! Updated regularly, this site can tell you where you can meet Robin in person throughout the West. As this is being typed, he's in El Paso, for example, but you can find Robin anywhere—especially when you check this site first to find his schedule.

http://www.edcampbell.com

Our technical editor, Ed Campbell, has his own Web site, too. Check it out—he has lots of information about palmistry to share with you.

http://www.palmistry.com

This is the Web site for Quebec's Palmistry Center, and among the many palmistry-related activities available here you'll find:

➤ Classes, including one on "how to change your hand"
➤ Readings
➤ Articles
➤ FAQ (that's online-ese for "frequently asked questions")
➤ Products

This site also includes links to other palmistry sites, and is a good place (after checking Robin's schedule, of course) to start your online search.

Other Sites

When we typed the word "Palmistry" into our search engine, we received over 1,000 matches. Among these were a fair number of skeptics' sites, which are worth reading to see just what those "rational" folks are saying. The vast majority of palmistry sites, however, were for books, products, and online readings. Which brings us to the next question.

Can You Get Your Palm Read Online?

The online reading sites that we looked at involved either scanning a picture of the palm and then attaching it to an e-mail so the palm reader could see it, or printing out an order form and attaching it to a picture to be sent via "snail mail." While experienced palm readers can see quite a bit through either of these methods, we'd recommend a real live palm reader for your first encounter. Unless, of course, your life line hugs your thumb so tightly that you're never going to leave your house. Then, by all means, try an online reading.

Products

Not surprisingly, the Web's hopping with folks selling palmistry products, from a ceramic hand with its mounts, fingers, and phalanges labeled, to CD-ROM lessons, to books, books, and more books. If nothing else, it's fun to see what's out there online, but once again, we'd recommend you patronize your local metaphysical bookstore and get more personalized service. It could be the beginning of a beautiful friendship.

Glossary

Your **active hand** is the hand you use to write longhand, stir the soup, hold the phone, punch someone's lights out, or honk your horn: your right, if you're right-handed; your left, if you're left-handed.

Your **active Mars**, located between the thumb and the life line, reveals your temperament—and your temper.

The **angle of eccentricity**, measured between the Mercury and Apollo fingers, determines how much, if any, a person's behavior departs from what society considers the "norm."

The **angle of generosity**, measured between the thumb and the Jupiter finger, reveals how you relate to others.

The **Apollo finger** is the third finger on the hand, also known as the ring finger. Your Apollo is where you'll find your approaches to creativity and all things artistic.

An **archetype** is a pattern of both the individual and collective psyches with a universal meaning, such as "hero" or "villain."

The **Camera's Eye** is a line that can be found curving down from the mount of Apollo to between the head and heart lines to a junction with the head line. This line shows a talent for visual balance and coordination that's often found in the photographer, hence its name.

The heart **chakra** is the center of the seven spiritual centers of energy in the body.

According to Eastern tradition, **chi** is the vital energy we generate and utilize on a daily basis. When the flesh at the tip of your thumb or any finger doesn't immediately spring back when you press on it, your chi may be low.

Dermatoglyphics is the study of fingerprint patterns, both on the finger and on the skin of the hand.

Dowsing is a method of finding something hidden using a special tool, such as a pendulum, rod, or wire. One can dowse for water, for example, by using a divining rod.

The **Girdle of Venus**, a line that curves from either Jupiter or the Jupiter-Saturn split to Mercury, shows an appreciation for the finer things in life.

The **head line**, the central of the three major lines on the hand, usually begins between the thumb and the Jupiter finger and travels in a gentle curve across the hand toward the percussion. Your head line reveals the nature of your thinking.

The **heart line** is the uppermost of the three most prominent lines on your hand, and can be found beneath the fingers on the palm. You can think of the heart line as a portrayal of your emotional inclinations and longings.

Intuition is a way of knowing something without a conscious thought process.

Your **Jupiter finger**, the first finger of the hand, is also called the pointer finger. It's where you'll find your social self, capacity for leadership, and your relations with intimate others.

The **life line** begins between the thumb and Jupiter finger and forms an arc to the base of the thumb. Your life line reveals your life and its impact on the world. Its length is not necessarily related to the length of your life.

The **lines** in your hand provide the plot details that make up your life.

The **lunar mount**, or **mount of the Moon**, is the area on your hand where you'll find your imagination and subconscious. It's located on the percussion of the hand below passive Mars.

The **Mark of the Teacher**, which shows profound skill in that arena, is comprised of two separate markings on the hand: a diagonal line on the mount of Mercury, and another, which is roughly parallel to the first, that lies between the head and heart lines under the mount of Mercury.

Medical stigmata, five parallel lines on the mount of Mercury, indicate a capacity for healing.

The **Mercury finger** is the fourth finger on the hand, also known as the "little finger." Your Mercury is where you'll find your approaches to communication, commerce, your capacity for healing and honesty, and impersonal relationships.

The **mount of Neptune** is concerned with foundations and dreams. It's located where the lunar mount approaches the lower center of the palm.

The **mount of Pluto** rules your potential for transformative experiences and your karmic connections to others. Seldom unmoving, it's found at the center of the palm where it meets the wrist. It migrates, rises, and falls in accordance with its use.

The **mount of Uranus**, at the conjunction of passive Mars, the lunar mount, and the plain of Mars, shows your capacity for idealism and invention, and how you use the media and the electron, the area of modern styles.

The **mount of Venus,** located at the base of the thumb, is where you'll find your heart chakra energy. You can think of it as a barometer of your love.

The **mounts of the fingers,** the fleshy area just below each finger, share a name with the respective finger. These are the mounts of yourself, the areas where your story will unfold.

The **mystic cross** or **cross of mystery,** found under the mount of Saturn or between Saturn and Apollo, used to be interpreted as a taste for the occult, and is today considered a mark of the gift of intuition.

A **myth** is a way of understanding something, told in the form of a story, that would otherwise be difficult to understand.

In palmistry, an **overlay** is any pattern that seems to be overriding a more typical one. More often found in the active hand, overlays can change rapidly and are therefore not read on their own, but with the passive hand pattern as well.

Pair bonding is a sociological term for any sort of cooperative relationship entered into by two or more people.

Palmistry, or **chiromancy,** is a means of understanding the macrocosm of the self through the microcosm of the hand.

Palm readers are people who have studied how the interrelationship between the palm and the self works and can help you better understand yourself by studying your hand.

Passive Mars, located between the head and heart lines on the percussion of the hand below the mount of Mercury, shows your ability to hold your own against the world.

The **percussion** of the hand is found on the Mercury-finger side of the hand, running from underneath the mount of Mercury toward the wrist.

Each finger is divided into three **phalanges,** the sections created by the finger's joints. The first phalange (the one with the nail) represents the intuitive, the second (middle) represents the mental, and the third (closest to the hand) represents the material.

You can think of the **plain of Mars** as the mount that reflects your ability to deal with slights and insults, real and imagined, and bounce right back to live another day. It's located between the head and heart lines, and active and passive Mars.

When a hand has a **psychic overlay,** you'll find certain features of the psychic hand, such as long, antenna-like fingers, a branching head line (as well as secondary lines), and very fine skin texture, overlaid on another hand type. Together, these features add sensitivity to the otherwise everyday hand.

Psychometry, a method of interpreting vibrations by feel, is a more dubious practice when it comes to reading the palm.

Palm readers always look at the **quality** of a line to determine its strength and vitality in the person's life. This includes its depth, clarity, and continuity.

395

A **rising line** is a line that begins in the lower portion of the palm and rises toward a specific mount of a finger. These lines show your inclinations and tendencies in certain areas.

The **rising line to Apollo** is a sign of success in the arts. It's found low in the hand and rises up into the mount of Apollo under the Apollo finger.

The **rising line to Jupiter,** found next to the life line and rising toward Jupiter, is the mark of the social critic and leader.

The **rising line to Mercury,** found along the percussion of the hand, rises from the center of the palm or the lunar mount up to the mount of Mercury. This line is all about communication.

The **rising line to Saturn,** or **destiny line,** is a line that begins in the lower portion of your hand and rises toward your Saturn mount. It's considered a barometer of your standard of living and potential for wealth, as well as your relationship with authority.

The **runes,** part of an ancient alphabet of Norse or Germanic origin, are often used for divination.

Your **Saturn finger,** the middle finger on your hand, is where you'll find structure, boundaries, and order. Saturn is also called the karmic enforcer.

The **set** of a finger refers to its placement along an imaginary horizontal line drawn across the base of the fingers. In an evenly set hand the bottom of each finger's third phalange is parallel to the other fingers'. Fingers that fall below this line are said to be low set, while fingers that begin above it are called high set.

The **Simian Crease** appears in the hand as a combined heart and head line. It can indicate single-mindedness and tenacity of purpose because feelings and thoughts are undifferentiated.

A **sister line** is any line paralleling the life line, found inside the life line (that is, toward the thumb). These lines are always good news, and are considered to have a strengthening capacity.

The **triangle of earnings** can be found where the head line meets the rising line to Saturn. If a Mercury line rises to form a triangle here, you can use it to assess your earning potential.

The **Via Lascivia,** which curves from the Jupiter-Saturn split no farther than the Apollo-Mercury split, is an indication of sensuality.

Whorls, which may appear in the form of bull's-eyes, ovals, loops, or tents, are dermatoglyphic (fingerprint) patterns on the fingertip or hand.

Index

Q

R

S